GAINING CONTROL

GAINING CONTROL

HOW HUMAN BEHAVIOR EVOLVED

Robert Aunger and Valerie Curtis

OXFORD
UNIVERSITY PRESS

OXFORD
UNIVERSITY PRESS

Great Clarendon Street, Oxford, OX2 6DP,
United Kingdom

Oxford University Press is a department of the University of Oxford.
It furthers the University's objective of excellence in research, scholarship,
and education by publishing worldwide. Oxford is a registered trade mark of
Oxford University Press in the UK and in certain other countries

Published in the United States of America by Oxford University Press
198 Madison Avenue, New York, NY 10016, United States of America

British Library Cataloguing in Publication Data

Data available

Library of Congress Control Number: 2014953421

ISBN 978-0-19-968895-1

Printed and bound by
CPI Group (UK) Ltd, Croydon, CR0 4YY

Oxford University Press makes no representation, express or implied, that the
drug dosages in this book are correct. Readers must therefore always check
the product information and clinical procedures with the most up-to-date
published product information and data sheets provided by the manufacturers
and the most recent codes of conduct and safety regulations. The authors and
the publishers do not accept responsibility or legal liability for any errors in the
text or for the misuse or misapplication of material in this work. Except where
otherwise stated, drug dosages and recommendations are for the non-pregnant
adult who is not breast-feeding

Links to third party websites are provided by Oxford in good faith and
for information only. Oxford disclaims any responsibility for the materials
contained in any third party website referenced in this work.

PREFACE

This book is an outgrowth of research we undertook not just to understand human behavior, but to change it. That's because we design health promotion campaigns in developing countries for a living, most of which require, in the current parlance, "behavior change." For example, modern lifestyles can lead to a wide variety of diseases, so many people would like to curb their smoking, limit their alcohol and calorie intake, and get more exercise. We are a long way from being able to understand behavior, much less helping people to change it effectively.

To make any headway on this difficult problem, we have had to adopt a number of strategies. First, experiencing human behavior from the "inside," with all of its complexity buzzing in our heads, is not, in our view, the place to start. Nor do we believe that the standard technique in psychology of explaining human behavior simply by isolating some bit has been that effective. Instead, we think it is more likely to be productive to start simple, with the behavior of other species, and build up a picture of human behavior from those less complex beginnings. In effect, we adopt an evolutionary approach that starts with the proposition that the human animal evolved from simple beginnings to have the qualities it does. We assume that current human behavior betrays its evolutionary history. By tracing that history, we think we can begin to see natural "parts" to the causal networks underpinning behavior production.

Our main argument is that what has been lacking from work on human behavior is an evolutionary story about how all of this could have happened. The present volume is a speculative reconstruction of that history, using an evolutionary logic that explains how, over the course of the phylogenetic lineage culminating in *Homo sapiens*, nervous systems could have moved step-by-step from living inside a creature with limited abilities to control its environment, based on a simple mental model of its world, to one with our present behavioral repertoire, which is causing massive changes to the globe's environment. It is a story of animals *gaining control* over their environments.

Second, we assume that brains (and the neurological systems that predated them) were designed by evolution to control behavior. We assume that these mental control systems are adaptations which were designed to solve particular problems in the niches in which those organisms evolved—and we assume that there were enough regularities in these niches for distinct adaptations to emerge. So, for example, to direct our behavior, humans still use simple cue-response reflexes that arose in invertebrates, the motivated reward system that arose in vertebrates, as well as the more recent deliberative, executive control system. Evolution did not do away with reflex when motivation was invented, nor did it do away with reflex and motivation when deliberative cognition came online. Further, by arguing that there are certain essential functions that behavior has evolved to execute, we believe that we can usefully classify behavior production mechanisms by what they do.

Third, we have not attempted to survey the ways in which all kinds of animals produce behavior, but only the ones in our own lineage—an unashamedly anthropocentric view. This is reasonable, since it is human behavior that we are trying to explain. We thus ignore the apparently complex behavior of bees or crows, but concern ourselves only with the behavioral innovations in the line that led to ourselves. This strategy might make it seem as if we were using teleological or *scalae natura* arguments, but we are not. There is no "great chain of being" leading necessarily from the simple to the complex, producing a ladder on which all life-forms can be ranked. Rather, if we look backward through evolutionary history using the lens of behavioral control and function and focus only on our own phylogenetic history, we see that complex behavior has simpler antecedents, and so on back to green slime. (The same would be true were we trying, for example, to trace the evolutionary history of the human eye.) There was no inevitable progression from simple to complex: in other lineages, adaptations such as eyes or behavioral control systems may not have changed, or even become less complex. However, in the case of our own species, over the long run, it did. Whatever the extravagant claims made by some behavioral scientists for the abilities of bees or crows or elephants or cetaceans, no one can seriously doubt that humans exhibit the most complex forms of behavior on this planet— such as writing books about our own behavior. Such complexity must have arisen from simpler origins.

Fourth, we have adopted the simplifying strategy, which relates to the second, of making some broad assumptions about the behavioral capacities of our ancestors. Of course we do not have extant examples of the animals that were actually our ancestors; we have only a few possible fossil candidates and no examples of fossilized behavior. How, then, can we unearth the behavior control systems of our ancestors? The best we can do is to look at the behavior of extant animals that are analogs of our progenitors. At a broad scale of generalization, the behavior of our single-celled ancestor must have been something like that of the extant class of bacteria; the behavior of the first mammal in our evolutionary history must have approximated that of the simplest extant mammal, etc. Of course any animal alive today has had many millions—and sometimes billions—of years to evolve since it first came along, so that it can be objected that extant animals are not a good proxy for our ancestors because they are out at the far end of their own branches of the Tree of Life; they have evolved for just as long as we have. But if their niches have not significantly changed, then their "way of life" can still be considered a model for the adaptations that were present in an earlier time.

Fifth, we have assumed that we can meaningfully chunk behavior into kinds. Progress in science depends on scientists being able to identify what exactly they are talking about. These fundamental units of analysis are what philosophers call "natural kinds." In the biological sciences, evolutionary natural kinds are adaptations that can be identified by their common history of selection for some function. However, in psychology there is major controversy over the definition of the fundamental units of analysis. Is behavior a response to environmental cues? Or internally generated to achieve mentally represented goals? Are there component constructs in the brain and, if so, how should they be labeled? To get around this problem we start by postulating that natural selection has created distinct adaptations in the brain for the control of distinct classes of behavior. To show that we are beginning from first principles we give them the agnostic name "behavior production units" (BPUs). Deducing the function, organization, and nature of these BPUs is the subject of this book. (In Chapter 7 we defend the view that what we have identified *are* psychology's natural kinds.)

Sixth, we have adopted a strategy concerning nomenclature. What names should we give to these natural kinds once we have identified them? Since our approach carves up the world of behavior into units somewhat different to those identified in other projects, to use terms such as "instinct," "drive," or "emotion" invites confusion. However, to coin neologisms is to ask an already charged reader to take on yet more cognitive load. We have therefore opted to use lay terms where they, more or less, cover similar concepts, but then have carefully defined them (see the glossary at the end of the book for our definitions of these terms). We believe that it is worth paying attention to our recast terminology because these definitions encapsulate the major conceptual shifts in the theory of behavioral control that we are proposing. In fact these may be the natural kinds that psychology has long been looking for. Were they to be widely adopted they might offer the promise of a unified and progressive approach in the behavioral sciences.

What is distinctive about our approach to behavior? One key difference is that we ground our study in the fundamental science of evolutionary biology rather than in the less fundamental discipline of psychology. And we will not simply argue, as does standard evolutionary psychology, that there must be structure in the brain because the brain evolved to produce categories of adaptive behavior. Rather, we are anxious to tell the story about how particular capabilities actually arose. Tracing the evolutionary developments culminating in contemporary humans through millions of years adds additional constraints to the kinds of explanations that are possible, and hence helps us to avoid telling "just so" stories.

We see the world of behavior in a functionalist/adaptationist light. We begin by asking what behavior evolved to do and then postulate the steps in the history of minds that produced that behavior. While other authors have attempted similarly broad explanations of behavior from other perspectives—neuroscience, neuro-economics, psychology, animal behavior, brain evolution, philosophy, evolutionary psychology—no one has yet attempted a synthesis from the perspective of the most fundamental of the life sciences, evolutionary biology. This is, as we have said, a first attempt at doing so. Because we cannot in one short volume (or indeed in a few life-times) collect all of the evidence required to support all of our claims, our survey is inevitably tentative and partial. We have tested some of the claims against published empirical evidence but have not, and cannot, examine all of our claims in the light of all of the subdisciplinary debates about brains and behavior. Such a complete examination we leave to the "holy grail" book that we—or more likely, others—will one day write. Our purpose is to tell a plausible evolutionary story of major steps in increasing complexity of the control of behavior and in its functions.

We believe the perspective put forward here will help scientists to frame more incisive and productive hypotheses about the causes of behavior. We also hope it will lead to improved means of changing behaviors that impact on health. This theoretical approach has proved enormously and robustly useful in clarifying our thinking about behavior in application to the real world of behavior change. We even find it helpful when we try to control our own behavior—for example, in weight regulation and in the management of our cooperative relationship. We hope that our approach will prove equally useful to others wishing to understand the anatomy of human behavior.

This project has benefited from the generous help of many people, including Tony Barnett, Adam Biran, Alison Bish, Kalina Christoff, Micheal de Barra, Barbara Findlay, Diana Fleischman, Carlos Gershenson, Katie Greenland, Jessie deWitt Huberts, Gaby Judah, Ara Norenzayan, John Odling-Smee, Miguel Rubio-Godoy, Thomas Reydon, Beth Scott, Mark Schaller, Szymon Wichary, and several anonymous reviewers, all of whom provided very thoughtful and helpful comments on earlier versions. We are grateful to them all. We also appreciate the efforts of Martin Baum and Charlotte Green which shepherded the book through Oxford processes. We are indebted to Douglas Vipond for very thoughtful and professional copy editing, and to Cherline Daniel for expert management. Thanks to Springer Verlag for allowing us to include (in modified form) an earlier paper from *Biology and Philosophy* as Chapter 6.

CONTENTS

Section 3 Philosophical Perspectives

Section 4 Concluding Thoughts

SECTION 1

THE BASIC ARGUMENT

Behavior is the quintessential adaptation of animals; it defines animals as a class of creatures. Behavior allows animals to seek out what they need, rather than waiting for it to arrive or drift past, and it allows them to actively influence their environments, and the other organisms in it, to their own advantage. Behavior comes in a vast range of forms, from the extremely simple to the unutterably complex. Some have very limited behavioral repertoires, with an influence that extends only locally and concerns only foods, wastes, safety, and reproductive opportunities. The microscopic aquatic rotifer, for example, moves randomly about its environment, avoiding or absorbing what it bumps into, and sometimes fissioning. Human behavior is at the opposite extreme. We eat in restaurants, buy branded toiletries, build skyscrapers, create legislative institutions, travel in flying machines, write poetry, and search for meaning in relationships, temples, and scientific books. Humans have discovered antibiotics, sent probes into space, decimated rainforests, shared a billion views of clips of kitten behavior, and decoded their own genomes.

But there is one thing that humans have singularly failed to do, and that is to properly understand their own behavior. Since the dawn of self-awareness we have struggled to understand the causes of our actions. It is testament to the complexity of the topic that we still do not have all of the answers. Yet such a project is urgent and necessary. Seeking a better understanding of human behavior is not just an intellectual exercise; it could help us to prevent obesity, infectious disease, violence, social inequality, deforestation, and anthropogenic climate change. In short, it could help us to enhance our own behavior.

Huge progress has been made—much of it in the last few decades—in psychology, neuroscience, philosophy, and artificial intelligence, but it is still not possible to take a single volume off the shelf and read a straightforward explanation of our own behavior. Lots of disciplines are working at the coalface of understanding behavior, and each brings its own tools—the brain scanner from neuroscience, lab protocols from psychology, questionnaires and interviews from sociology, field diaries from zoology, games from economics, and logic from philosophy. But each discipline has been mining independently with no unified map as to where the coal seams lie—indeed, in some cases they do not even agree on what they mean by "coal." There remain many unknowns, many different perspectives, and little agreement as to the component parts of the "machine" that produces human behavior. In our view a unified, explanatory perspective on behavior is still several decades away.

To get a start on this ambitious project, we have taken a radical approach: to argue that one must start at the beginning, with the evolution of human behavior from simpler origins, because only by doing so can the functional nature of that behavior become clear.

We start with the proposition that behavior is designed to solve problems— evolutionary problems, such as how to find food, or a mate, or a place to sleep safely. Further, we suppose that these problems are "set" for an animal by its environment, and determine the way that it draws a living from that environment. In simple terms, we propose that the evolutionarily significant tasks that an organism must perform to maximize its inclusive fitness are defined by the dimensions of its niche. A niche can be considered to consist of the aspects of the animal's environment that pose evolutionary problems, and to which the animal must find means to respond effectively in order to survive and reproduce. Each problem can be considered a "dimension" of its niche, so an animal's niche is considered multidimensional (Hutchinson, 1957). More complex niches therefore have more dimensions. The "hypervolume" defined by this multidimensional niche is the actual life-space to which the animal is adapted, and which defines its "way of life."

We assume that early in the history of life, niches were relatively simple. Early animals could therefore survive and reproduce using a small behavioral repertoire. However, through niche competition or drift, some animals entered a new way of life. Such changes sometimes involved performing new tasks, such as reproducing sexually, broadening feeding strategies, competing with new species, or cooperating with conspecifics. These changes in behavior made the niches of such species more complex than those of their forebears. For example, the niche of the nematode (*Caenorhabditis elegans*) is a liquid surface containing oxygen, nutrients, prey, bacterial and viral parasites and, sometimes, predators. The nematode's behavioral repertoire therefore includes dynamic responses (reflecting its morphological qualities) to odors, thermal gradients, feeding aggregation, avoidance of bacterial parasites, and predator escape behavior. The niche of the nightingale (*Luscinia megarhynchos*), on the other hand, has further dimensions (because it is social), so its behavioral repertoire also includes the manipulation of other nightingales via song, and finding a mate with which to reproduce and to help care for the young.

The relationship between behavior and niches can be considered coevolutionary: sometimes, an animal behaves in a new way, creating a new niche dimension—such as when sexual reproduction evolved. Other times, it is the environment that changes, posing a new problem to a species—such as when the atmosphere gets colder, or the animal's primary food species dies out. We thus are agnostic about whether it is the behavior or the environment that changes first, requiring the other to "adapt." What is important is that the animal (its physiology, morphology, and behavior) is adapted to its niche, the aspects of its environment to which it must respond.

An increase in "task repertoires" (the kinds of fitness-important tasks an organism must perform) required an animal to be able to produce new kinds of behavior. Such capacities required new kinds of control systems for producing behavior, which consequently become more complex themselves. Hence, animals in some evolutionary lineages (e.g., that leading to *Homo sapiens*) underwent a series of steps toward increased complexity—in niches, in task repertoires, and in the accompanying psychological systems for producing behavior.

We hasten to add that we are not engaging in the argument that evolutionary processes are teleological or purposive in any sense—that is, striving toward particular goals. There is no "great chain of being" leading necessarily from the simple to the complex, producing a ladder on which all life-forms can be ranked. Rather, we make what is—we hope—the much less controversial claim that looking *backward* through evolutionary history with a particular lens, focusing only on an individual lineage in the phylogenetic tree, we see that there have been points at which behavior has become more complex on the way to humankind. This need not be the case in other lineages, where behavior may have not changed, or even become less complex. The reason for increasing behavioral complexity is, we argue, that the niches within which our ancestral species lived have, at particular points in time, themselves become more complex—more multidimensional—and that behavior has responded by becoming equally complex to cope with increased demands. Had this kind of environmental stimulus not been present, evolution would not necessarily have led to greater control over the production of behavior. It's just that, in the case of our own species, it did.

The organizing theme in this story is thus that of gaining control over the production of behavior, as this is the way in which increasingly sophisticated forms of behavior—and the increasing *variety* of behaviors—come about. Control in this context refers to the psychological ability to develop "command sequences" for the motor system to execute as a stream of behavior—which may last or shorter or longer time, and consist of more or fewer actions—and to select among alternative command sequences based on some criteria. These commands are then passed to the motor control system for execution.

This idea of control is central to the story for another reason. Progress in science depends on scientists being able to identify what exactly they are talking about. These fundamental units of analysis are what philosophers call "natural kinds." In the biological sciences, evolutionary natural kinds are adaptations that can be identified by their common history of selection for some function. However in psychology there is major controversy over the definition of the fundamental units of analysis. To get around this problem we start by postulating "behavior production units" (BPUs). Through natural selection, BPUs evolved to produce behavior that solved problems regularly arising over the course of the evolutionary history of animals. Deducing the function, organization, and nature of these BPUs is the subject of this book. (The next chapter develops the BPU concept; Chapter 6 is a defense of BPUs as the "natural kind" of psychology.)

Time will tell whether the sketch that we outline here, based on this theoretical strategy, has been able to correctly describe the landscape of behavior. Even if it is only half right it will have been worth setting out the sketch so as to encourage others to fill in missing parts of the picture. Should our map prove nearly right, then it should offer some real hope of unification in the behavioral sciences and hence accelerate our project to understand the complexities of our own behavior.

We begin the story with two chapters setting out more fully our general framework for the evolution of behavioral control. These chapters provide the set of concepts we use to describe advances in behavior and human psychology. We follow this, in Section 2, with the story of how complex human behavior evolved.

CHAPTER 1

PRODUCING BEHAVIOR

When we ask our students to define "behavior" they find the task surprisingly difficult. Their definitional attempts often include thoughts, feelings, plans, actions, reflex responses, and objectives. In this book we define behavior as *self-propelled movement producing a functional interaction between an animal and its environment*. Behaviors therefore include actions such as finding a mate or fleeing a predator, but do not include heartbeats or peristalsis because such motion does not interact with the environment; it is rather physiological in nature. Further, behavior is locomotory or self-powered rather than being dependent on external forces, like drifting in a current of water or air; movement can be of the whole body or of body parts, or can involve ejections into the environment from inside the body (for example, speech or defecation).

Because behavior is a functional interaction with the environment it must, at its simplest, involve three component parts. First, animals must be able to perceive what is going on in the world and to recognize when these present threats or opportunities. Second, they must then determine what to do about these phenomena. And finally they must organize their response—the musculatory-skeletal system must be mobilized into taking some relevant action. The first, the perceptual system, and the last, the motor control system, have already been well described in the literature (Carlson, 2013; Purves et al., 2011). The system of interest is in the middle box, in-between these two. In this, we follow William James, who said "The whole neural organism, it will be remembered, is, physiologically considered, but a machine for converting stimuli into reactions; and the intellectual part of our life is knit up with but the middle or 'central' portion of the machine's operations" (James, 1890, Chapter 23 on 'The production of movement'). This middle box has been described as "cognition," "information processing," or "central processing" (Harnish, 2001; Mesulam, 1998; Sloman, 2001) and it is where scientific contention still lies. We dub the content of this middle box "the behavior production system" and it is the subject of this book.

Behavior Production Systems

Behavior production systems in animals came about through a process of evolutionary tinkering. Species in a line of descent tend to have the same genotypic and phenotypic qualities as their ancestors, with a few added changes, which are cobbled together out of pre-existing parts. More complex organisms come about through the incremental accumulation of functionality where new features and abilities evolve by co-opting existing structures that previously served other adaptive functions (Elena & Lenski, 2003). For example, the jaws of early vertebrates evolved from skeletal rods called pharyngeal arches which originally served to keep gill slits open in a species ancestral to this group (Mallatt, 1996).

The architecture of the human brain similarly reflects its evolutionary history: some control mechanisms are similar to those present in unicellular animals, some structures are similar to those of invertebrates, and others are mammalian in origin (A. B. Butler, 2001; Rubenstein et al., 1999; Streidter, 1998). Indeed it seems likely that the brains of all bilateral animals may have originated from a single ancestral species (Reichert & Simeone, 2001), with the same central nervous systems being characteristic of all bilaterians (Holland, 2013). More than 95 percent of the genes expressed in the brains of planarians (flatworms) are also found in the fruit fly, nematode, and human (Mineta et al., 2003). It should therefore be possible to trace the development of the behavior production systems of humans by using information about developments in the phylogeny of animals in our evolutionary history.

We propose that what lets animals turn salient external and internal stimuli into adaptive outputs, or behavior, are accreted brain mechanisms which we will call BPUs.

What are these BPUs? Though it is helpful to imagine them as specific organs in the brain, they certainly need not be spatially distinct or physically encapsulated. Any given region of neural tissue can respond to a broad range of stimuli, and can produce a broad range of outputs. For example, the insula—which is anatomically distinct—is associated with a wide range of stimuli and has been reported as being differentially activated in nearly a third of all published fMRI studies (Yarkoni et al., 2011). Brain structures are known to multitask—even down to the level of individual neurons, which can be excited by faces, cars, social situations, or patterns of lines. Nevertheless, given our state of ignorance about brain organization and function, it is still a useful abstraction to argue that there must be certain *functionally* distinct networks, in a dynamic, stochastic sense, which achieve certain kinds of control over behavior, as that is the primary job the brain must do. We therefore expect there to be organized suites of activated neurons that accept relevant stimuli and organize the production of appropriate behavior. Finding a suitable mate requires different skills from increasing status, which requires different skills from escaping a predator. It seems unlikely that a single perfectly integrated, topologically random network can achieve each of these as efficiently as three differently structured networks (Tooby & Cosmides, 1992). To this degree, then, we believe the brain is modularized in a way that makes the BPU concept meaningful.

Our purpose in in identifying distinct BPUs is not, then, to postulate that certain areas of the brain do specific things across a range of animals (such a task, if indeed it is possible, we leave to comparative neuroscientists). Our plan is rather to seek a general classification system for BPUs which can illuminate how the behavior capabilities of species have evolved over time. For this purpose, it is enough to propose classes of BPUs which are distinguished by their fundamental properties.

As we have said, we are not here concerned with the organization of perception, nor with the organization of motor responses; these are relatively well understood. Neither are we concerned with the thorny issue of how competing proposals for control of behavior from the multiple BPUs are adjudicated (the so-called action selection problem; Prescott, 2007). This is still very poorly understood (Redish, 2013). Finally, we do not concern ourselves here with issues such as temperament, mood, expression, and the role of culture in human behavior. For the most part, these either modulate processes we *do* discuss or are late additions to behavior production which fall outside our scope.

As with any historical phenomenon, the way in which things work can change over time. Just as cilia can become fins, which can evolve into legs (Coates et al., 2002), so early mechanisms in brains for producing beneficial behavior can be elaborated and improved upon in later descendants. Brains have shown remarkable increases in size and complexity in the lineage between early multicellular animals and our group of primates (Allman, 1999; A. B. Butler & Hodos, 2005; Northcutt, 2002; Streidter, 2005). What could have been the selective pressure responsible for this increase in investment in brains by later species in our lineage? One advantage of devoting greater neural resources to the production of behavior is that it increases the time horizon over which responses can be controlled. A simple animal that can only respond instantly to an immediate cue may miss the opportunity to recognize a pattern of cues that implies a larger benefit or danger in the medium term. And an animal that can make a long-term plan can reap far greater evolutionary rewards beyond the imaginative scope of the simple reflexive animal. Animals that can forgo a present benefit can thus enjoy a higher return over the longer term by pursuing a different sequence of behaviors than would be dictated by responding to current conditions at each moment. The adaptive value of behavior can thus be increased by calculating responses over longer time frames—that is by *gaining control* over their own behavior.

Three Levels of Control

We propose that there have been three major evolutionary innovations in behavioral control in the lineage leading to humans. (In Chapter 7 we argue that these are in fact "major evolutionary transitions" in the sense of Maynard Smith and Szathmary (1995), but that is a technical argument of interest primarily to evolutionary biologists, so we leave it to later.) The first transition produced the invention of the reflex arc in simple unicellular animals, which enabled behavior that had immediate benefits. The second was the invention of the motivational behavior production system in vertebrates. This system allowed animals to pursue goals that helped them meet their needs, integrated over a longer time horizon than simple reflexes. The final major transition produced the executive control of behavior in higher mammals. This brain system allowed such animals to plan a sequence of behaviors over a long period and so reap even greater rewards from their interactions with their environments. These three types of behavior production systems are all recognizably present in the human brain (A. B. Butler & Hodos, 2005; Rubenstein et al., 1999; Streidter, 1998).

These three transition points will be described at length in the second section of the book, where we discuss *how* they evolved. Here, we explain *why* they evolved, by drawing out the distinctive functions of the three main types of human behavior.

Table 1.1 shows the characteristics of the three types of behavior production systems. The oldest type is the reactive system, which causes quick responses to cues (often features of the local environment). This system arose in the earliest animals and is still responsible for reflexive responses in humans such as the eye blink and for habitual responses such as walking. The motivated system came along with early vertebrates and allowed animals to pursue goals such as finding food or mates. Executive control is even newer, being a faculty arising with primates, that enabled even longer-term planning of behavioral responses to environmental conditions.

A variety of new faculties—such as types of learning and memory, and abilities to mentally represent phenomena in the external world—can be associated with each level of control (described at length in Section 2). An important consequence is the ability to control behavior over increasingly long periods of time. On the other hand, these more sophisticated forms of control tend to take longer to process information prior to a response. Conscious control is probably associated only with the most recently evolved kind of behavior: that which is under executive control.

The academic scholars stressing the existence of each level are quite different. The tradition of ethology can be associated with an emphasis on the reactive nature of

Table 1.1: Characteristics of the Levels of Behavioral Control

	Reactive	Motivated	Executive
Types of behavior	Reflexes, instincts, habits	Drives, emotions, interests	Implicit/explicit plan execution
Stimulus	Specific cue	Opportunity, internal indicator	Opportunity, internal reflection, decision to act
Speed of reaction	Rapid	Medium	Slow
Time horizon*	Short	Medium	Long
Target of attention	Cue	Goal	Objective
Mental representation	N/A	Goal-state	Meta-representation: the manipulation of symbols, tokens
Brain system type	Multiple hardwired systems	Modular	General-purpose
Origin in our lineage	Metazoans (hydra)	Vertebrates (bony fish)	Primates (monkeys)
Location	Striatal brain	Limbic-midbrain	Prefrontal cortex
Purpose	Accomplish specific tasks	Meet needs	Achieve objectives
Composition	Dedicated neural pathways	Reward system	Deliberation, theory of mind, language abilities
Learning	Habituation, sensitization	Reinforcement learning	Simulation of actions and outcomes
Memory	Procedural	Affective encoding	Declarative/episodic
Consciousness	Unconscious	Unconscious	Conscious and unconscious
Examples	Eye blink, shiver, walk, spit out, scratch, groom	*Hunger, status, justice, play, nurture, exploration*	Cultivate a garden, trade a commodity, study to pass an exam
Individual variation	Degree of motor coordination	Personality types	Reflective styles, impulse control, deferred gratification
Historical proponents	Ethologists (Lorenz, Tinbergen)	Pavlov, Freud, Garcia	Cognitive psychology, economics

* Includes time before response (from time of stimulus), future time horizon over which response is calculated prior to enactment, and length of time over which behavioral response is controlled.

animal behavior. A number of early-to-mid-twentieth-century figures were important in identifying the importance of unconscious motivations in human behavior
(e.g., Freud). The cognitive revolution in the 1960s (Gardner, 1986) brought about
a near-pathological focus on high-level information processing such that the disciplines of psychology and economics can be linked to this kind of explanation for
behavior.

Of course, we are far from first to propose that the human brain has a variety of
different control systems operating in parallel. Table 1.2 shows some of the main

Table 1.2: Multilevel Control Models*

Model	Reactive	Motivated	Executive	Discipline
Dual process	1	0	1	Psychology
Ortony et al. (2004)	2	0	1	Psychology
McDaniel/Einstein (2007)	1	0	1	Psychology
Sloman (2001)	1	0	2	AI
Newell (1990)	1	0	2	AI
Minsky (2006)	2	0	4	AI
Dennett (1996)	2	0	2	Philosophy
AuRA	1	1	1	Robotics
3-Tier	1	1	1	Robotics
ATLANTIS	1	1	1	Robotics
Stanley	1	1	1	Robotics
MacLean (1990)	1	1	1	Neuroscience
Rolls (2005)	1	1	1	Neuroscience
Redish (2013)	1	1	1	Neuroscience
Cooper/Shallice (2006)	1	1	1	Cognitive Neuroscience
Reason (1990)	1	1	1	Applied Psychology
Kielhofner (2007)	1	1	1	Occupational Therapy

* Numbers in cells refer to the number of levels in a given model that conform to our definition of
reactive, motivated, and executive kinds of control.

proposals in the literature, which range from two to six systems operating in parallel. Dual-process models (Norman & Shallice, 1986; Schneider & Shiffrin, 1977; Shiffrin & Schneider, 1977; Stanovich, 1999) have been common in psychology for describing a range of phenomena, from perception to planning. The psychologist Daniel Kahneman popularized this idea as thinking "fast" and "slow" (Kahneman, 2011). These models distinguish between automatic and controlled behavior, which correspond roughly to our *reactive* and our *executive* control systems.

Other models make additional discriminations. For example, Ortony and colleagues (2004) advocate a tripartite division of affective systems: "reactive" (the hardwired release of "proto-affects" or fixed action patterns), "routine" (automatic, unconsciously controlled "emotions"), and "reflective" (higher-order, cognitively elaborated emotions). Similarly, the three levels of Sloman's (2001) CogAff framework are reactive mechanisms, deliberative reasoning (requiring the ability to construct hypothetical representations of alternative futures), and reflective meta-management (requiring language, enabling monitoring and reflection). Newell (1990) argues for three levels of control over behavior, which he calls "scales of human action," based on the time over which they are controlled: "biological" (10 milliseconds), "cognitive" (10 seconds), and "rational" (hours). Minsky (2006) devised a model with six levels of control: instinctive reactions, learned reactions, and then four subdivisions of our planning level: deliberative thinking, reflective thinking, self-reflective thinking, and self-conscious emotions. Dennett (1996) argues that there are four stages in cognitive evolution: "Darwinian" creatures exhibit innate, instinctive behavior hardwired into their genotypes, and hence cannot adjust their behavior when circumstances change; "Skinnerian" creatures exhibit phenotypic plasticity in the form of trial-and-error, associationist learning; "Popperian" creatures are able to represent and select behavioral options based on an internal model of the external environment prior to action; and "Gregorian" creatures have world models in their heads and a variety of novel mental tools (symbolic representation, language, the ability to transmit information efficiently, social facilitation, conscious mental contents, "thinking," life story, and culture).

All of these approaches in psychology, AI, and philosophy identify one or more levels similar to our reactive system, and then jump directly to one or more levels of cognitive control. None of these models has an explicit motivation level.

Interestingly, it is roboticists and neuroscientists who are nearest to us in approach. Roboticists have found that they need three levels of control for sophisticated mobile robots, such as AuRA (Arkin et al., 2003; Stoytchev & Arkin, 2001), 3-Tier (Bonasso et al., 1997), ATLANTIS (used in NASA rovers to explore other planets; Gat, 1998), and Stanley, the robot that won the DARPA Grand Challenge to traverse unrehearsed off-road terrain (Thrun et al., 2006). These architectures consist of three layers:

- *reactive*: a feedback mechanism that controls primitive (routine) activities, relating sensors to behavior actuators (e.g., motors)
- *sequencing*: a special-purpose operating system that controls conditional execution and parameterization of primitive activities (i.e., it selects which primitive behaviors are active, while responding conditionally to situations)
- *deliberative*: a mechanism for performing time-consuming computations (e.g., searching, world modeling) and the construction of ordered plans

Tripartite systems similar to reactive, motivated, and executive control have thus been found necessary to guide the production of complex behavior by machines in the physical world. This suggests that not just a functional but a mechanistic division into these levels is a reasonable hypothesis for human agents as well.

Prominent neuroscientific models of the brain also suggest three levels of control similar to ours. For example, MacLean's (1990) "triune brain" hypothesis—an "Archipallium" brain in the brainstem and cerebellum, a "Paleomammalian" brain in the limbic system, and a "Neopallium" brain in the neocortex—is similar in many ways to ours. Similarly, Rolls (2005) finds three routes to the initiation of action: reflexes, which are under genetic control (implemented in the brainstem and spinal cord), "implicit behavioral responses," which are goal-based and motivational (in the thalamus and striatum), and "explicit behavioral responses," which are implemented using language (in the cortex). Implicit decisions use the reinforcement-related value of a stimulus based on dopamine, working as a currency for behavior selection; explicit decisions operate via multistep syntactic planning, based on language and consciousness. Redish (2013) also has a system much like ours, except that he divides the reactive into reflexive and habitual (based on whether the response is hardwired or learned).

Neuroscientists have further identified structures in human brains that correspond to our reactive, motivated, and planned types of behavioral control. They have described simple circuits or columns (Hebb, 1949; LeDoux, 2000; V. Mountcastle, 1957), modules (Damasio, 2003; Freeman, 2000; Panksepp, 1998), and systems (Kelso, 1995; Thelen & Smith, 1994), each of which probably instantiate one level of control (i.e., reactions are probably executed by circuits, motives by modules, and planning by neural systems). Recent work in brain "connectomics" has provided evidence for large-scale neural networks subserving behavioral control at each of the three levels (Bressler & Menon, 2010), and there is evidence for specific pathologies in each (Cole et al., 2012; Menon, 2011).

It is also interesting to note that one of the primary authors of the dual-process view of mind now suggests it is time to switch to a triple-process theory. Stanovich (2009) argues that System 2 needs to be partitioned into two mechanisms, which he calls "algorithmic" and "reflective," based on studies of individual differences in reasoning processes and a taxonomy of cognitive errors made on tasks in the heuristics and biases literature.

The history of thought about the brain's architecture—whether from an embryological, segmental, or evolutionary perspective—has often suggested three divisions. The schemes differ in which structures get assigned to which part of the triplet (Swanson, 2000). For example, the segmental view chops the brain into front, middle, and back regions, while the evolutionary view is concerned with layers (the human neocortex is considered to have six layers, based on morphological traits). The tripartite segmental model of a forebrain, midbrain, and hindbrain (first proposed by Varolio in 1573) remains the simplest for mammals, but a concern with layers is more dominant in contemporary neuroscience (Swanson, 2000).

Similar views can also be found outside psychology. The philosopher John Dewey argued there are three faculties in the mind: habit, impulse, and intelligence, which roughly conform to our schema (Dewey, 1922). Habit is the present of past things (reaction from memory); impulse the present of present things (perception as stimulus); intelligence the present of future things (imagined plans). In fact, the three-part distinction goes back to Aristotle who, in his *De Anima*, proposed that plants have a vegetative soul, animals a vegetative and sentient soul, and humans a vegetative, sentient, and rational soul. We are happy to be in a long lineage that begins with Aristotle.

Finally, it is interesting to note that the Anglo-American legal tradition also encompasses an implicit three-level model to determine culpability. In the case of homicide, for example, three levels of culpability are distinguished: "involuntary manslaughter" is judged where the cause was reactive (when a person kills but "without the intent to kill or cause grievous bodily harm"), "voluntary manslaughter" for motivated, but not planned killing, and "murder" for premeditated behavior ("Murder occurs when the premeditated or malicious intent to kill another person is acted out and results in the death of the intended person"; see <http://en.wikipedia.org/wiki/Manslaughter_in_English_law>).

Learning and Memory

Each episode of behavior has physiological consequences for the animal (behavior requires energy to perform but can also result in resources being acquired, such as food), as well as psychological rewards and punishments that lead to changes to the nervous system itself. These latter forms of changes are typically classified as learning and memory (Kandel et al., 2014). Simply put, learning modifies neural systems according to experience, and memory stores such information for future use. Learning and memory are essentially an adaptive system for acquiring and storing information relevant to survival and reproduction. Animals are thereby able to modify their actions according to what has happened previously (Nairne et al., 2007).

Multiple kinds of specialized memory are likely to evolve because no one system can meet disparate demands (Sherry & Schacter, 1987; Tooby & Cosmides, 1992). For example, the graceful and gradual acquisition of habits is contradictory to the one-shot learning needed to remember particular events (these various types of memory are described later). Hence, specific forms of memory can be argued to have evolved to solve particular kinds of functional problems associated with specific classes of behavior. (Note that we ignore perceptual memory here—it is adapted to the recognition of regularly encountered features of the environment, and hence, as the name suggests, an aspect of perception, which takes place prior to behavioral control.) Thus we argue that memory and learning take a number of forms, each of which has arisen to serve a particular evolutionary function related to behavior production. Like behavior itself, new forms of memory and learning have become more complex with time. How each of these systems evolved is described along with the evolution of behavior production systems themselves in Section 2. Here, we present an overview of learning and memory as systems.

Generally speaking, memory requires alterations in brain structures (Squire, 1986). The most popular candidate site for memory storage is therefore the junctures, called synapses, that connect neurons. Changes in the transmission efficacy at the synapse or growth of new connections ("synaptic plasticity") are generally considered to be the cause of memory, and a particular pattern of synaptic usage or stimulation is believed to induce synaptic plasticity.

Memory is generally categorized into short- and long-term forms. Long-term memory is mechanically different from short-term modifications of neural networks, and probably evolved from short-term memory (Ginsburg & Jablonka, 2007a; Wells, 1968). Thus, a second step in memory evolution involved long-term stabilization of new associations via molecular consolidation at synapses (Kandel et al., 2000). A long-term memory passes through at least three steps in its life span: first it is encoded, then consolidated, and finally it is retrieved. During consolidation a memory can undergo both quantitative and qualitative changes in its neural connectivity. Quantitative changes involve modulation of the "strength" of existing connections between neurons, as they are repeatedly stimulated (called "habituation" or "sensitization"). However, such temporary modulations can also be fixed relatively permanently by molecular modifications at synapses, making the memory persist long-term.

Two basic types of long-term memory can be distinguished. The first class involves consolidated (i.e., chemical) changes to existing connections between neurons (the long-term versions of habituation and sensitization). A second class of long-term memory involves the formation of novel synaptic connections that link together neurons that previously were unconnected (hence the name "associative"; Hebb, 1949). This psychological association can link two sensory stimuli, or a sensory stimulus and a behavioral response, brought about by reinforcement. Inherent in the notion of associative learning is the assumption that the reinforcement of new behavior depends on internal evaluation. This is typically based on quantities of dopamine being released. This kind of so-called associative learning has been documented only in organisms with a central nervous system—that is, among nematodes and their successors, but not in sponges or placozoans, which came earlier (Abramson, 1994).

There are commonalities among these learning and memory systems due to shared evolutionary history, niche overlap, and general principles of information processing (Staddon, 2003). This is likely because neurons, even in the earliest animals with nervous systems, exhibit fundamental physiological properties common to those in all later animals, including excitatory and inhibitory postsynaptic potentials, and calcium-dependent release of neurotransmitters at synapses (Spencer, 1989). This implies that we can tell a coherent evolutionary story about developments on the input side of behavior—in these abilities to acquire and store new information—just as we plan to do with the output side, which consists of systems to control motor output from mental processing.

The Behavior Production Process

We can now put all of these insights together to describe how behavior production takes place. Figure 1.1 shows a simplified schematic of the essential elements. At the front end we have inputs and decoding—a process by which opportunities and threats are recognized and classified, and internal states computed (sometimes using stored memories), which we do not further explore here. These systems provide inputs to our three behavior production systems, the reactive, the motivated, and the executive control systems. An action selection process then picks a response to implement, depending on which behavioral option has the highest valuation (by a process not yet understood) and then the motor system is mobilized to produce behavior—again systems that we do not discuss here. Learning is loosely pictured as the psychological consequence of feedback from the resulting behavior. This cycle happens repeatedly to produce the behavior we see an animal exhibiting over time.

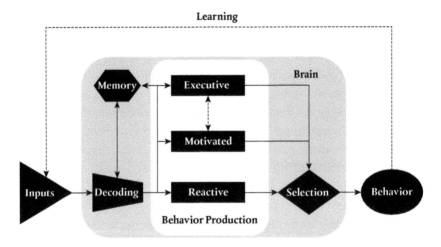

Fig. 1.1. The Behavior Production Process

With the overall process of behavior production now described, we can move to a consideration of what kinds of consequences behavior can have.

The Functions of Behavior

So far in this chapter we have set out how behavior is produced and controlled by three types of behavioral production system, using arguments not unlike those of many behavioral scientists. However, it was not just the behavior production systems that evolved; the adaptive functions that could be served by behavior have also evolved. Here we propose a new means of carving up the world of behavior via its ultimate function. We suggest that behavior has been designed by evolutionary processes to put animals into new situations with respect to the world, with three sorts of functional advantage. (As we will see later, these distinctions are independent of the levels of control.) First, animals could improve the state of their own bodies—for example by consuming foods, avoiding predators and parasites, keeping themselves warm and hydrated, and by engaging in reproduction. Such behavior produces immediate survival and reproduction benefits.

The second sort of state that animals can get themselves into is one where they have changed their relationship with the world such that they are better able to get evolutionary benefits in the future. They might, for example, invest in a pair-bond so as to be able to bring up offspring more successfully, fight to establish a territory such that they can benefit from its produce, or invest in improving their status so as to get access to resources in future.

Finally, animals can act to change the state of their own abilities. They can invest in learning about the world and their own influence within it, thus gaining skills and abilities that can eventually also be parlayed into functional benefits. We call these three types of end-state that animals can seek physiological, situational, and aptitudinal (Aunger & Curtis, 2008). Table 1.3 sets out these three types of behavioral functions in terms of the end-states that they produce.

Our first category of "physiological" end-states provides reproductive or survival benefits directly. These end-states tend to be focused on the condition of the body, because gaining immediate evolutionary benefits involves the acquisition of some resource, or improves the survival chances of the body. This first level of behavioral function is thus aimed at getting resources into the body and wastes out (eating, drinking, excreting), keeping the body within a range of conditions for optimal functioning (move to suitable air, temperature, light, humidity conditions), avoiding physiological damage (projectiles, cliff edges, parasites), and exchanging gametes (copulation).

The second way to use behavior to get adaptive benefits is to manipulate one's environment so as to put oneself into a "situation" where the acquisition of benefits becomes more likely in the future. Effort can be directed at improving the physical world (e.g., by finding or building safe, productive habitats), the biological world (e.g., by caching food or by cleaning up pathogen habitats), or the social world (e.g., by investing in offspring, by investing in a mate so they will help rear children, or by investing in improving social status so as to get better access to resources). Biologists refer to this type of behavior as "niche construction" (Odling-Smee et al., 2003).

Our third category of behavioral function is "aptitudinal," and is even more indirectly related to evolutionary benefits. In this case behavior serves to improve the

Table 1.3: Categories of Behavioral End-states

End-state	Behavioral function	Focus
Physiological	Changes evolutionary benefits themselves (i.e., provides benefits directly, such as offspring or resources for survival)	Body
Situational	Changes relationship of agent to the world such that its ability to secure future evolutionary benefits is increased (e.g., access to territory or increased status)	World
Aptitudinal	Changes capability to carry out tasks more effectively in future (e.g., gain future situational or physiological benefits by acquiring knowledge or skill)	Brain

actor's own skills and abilities to carry out physiological or environmental tasks more effectively in the future (for example, through practising skills like play hunting). The focus of aptitudinal behavior is thus on changing the state of the brain, where memory and skill-based knowledge resides (Deci & Ryan, 1985; Maslow, 1943; White, 1959). (It is true that almost any behavior is likely to be accompanied by learning. However, this does not make all behavior aptitudinal because the primary function of those behaviors is to achieve other kinds of end-states, rather than learning as an end in itself.)

This analysis suggests, then, that behavior improves any of three kinds of end-states: those that improve the state of the body, the state of the world, or the state of the behavioral control system (i.e., brain). These three sorts of end-state define the ways in which behavior can be distinguished functionally, and therefore should reflect differences in the ways they have been naturally selected over time.

This approach thus postulates three types of behavior, valued according to their past history of contribution to biological fitness. This approach is in accord with expected utility theory in economics (Savage, 1954; von Neumann & Morgenstern, 1944) and expectancy value models in psychology (Bandura, 1986; Fishbein & Ajzen, 1975), where the value of a behavior is determined by the odds that the behavior will put an animal in a particular state, multiplied by the value it attaches to being in that state. In our case, value is measured not in terms of utility or perceived costs and benefits, but in terms of *evolutionary* benefits. We argue that end-states can be categorized by the nature of their relationship to evolutionary benefits: direct provision (physiological), indirect provision (situational), and even more indirect provision (aptitudinal).

Of course, the value calculation that animals use when choosing a particular kind of behavior cannot be evolutionary fitness. Rather, evolution has provided a reward system to guide animals toward those kinds of behaviors that enhanced the fitness of their ancestors: unsurprisingly, natural selection has tuned brains to prefer adaptive over maladaptive behavior. Reward reinforced behavior that tended to get animals into end-states that led to enhanced fitness in their evolutionary past (what those pasts were is a topic for later in this book).

The distinction between physiological and other end-states can be seen in brain imaging studies in humans. Separate systems evaluate choices between immediate biological rewards and those delayed in time (McClure et al., 2004), even when the delay is only a few minutes (McClure et al., 2007). Different brain systems are involved in valuing these different rewards, so, at any remove from the present, there is a clear demarcation in the brain's calculations between immediate and future benefits. The result of this bias, in behavioral terms, can be seen in the paradox of temporal discounting: faced with a choice of $10 today or $11 tomorrow, people tend to choose the lesser quantity today. However, when the same individuals are faced with the choice between $10 a year from now and $11 a year and a day from now (the same time difference), they choose to wait and consume the greater quantity (Frederich et al., 2002).

Similarly, the division between aptitudinal and other kinds of end-states is supported by the literature on human intrinsic motivation (Deci, 1975; Ryan & Deci, 2000). Intrinsic motivation occurs when behavior is performed for its own sake rather than to obtain material or social reinforcement (i.e., extrinsic motivation). Internally motivated behaviors tend to be felt as pleasurable, and are typically called playful, creative, or curious (Lepper et al., 1973). Tangible rewards tend to have a negative effect on intrinsic motivation—that is, providing people with money, food, or other inducements to do a task they find pleasurable in and of itself tends to reduce their willingness to perform it (Deci, 1971; E. L Deci & Ryan, 1985; Lepper & Henderlong, 2000) or to do so less creatively (Amabile, 1996). This suggests that some behavior is performed for the functional reward of skill-based learning for learning's sake—just the function we have postulated for aptitudinal behavior.

Our proposal that there are three types of behavioral function that serve to get organisms into three types of end-state has similarities with a number of approaches in the literature. First, splitting types of behavior production into different kinds of end-states has been common in psychology since the beginning. Murray (1938), for example, argued that primary (or viscerogenic) needs are biological or innate, while secondary (psychogenic) needs either derive from these biological needs or are learned. Examples of primary needs included food, water, air, sex, and avoidance of pain, while achievement, power, recognition, acquisition, dominance, aggression, autonomy, affiliation, rejection, nurturance, and play were considered secondary. Similarly, Dollard and Miller (1950) argued that secondary needs are associated with satisfying primary needs. In educational and occupational psychology, intrinsic motivation is distinguished from extrinsic ("instrumental") motivation, contrasting inherent pleasure with extrinsic rewards or incentives (such as money). Intrinsically motivated action directly satisfies the need, while in the extrinsic case, behavior satisfies an intermediate goal, which can indirectly lead to the satisfaction of a need (Deci, 1975).

We argue, however, that the important difference between classes of end-states is not one of innateness versus learning (Deci, 1975; Logan, 1999; Murray, 1938), nor is it one of different learning mechanisms (Dollard & Miller, 1950). Nor do we believe that all behavior is motivated (as suggested by both the occupational and educational psychology literatures). We suggest that *the fundamental distinction between production types is their evolutionary function*, not some aspect of their psychological mechanism. Whether the information used to produce the behavior is innate or learned is not the issue. The difference between kinds of end-states lies in the types of selection process that caused the different kinds of behavior to evolve in the first place: one class is based on a direct association between the behavior and a fitness benefit, the others via more indirect relationships.

We have now presented our approach to understanding how behavior is produced, in terms of three kinds of control systems and three kinds of functional benefits of behavior. Putting these together will provide us with the BPUs we seek. But to do this correctly we have to uncover the actual history of behavior production in animals that gave rise to humans. Our psychological facilities did not arise de novo; they are the result of a long process of evolution in our phylogeny. The steps we took to reach our current level of behavioral complexity must be uncoverable, not through archaeology, but through examining the behavioral capacities of species ancestral to ourselves. Since we cannot actually meet and test these ancestors, we need at least to be able to tell a plausible story that fits with the evidence we do have. The story of these adaptive increases in complexity is what we tell next.

SECTION 2

AN EVOLUTIONARY NARRATIVE

With these preliminaries now out of the way, we can tell the evolutionary story of the transitions that have led from a simple way of life to the complex niche that contemporary humans inhabit. Much of the remainder of this book consists of a description and justification of these steps in the history of behavior production. We shall see that this offers us principled ways of carving up the various classes of behavior, and hence of predicting the existence of corresponding behavior production units (BPUs) in brains. At the same time, we will tell the story of the how learning and memory changed at each step to support these developments.

Chapter 2, "Living in the Moment," deals with the evolution of reactive behaviors; Chapter 3, "Getting Directions," tells the story of motivated behavior; Chapter 4, "Changing the World for the Better," discusses the executive control of behavior.

Of course, as we have said, because behavior does not fossilize, we cannot reconstruct the behavioral abilities of our ancestors directly. We can only make inferences based on extant animals that may or may not be representative of the behavioral capabilities of animals at a certain point in our evolutionary past. The sequence shown is therefore hypothetical. It is, however, consistent with the evidence from the behavioral repertoires in extant animals with ancestors at various points in phylogenetic time and with major developments in the evolution of brains. Given that contemporary species have had many millions of years (in some cases) to evolve new abilities since that point of divergence, our argument regarding the timing of new types of production systems is based not on the most advanced contemporary exemplar in some clade, but rather on the inferred qualities of a prototypical ancestral species in that group.

This section of the book consists of a description of these steps in the history of behavior production, summarizing the way in which the animal lineages leading to humans gained increasing control over the production of their behavior.

CHAPTER 2

LIVING IN THE MOMENT

Because behavior is work, in the classic physical sense of being energy-expending, there will be selection pressure on any behavior to make that behavior energy efficient—that is, to achieve evolutionary benefits at minimum cost. An animal's default state is therefore no behavior—that is, a state in which there is no active involvement with the environment (i.e., "resting"). This section is about how behavior has evolved additional complexity over time. Our account of the steps in increasing sophistication of control and achievement of different functional end-states is represented in Table 2.1. Indeed, this table summarizes our primary claims about the history through which the animal lineages leading to humans gained control over production of their behavior. Each step is associated with the behavioral novelty that identifies it, along with the animal group that first exhibited that type of behavior classified according to the level of control through which it works and the end-states it achieves. We provide examples of proposed BPUs in italics. The table also provides information concerning the kind of nervous system exhibited by the animal group associated with that development, relevant developments in learning or memory, and the date that group arose in evolutionary history.

The earliest form of animal movement was passive motility (e.g., in sponges). This is not behavior, by our definition, since there is no controlled interaction with the environment. Being buffeted around in wind or water currents has some adaptive advantages over a sessile way of life, yielding a greater likelihood of encountering nutrients and of leaving waste products behind, but can also put animals in danger of ending up in unsuitable or hostile environments, or prey to predators and parasites. Thus, even passive movement induces selection for an ability to respond appropriately to opportunities and threats. Further, even in a state of rest, an animal's energy stores will become depleted by metabolic activity. For this reason, too, an animal will face selection pressure to increase its rate of contact with food—that is, either to propel itself through the environment, or to have the environment move through its body (e.g., sponges sucking in ocean water) until an opportunity to eat affords itself.

The selection pressure for locomotion led to the advent of specialized organs such as villi and flagellae. These appendages provided the ability to direct movement,

Table 2.1: The Evolution of Animal Behavior in the Human Lineage

Type (or Level) of Control	Production Class (with example BPUs)	End-State	Origin*	Learning/Memory	Nervous System	Behavioral Novelty
Reactive	Reflexes (startle, suckle)	Physiological	Bilateria [Cnidaria] (650 MYA)	Habituation/sensitization	Nerve net	Algorithmic responses to stimuli
	Exploration	Aptitudinal		Classical conditioning		Movement without external stimulus
	Instincts (shoaling, migration)	Situational	Protostomes [Annelids, Arthropods, Mollusks] (550 MYA)	Operant conditioning	Center/periphery (nerve cord with ganglion + transverse nerves)	Cue-induced behavior complexes (i.e., "chunked" sequences)
Motivated	Drives (lust, hunger, disgust, fear)	Physiological	Chordates/Vertebrates [Bony fish] (450 MYA)	Affective learning/Emotional memory	Myelinated, lobed brain, 1) three-layer cortex	Controlled responses to local circumstances (goal-direction)
	Interests (nonsocial-play, curiosity)	Aptitudinal		Procedural memory		Skill acquisition/Motivated search
	Ecological Emotions (hoard, create)	Situational	Amniotes [Reptiles] (400 MYA)	Cognitive maps	Enlarged, differentiated forebrain	Territory-related (proto-social) behaviors

Table 2.1: (continued)

Type (or Level) of Control	Production Class (with example BPUs)	End-State	Origin*	Learning/Memory	Nervous System	Behavioral Novelty
	Social Emotions (love, affiliation, status)	Situational	Mammalia (250 MYA)	Vicarious conditioning	Neocortex (six neuronal layers)	Behavior contingent on other agents (strategic goals)
	Interest (social play)	Aptitudinal				
Executive	Implicit Planning	Physiological and situational	Primates (60 MYA)	Abstract concept learning/declarative (episodic/semantic) memory	Expanded prefrontal cortex, well-developed hemispheres	Ordered goal-achievement sequences (plan execution)
	Explicit Planning		Humans (7 MYA)	Reflective learning/Autobiographical memory	Brodmann area 10	Symbol-based behavior (language, art, music, ritual)

* MYA = million years ago

enhancing the likelihood of coming into contact with nearby resources or cues (biologically salient stimuli). These enabled the most primitive forms of behavior produced by simple systems in which an animal perceives a cue and reacts to it using motor control. The behavior produced in this way comes in three classes, depending on the end-state produced, which we label "reflex," "exploration," and "instinct."

In what follows, we present the evolution of behavior using a common format. We begin each section by identifying the animal clade that first exhibited the new psychological and behavioral features of interest; next we say something about the state of life-forms at that stage; and then move on to descriptions of the new classes of behaviors as well as the novel types of learning and memory associated with these new BPUs.

Bilateria

In the waters of the Earth about three-quarters of a billion years ago, a primitive form of life, having a body shape with a particular orientation (i.e., not spherical), but that was the same on both sides (i.e., radial symmetry), was either swimming about or attached to some underwater surface. These were hydra and related organisms like jellyfish and sea anemones, collectively known as Cnideria. These organisms controlled movement using a simple nerve network without any higher-order structure.

Reflexes

By the time these early Metazoans evolved, animals could perform random, self-propelled searches of their local environment. Of course, moving around will eventually lead an animal to come into contact with objects. Fast-acting responses therefore must have been present in the first metazoa, probably as an inheritance from unicellular forms of life. For example, Cnideria, the earliest class of animals with a nervous system, convulse their bodies rapidly after bumping into solid objects. This type of behavior is produced by a system called a reflex. Reflexes are a class of BPUs that, in later-evolving animals, cause behavior such as the annelid escape reflex, the emetic reflex in a crocodile, the cervical contraction and the suckle reflex in mammals, and the human blink reflex.

Reflexes are simple reactive algorithms: detect an opportunity or threat and act appropriately. They result in a primary benefit such as the ingestion of resources, the avoidance of bodily damage, or the duplication of genes (e.g., through fissioning or cloning). Reflexes are thus cue-generated behaviors that allow an animal to attain physiological end-states (as discussed in Chapter 1). Evolution will tend to build in such rigid responses when a situation can be identified with precision in which there is a unique solution, and when the risks associated with rigid responses are negligible and/or the costs of error are high (Staddon, 2003). Single, stereotypical motor responses to specific stimuli can be performed through the three-step "reflex arc" of sensation, conveyance, and response (Dewey, 1896). There is also a tight relationship between the intensity and duration of the stimulus and the intensity and duration of the response (McFarland, 1998). Repeated reactive behavior in the presence of an external attractive or aversive gradient results in what behaviorists call "taxis," or a simple change in direction in response to an environmental gradient (Staddon, 2003).

Many invertebrate behaviors qualify as reflexes. The behavioral repertoire of the earliest multicellular animals typically consisted of random movements plus reflexive behavior. Animals would begin randomly moving about and when contact with a resource (e.g., food item) was achieved, reflexes could operate (e.g., consumption). Lack of food stimulates random searching behavior in medusas (a type of jellyfish), for example (Ginsburg & Jablonka, 2009). Contact with dangers cause withdrawal movements. The relationship between the action and the evolutionary benefit is immediate and clear. Reflexes are thus the starting point for the evolution of behavioral complexity, and the baseline in behavioral control.

Reflexes in invertebrates are limited by the simplicity of their neural systems, where neurons have mostly fixed roles (Swanson, 2003). However, reflexes persist as a means of producing behavior in even the most complex animals. For example, the diving reflex is a BPU that involves peripheral vasoconstriction, anaerobic metabolic activity, and stored oxygen use; it lasts for as long as a mammal is underwater (P. J. Butler & Jones, 1997).

Reflexes are thus a class of reactive BPUs that arose in bilateria to put animals in improved physiological end-states.

Habituation and Sensitization

Even the simplest forms of response to stimuli need not always be the same, thanks to learning. The mechanisms of habituation and sensitization are temporary, quantitative modulations of existing neural connections, resulting in transient selective stabilization of recently used neural pathways. This kind of synaptic plasticity is found even in early bilaterians such as the cnidarians we have been discussing (Haralson & Haralson, 1988; Johnson & Wuensch, 1994). If contacts with environmental objects occur multiple times within a relatively short period of time, the response can be deadened, or "habituated" (i.e., learning *not* to respond to an irrelevant or unimportant stimulus). Habituation can be discriminated from simple motor fatigue by being specific to a particular kind of stimulus, dishabituation by a strong contradictory stimulus, and by a savings effect (i.e., a quicker reduction in responsiveness after repeated sessions of habituation; Kandel et al., 2000). This kind of learning is adaptive because quickly repeated stimuli of the same kind are likely to be due to the same cause, which, if it hasn't caused a harm or benefit already, is unlikely to do so in subsequent contacts. Conversely, with sensitization the magnitude of a response to a repeated stimulus is increased, or its threshold is lowered. Following sensitization, very little stimulation is then required to produce large effects. Presumably this is because repetition in this case suggests an increased threat or benefit. For example, irritation of one's skin can become painful with continued repetition, suggesting the possibility of real damage. Similarly, withdrawal from a predator becomes more rapid, and movement toward a food source becomes faster (Ginsburg & Jablonka, 2007a).

Exploration

The second type of BPU in Table 2.1 is *exploration* (we will italicize the names of individual BPUs throughout the book). Even during times when there was no biologically significant situation present, animals could acquire some benefits from simply moving through the environment. Cnideria accomplish this by continuously engaging in gentle whole body convulsions. In this way, they could acquire information about their local surroundings for later use. *Exploration* is a BPU that is random with respect to resources or dangers, so it is relatively inefficient at producing end-states that provide immediate benefits. However, *exploratory* behavior can have benefits in the future. In complex, stochastic environments, *exploration* can reduce uncertainty about the amount or location of resources, or the presence of dangers or escape routes through information gathering in animals that can store memories (Inglis, 2000) This is shown by the fact that when an animal is put in an unfamiliar environment, it engages in *exploratory* behavior until it gets a good knowledge of the area within its range (Nissen, 1930; Shillito, 1963; Wolfe, 1969; Wood-Gush & Vestergaard, 1991). Interest is shown in things that are new, complex, and unfamiliar (Berlyne, 1960).

But as the degree of uncertainty about the environment is reduced by each new unit of information, additional units produce less improvement in knowledge about local conditions. Additional effort expended on *exploration* is thus associated with decreasing marginal returns. Eventually, reduced energy stores will also lead to a cessation of *exploration* (Huber et al., 2011; Toates, 1986). *Explore* can be regarded as a behavior production system that puts animals in an aptitudinal end-state. It is enacted when animals have sufficient energy stores and no pressing emergencies (Nissen, 1930; Panksepp, 1998).

Exploration evolved in some cases into a positive preference for new stimuli. For example, earthworms (Annelids) exhibit a tendency to *explore* in the sense that when placed at a T-junction in a maze, they will on the first opportunity make their way down one arm, but when presented with the same opportunity again, show a high probability of taking the other option (Dember & Richman, 1989). This neophilic tendency disappears when the worm's circumpharyngeal ganglia are removed, suggesting that this level of behavioral control is associated with centralized nervous systems (Wayner & Zellner, 1958), and so probably occurred in evolution after the original appearance of random *exploration* in animals with more simple neural nets such as Cnideria. *Exploration* is thus a reactive BPU that arose in bilateria to put animals into improved aptitudinal end-states.

Classical Conditioning

Exploring one's environment brings one into contact with new information that could be adaptive to store for later use. Classical conditioning enables learning about relationships among features of the environment, such as a bell ringing and the presentation of food in Pavlov's classic experiment with dogs (Pavlov, 1927). (Although we are arguing that this ability arose early on in animal evolution, it has been studied most in mammals, so many of the examples here will be from these later-evolving animals.)

In this relatively simple kind of learning, the "naïve" animal begins with no particular response to presentation of a stimulus, but comes to pair one external event with another through the repeated experience of one being temporally closely related to the other. This relationship would initially be unexpected, but once the connection has been made, the animal makes a similar response to presentation of the first stimulus as it would normally to the second. In Pavlov's classic experiment, dogs initially began to salivate when food was presented, but through an experimental protocol, heard a bell ring just before the food was presented, until salivation began with hearing the bell rather than presentation of the food itself. In this way, a stimulus that previously had little effect on behavior (a "neutral" stimulus) becomes able to produce a reflexive response. This is a simple means by which long-term associative memories can be formed.

An alternative means is imprinting, a specialized form of biologically prepared, one-shot, critical-period learning. For example, the first large active object perceived thirteen to sixteen hours after hatching is taken by young geese to be their "mother." This kind of rapid learning, apparently independent of the consequences of behavior—as when hatchlings imprinted on the ethologist Conrad Lorenz—has been documented in invertebrates such as insects (Lorenz, 1937). Obviously this quicker kind of learning is more likely when the conditions are stable in natural environments, thus lowering the likelihood of imprinting on the wrong stimulus.

Simple animals exhibit the same behavior. For example, aquatic planaria (flatworms) exposed simultaneously to the scents of injured planaria and sunfish for two days learned thereafter to avoid the scent of sunfish when exposed only to that scent (Wisenden & Millard, 2001). A common example is fear conditioning, in which an animal acquires fear responses to a previously neutral stimulus which has been paired with an aversive stimulus, such as an electric shock to the foot.

This conditioned response is often generalized, such that the animal will respond in similar fashion to a stimulus that resembles the original one. In Pavlov's dogs, for example, an animal trained to salivate to a particular tone also salivated to tones of other frequencies, but the more different the frequency from the original conditioned stimulus, the less the dog salivated to it. Thus, the magnitude or likelihood of the generalized response depends on the degree of similarity to the original.

However, Pavlov also discovered that a dog will not continue to salivate to the sound of the bell if the bell is heard many times without any food being presented afterwards. (In animal behavior terms, the conditioning is extinguished.) Obviously, this kind of learning is desirable when a behavior is no longer necessary, due to changed conditions in the environment. Planaria can do this too (Baxter & Kimmel, 1963; Jacobson et al., 1967). Although it is not yet clear whether Cnidaria can do associative learning (Papini, 2011), they have the genes for neurogenesis, suggesting that they may be able to acquire new associative connections during their lifespans (Galliot et al., 2009).

Protostomes

The next major development in animals was a body that was not only bilateral, but which has a central, fluid-filled body cavity in which organs are suspended. These were the protostomes (e.g., arthropods, roundworms, mollusks, and chordates), which first evolved roughly 550 million years ago. Protostomes tend to have a concentration of nerves at one end (i.e., a ganglionic mass or simple brain) and a nerve cord running the length of the body. They also have a circulatory system, various sensory systems (e.g., for touch and sound), organs (muscles), and a mouth at one end and an anus at the other; some could even reproduce sexually.

Instincts

We define instincts as an ability to accomplish behavior that puts an animal in a better position for survival or reproduction, without a directly linked physiological benefit. We suggest they arose around the time that the early protostomes appeared. We have chosen to use the word "instincts" for BPUs associated with cue-generated behaviors that leave the animal in a situational end-state, because such BPUs provide evolutionary benefits only indirectly. For example, flatworms (early protostomes) "know"— without previous learning—to use chemical cues from injured conspecifics to warn them of a risk of imminent predation, a situation from which they flee (Wisenden & Millard, 2001). Similarly, shoaling fish instinctively follow their nearest neighbors more closely when predators are nearby, probably because such defensive maneuvers have tended to reduce predation rates in the past (Tien et al., 2004). Instincts were apparently harder to evolve than reflexes or *exploration* (which evolved earlier), probably due to the lack of a physiological signal on which natural selection could act.

Sometimes getting into a better position or state requires engaging in a number of behaviors in sequence. For example, cuckoo chicks, on finding themselves sharing a nest with eggs of the host species, respond by pushing them out by means of a complex series of actions, thus improving their state by eliminating the competition for food. Winter migration in a variety of perching birds—a very lengthy sequence of behaviors in some cases—comes at an energetic cost, but it puts the bird in ecological circumstances where it is better able to acquire evolutionary benefits such as food and improved survival. Migration is triggered by the environmental cue of photoperiod (the ratio of light to dark during the day). As photoperiod falls, birds prepare by accumulating fat reserves; when wind conditions are good and fat stores sufficient, their flight begins (Wiltschko & Wiltschko, 2003).

Landing after a long migratory flight is a consequence of conditions in a prior environment at some potentially considerable remove in time. To achieve this end, behaviors must be chunked, with the entire sequence being automatically executed once initiated by a cue. This represents a new level of behavioral control.

How could costly behaviors that lead to an end-state without immediate evolutionary benefit have evolved in the first place? We can think of two mechanisms. First, a new genetic variant could have arisen which modified a brain such as to introduce a behavioral bias that happened to leave a coelomate in a situational end-state. Because such a state was advantageous compared to alternatives, animals with that variant were naturally selected. Second, the environment could have changed without an accompanying change in the behavioral phenotype. By chance the old behavior still produced indirect benefits, so selection was maintained in the new environment for the old behavior—the process known as exaptation, or the chance substitution of a new adaptive function for the one that originally caused the behavior to evolve (Gould & Vrba, 1982).

Compound instinctual behaviors, like the "hygienic" removal of diseased brood in honeybees (Arathi et al., 2000), probably arose through the accumulation of genetic mutations attaching a new behavior to a stimulus from a previous behavior. Over time, genes to support additional behaviors could be stuck together to form complex sequences (Avital & Jablonka, 2000). Similarly, reflexes can be compounded to form instinctual behaviors. For example, fish can learn to associate cues of danger (e.g., conspecific injury signals) with predator cues (Brosnan et al., 2003). They can also learn to associate habitat cues (e.g., water temperature) with presence of the predator (i.e., predator habitat recognition). Both of these mechanisms lead to flight strategies (a predator escape reflex). In combination, they produce an instinct to evade risky habitats, whether predators are present or not (Kelley & Magurran, 2003). Through either of these simple learning mechanisms, instincts appear to be modifications of individual reflexes or chunkings of reflex chains—executed to achieve a new kind of end-state, acquired through a form of biologically prepared learning. These chains, originally linked by psychological tendencies, can, over generations, be assimilated into rigorously performed, genetically informed strategies (a process called the Baldwin effect; Baldwin, 1896).

Instincts are thus a class of reflexive BPUs that arose in protostomes that put animals into improved situational end-states.

Operant Conditioning

What sorts of learning mechanisms are associated with instincts? Reactive behavior depends heavily on environmental regularities to ensure that the animal winds up in a beneficial situation. The internal representation of end-states is relatively simple, so the animal can be readily tricked by a change in circumstance. Novel situations can therefore lead to maladaptive outcomes as, for example, when graylag geese become imprinted on an ethologist (Lorenz, 1937). If the animal keeps winding up in the wrong kind of situation, such less-than-adaptive outcomes can eventually modify the mechanisms producing reactive behavior.

The formation of instinct chains—complex behavioral sequences, each of which is triggered by performance of the previous one—requires this novel form of associative learning: operant conditioning. While classical conditioning is about learning associations between facets of the environment, operant conditioning is learning about what follows from a behavior. The organism acts, and that action has effects: these consequences—positive or negative in terms of the animal's fitness—determine whether or not that response is more or less likely to occur again. To create a complex instinct, completion of each step of the chain of events needs to be rewarded so that the prior action serves as the reinforced cue for the next.

This in turn required the development of a psychological "reward" system (Rolls, 1999). Rewards provide a proximate signal of the adaptive utility of the behavior, even when the eventual benefit is beyond the perceptive ability of an animal. Likewise, negatively valenced rewards (possibly perceived as punishments) discourage maladaptive action (Wise, 2004). The consequence is Thorndike's law of effect, which states that a rewarded behavior is likely to be repeated (Thorndike, 1901). Operant conditioning provides the mechanism: using reinforcement (or punishment) to increase (or decrease) a behavior. Note that such learning is not based on a cognitive understanding of the situation, or on one-shot problem solving (e.g., an "aha" moment involving reasoning). Rather, it is a more gradual process like its counterpart, classical conditioning. In effect, the animal has to learn what behavioral response in a given situation is most likely to produce beneficial outcomes through repeated experience.

A number of factors can influence how quickly and strongly an operant association is made. For example, fast feedback is more effective than slow, and if the consequence follows the response more consistently after successive instances, then the ability of that situation or stimulus to induce conditioning is increased. An association is also more likely to persist (i.e., become habitual) if it has been created by unpredictable periods between performance and the reward or punishment (Dickinson, 1985).

The sea hare—an extremely well-researched invertebrate (*Aplysia californica*)—is known to exhibit habituation and sensitization, but also both classical conditioning and operant conditioning (Brembs et al., 2002; Kupfermann, 1974). When searching for food, the sea hare takes random bites, even when no external stimuli are present to trigger a bite (Kupfermann, 1974). When the animal fails to grasp food, the esophageal nerve shows little activity. However, when the animal grasps and swallows seaweed, bursts of electrical activity in the esophageal nerve accompany the ingestion of food. The activity is rewarded with a dose of dopamine (Brembs et al., 2002), the transmitter for the reward signal (Nargeot et al., 1999). Dopamine is also considered to be the prime transmitter for reward-related signals in humans and other mammals (O'Doherty et al., 2001).

One of the significant consequences of the ability to learn from experience via operant conditioning is that habits can be formed. Habits are learned automatic responses to environmental or psychological cues to action (W. Wood & Neal, 2007; Yin & Knowlton, 2006). Habits are important in the description of human behavior: up to 50 percent of everyday activity has been attributed to habitual performance (Ouellette & Wood, 1998). The considerable reliance upon learning in humans, even for acquiring basic life skills (Robert Boyd et al., 2011)—extending to the development of a novel stage of continued dependence in the life history, adolescence (Bogin, 2009)—means that humans tend not to exhibit many instinctive behaviors, but rather cope via a wide variety of habits, which can be thought of in this context as "learned instincts." Many everyday activities, around commonly arising situations, are likely to be habitual: brushing our teeth, driving a car, repetitive tasks at work, and so on (W. Wood et al., 2002).

The behaviors that we have covered so far—*exploration*, reflexes, and instincts—are all reactive, that is, they were designed by evolution to respond directly to the environment in which they evolved, and have only limited flexibility via biologically prepared associative learning (Seligman & Hager, 1972). However, if environments change more rapidly than genes can accommodate through mutation, or in directions for which learning is not prepared, behaviors can become maladaptive. Natural selection would have put pressure on species living in dynamically changing niches to find more flexible means of controlling their behavior. As we will see, this means was goal-direction.

CHAPTER 3

GETTING DIRECTIONS

Thus far we have been discussing animals that produce behavior by reacting to cues that an evolutionarily important situation is present. However, sometime during the evolution of the first vertebrates around 450 million years ago, a new, more complex form of behavior production arose. Animals became able to persist in a particular course of behavior in the face of cues to respond otherwise. For example, gravid snakes bypass opportunities to eat, even when hungry, to continue to bask and so maintain a high internal temperature suited for gestation (Gregory et al., 1999; Lourdais et al., 2002). The ability to initiate or maintain a course of action toward a goal, independent of external cues, requires motivation (Berridge, 2004; Franken, 2001; Kleinginna Jr. & Kleinginna, 1981; Weiner, 2013). A motivated action differs from a reflex or instinct because it is not a reaction to an external stimulus; it is the result of an interaction between stimuli and internal states, or what we call indicators (often a psychological or physiological state; Bindra, 1978; Toates, 1986; Wong, 2000). Motivated action implies the ability to ignore immediate benefits in favor of pursuing longer-term goals. Such goals can be physiological, situational, or aptitudinal (see Table 2.1). To pursue a goal an animal must be have mental representations of at least some aspects of the world (J. Wood & Grafman, 2003). One kind of mental representation is a goal, or conception of a desirable state of the world (what we gloss as an end-state achieved through behavior). Because motivated animals can work to meet goals, motivated behavior exhibits a new degree of flexibility. Whereas *exploration*, reflexes and instincts are reactive, motivated behaviors are *proactive* because they are performed to some degree independently of the local causal environment (Adolphs, 2005). Goals are thus internal representations of the end-states animals seek to achieve, and for which they will work (although they need not be conscious of having such goals; Rolls, 1999). In most cases, goal achievement should satisfy one of the animal's needs—that is, one of its evolutionary requirements (as set by its niche) for survival or reproduction.

Although the dopaminergic reward system was invented earlier (as we saw in Chapter 2), it was at first coupled with nervous systems that didn't allow for the internal representation of end-states; reward was simply coupled with an association to current behavior or the current situation in early forms of operant conditioning.

The time frame for association making was limited to the immediate context. With a true motivational system, the reward system is coupled to a more sophisticated ability to mentally represent the world, in the form of psychologically "present" but temporally distant end-states toward which an animal might put forth effort to reach.

Goal fulfillment is thus an experience for which an animal will work, while a punishment is an end-state which an animal will work to avoid (Rolls, 2005). Animals pursue goals that are valued by the dopaminergic reward system, and particular end-states are valued because they have been successful in promoting survival and reproduction in the past (Tooby & Cosmides, 1992). In effect, what is psychologically valued is what has been selected for in the animal's lineage (Wong, 2000). We argue that the evolution of rewards coupled to goals allowed goal-directed behavior to become physically possible: organisms became willing to persist in behavior without immediate physical benefit because they were provided with psychological rewards (Rolls, 1999; Schultz, 2002). These rewards could change the value of indicators (internal states associated with particular situations), suggesting that the gap between a need and the animal's current state was decreasing. The reward system thus now functions as a system for tracking progress toward a goal, rather than simply a signal of whether an individual behavior was beneficial or not.

Further, once animals had the ability to pursue goals, it was a natural extension to use the reward system to predict returns from future behavior, based on prior experience with that behavior in similar circumstances (Montague & Berns, 2002). For behavior to be guided by future outcomes, an animal must be able to value expected consequences by their likely contribution to biological fitness. But fitness-related benefits come in many forms, such as reproductive opportunities, food, territory, and money. To evaluate behaviors that may return any combination of these (e.g., immediate copulation versus nest building), it is necessary to have a common psychological "currency" (Cabanac, 1992; Rolls, 1999).

In humans, dopamine activations in the striatum and dorsolateral and orbital frontal cortex are known to discriminate between different kinds and amounts of reward, and therefore might serve as this currency (Montague & Berns, 2002; Sugrue et al., 2005; Z. M. Williams et al., 2004; Yamada et al., 2013). Since dopamine activation can arise from actual receipts of rewards and well as the mere *expectation* of rewards, the behavior selection system can compare the consequences of potential behavioral choices with respect to their likely rewards. Then, through discrimination learning, the behavioral option associated with the greatest likelihood of reinforcement would be chosen (Logan, 1999).

Predicted rewards can also lead animals to prepare for movement. In this way, dopaminergic activity may guide behavior toward rewarding activity that ameliorates *needs* (Schultz, 2002). The motivational system thus functions to inform the animal about its present deviation from a desirable end-state, and guides it toward reaching this state by directing adaptive behavior based on past history and information stored in long-term memory. It evaluates inputs on the basis of the animal's previous history of learning, which includes past triggers of response, the route taken, and the end-states attained by such behavior. Neuroscientists now call this the "predictive" brain, because it acts to minimize, with every action, the difference between the state it currently perceives itself to be in and that it expected to achieve via its most recent behavior, thus keeping the animal efficiently on track to achieve goals (Friston, 2010; Hawkins & Blakeslee, 2004).

In sum, the ability to pursue goals, coupled with the dopaminergic reward system, enabled vertebrates to simulate the consequences of different actions, prioritize possible actions based on their expected returns, and select the one likely to produce the highest return, even if that outcome could only be achieved through a sequence of actions. Motivated animals thus have the ability to make use of stored information about past conditions (i.e., an indicator) to determine their current behavior. The action selection mechanism constantly compares the current state of the animal against an abstract standard: an internally represented, remembered goal to achieve a desired end-state, toward which the behavior of the animal is aiming.

We argue that motivated control over behavior must be restricted to animals with hierarchically organized nervous systems, that is, vertebrates. Only vertebrates have brains with multiple centralized ganglia as well as peripheral nerve circuits (Streidter, 2005; Swanson, 2003). Indeed, the basal ganglia may have evolved in vertebrates to enable selection among needs (psychological representations of tasks related to an evolutionarily significant aspect of an animal's ecological niche); this selection requires goal-directed behavior (Redgrave et al., 1999).

Animals with hierarchically structured nervous systems thus acquired the ability to internally represent end-states, leading to the first "mental Rubicon" for behavior production: goal-direction. This allows some kinds of information (stimuli) to be ignored, but also allows new ways for information inherited from the animal's own past (i.e., remembered states) to be put to use in determining current behavior (Ginsburg & Jablonka, 2007a, 2007b).

Vertebrates

We think that this new kind of motivated behavior—attempting to make the world resemble internally represented end-states (goals) through concerted activity—began with the evolution of vertebrates. Such animals, which include bony fish, amphibians, reptiles, birds, and mammals, first arose around 450 million years ago. Vertebrates have differentially segmented bodies, bones, a skull, and appendages; they also have more complex brains than invertebrates, which simply collect nerves at one end of their body (the cerebral ganglion). A reptile brain, for example, is divided into recognizable organs, including a cerebrum, cerebellum, and optic and olfactory lobes. This enhanced structure supports more sophisticated forms of behavioral control, as we will see. More complex brains (and bodies) can support a broader range of flexible strategies for dealing with evolutionary problems.

Drives

We argue that the first form of motivated behavior to evolve was a "drive" (the fourth category of behavior production in Table 2.1). Drives cause goal-directed sequences of behavior that result in the attainment of physiological end-states. It only becomes necessary to pursue a goal that provides benefits when current conditions are not optimal. Drives are therefore concerned with achieving optimal levels of resources in an animal's body or within an animal's immediate control, because these actions provide direct evolutionary benefits. In effect, they are responses to *indicators* of an evolutionarily significant problem or *need*. The regulation of the internal milieu may involve consumption, or bringing external resources inside the body such as would occur from *hunger, thirst,* or *acquiring male gametes* (if female); however, sometimes it involves expelling materials such as gametes (if male) or waste products. Drives thus typically involve resources bridging the body boundary. Some drives, such as those associated with the location of appropriate ecological conditions such as temperature, pH, or moisture, do not involve consumption or expulsion per se, but require that conditions like heat, pressure, or moisture be balanced to ensure the optimal operation of internal processes.

Drives manage internal resource levels, whether the relevant cue comes from inside or outside the body (the signal for thirst is internal; of an opportunity for sex, environmental). For example, *hunger* is regulated by the level of glucose in the bloodstream (Melanson et al., 1999), where the glucose level can be interpreted as a cue for the animal's nutrient balance. The animal's goal, toward which it will work, is to bring glucose levels within an optimum range. Drives like *hunger* differ from reflexive ingestion because they allow an animal to actively pursue an end-state, rather than relying on recognizing items in its immediate perceptual environment as edible and incorporating them. Instead, search and capture can take place prior to consumption.

We argue that drives evolved around the time vertebrates began to appear. Fish are able to exhibit the persistent or prioritized behavior indicative of motivation. For example, hungry fish are more likely than satiated fish to risk predation in order to find food (Vehanen, 2003). Hungry guppies will find their way through a novel maze to find food faster than satiated guppies, suggesting that they engage in a motivated search of their environment (Laland & Reader, 1999).

Though they may have similar outcomes in terms of benefits, drives are more sophisticated than reflexes because they require finding a route to the desired end-state. Thus ethologists (Hinde, 1970; McFarland, 1998) and neuroscientists (Everitt et al., 1999; Kumar et al., 2014), based on original work by Craig (1908), commonly distinguish two phases of drive-related behavior—appetitive and consummatory. In the appetitive phase, an animal actively seeks to procure the object of a goal (i.e., a resource) to reduce the intensity of the drive. It does this by engaging in goal-driven investigation of its local environment. That is, it searches for cues of a specific resource. Once the desired object has been perceived, the consummatory phase begins in which the resource is acquired (Watts, 2003). So an animal will first sense that it is hungry, then engage in a search for food, and then consume it. Similarly, search for a mate can result in copulation, which achieves a successful fertilization, an immediate indicator of likely reproduction.

We therefore speculate that drives arose from the combination of two older kinds of production system: the exploratory behavior, seen in all Metazoans, together with a reflex. The two are joined in order to achieve the function of managing resource levels appropriately and reliably. This need-directed search, when followed by a reflex, is commonly recognized as a "drive" (e.g., hunger, thirst). The concept of two phases in drive execution is supported by the evidence that "wanting" (incentive salience or motivational value) is separable from "liking" (hedonic reaction; Berridge & Robinson, 1998). While animals tend to want what they like and like what they want, the two can be dissociated, so that drive-based behavior need not work homeostatically, although it tends to in most evolutionarily relevant situations. This kind of cobbling together of available production systems to make something more complex is just what one would expect of an evolutionary process.

Experimental psychologists nowadays avoid use of the word "drive," largely because a number of results have been interpreted as refuting Hull's classic drive reduction theory (C. Hull, 1943). However, in each case, these experimental results can be reinterpreted as demonstrating a "tricking" of the reward system in a way natural selection cannot be expected to have foreseen. First, rats will work to obtain saccharine rewards even when not calorie deficient (i.e., not in a state of "hunger"; Sheffield & Roby, 1950). However, saccharine constitutes an artificial, non-nutritive source of sweet taste, which is a proximal cue of ripe fruit in the animal's evolved niche, so rats will continue to seek the reward from the taste even when sated, because saccharine doesn't cause the "full" feeling from calorie consumption (Berridge & Robinson,

1998). Second, hungry rats will work to obtain direct electrical stimulation of their mesotelencephalic dopamine system, even over the option to receive food (Olds & Milner, 1954; Routtenberg & Lindy, 1965). This surgical procedure tricks the evolved reward system to respond in the absence of real benefits. Showing that maladaptive outcomes can be obtained through such artificial procedures does not refute the validity of the general claim that drives evolved to produce need-directed behavior that improves an animal's fitness, and that such behavior tends to appropriately manage internal resource levels under natural ecological conditions.

In sum, the possession of drives allow animals to pursue end-states through multiple bouts of behavior, always gauging how close they have come with each action to the end-states they are after, and redirecting their efforts should the "error" or discrepancy between their expected state and that they perceive themselves to be in be judged significant.

We can identify a number of independent drives that must have arisen early in vertebrate evolution to cater for fundamental physiological needs.

Lust. Some needs concern the physiological requirements of reproduction and somatic survival. In particular, vertebrates reproduce through sexual intercourse. Thus the motive to meet the need to maximize gene copy production is the pan-vertebral drive to engage in copulatory behavior. This requires a search for and pursuit of appropriate candidates and the consummation of sexual union. We label this motivated mating BPU *lust*.

Hunger. Vertebrates, like all organisms, have basic metabolic needs to sustain life. The body's metabolic and physiological needs are met in two ways by vertebrates: first, through the acquisition of resources such as nutrients, water, oxygen, and sunlight. This BPU drives both search and consumption; we label it *hunger*.

Comfort. Second, because terrestrial niches vary in terms of essential physical conditions such as temperature, elevation, and moisture levels, maintenance of the body's physiology also requires behavior. We label this BPU *comfort*. *Comfort* produces tactics such as relocating to shade when the sun is hot; covering the body with warm, dry clothes and finding shelter when it is not; removing thorns, tending wounds, consuming medicated plants; saving energy by sleeping or resting; and voiding wastes. Feelings of discomfort or pain may accompany motivated efforts to attain a state more conducive to physiological flourishing.

Fear and disgust. Vertebrates, like most animals, face two significantly different kinds of biological threats from the environment—those able to sneak undetected into body sites, and those that attack from outside the body (predators). These problems require different kinds of defensive and offensive strategies. Hence vertebrates have two drives to organize behavior that meets the need to minimize bodily damage from these threats. First, *fear* drives motivated behavior that avoids hurt-from-without threats, including predators, but also aggressive conspecifics and accidents (Ohman & Mineka, 2003). Tactics include aggregating in a group, fleeing, hiding, and avoiding environmental dangers such as fires and floods. Second, *disgust* drives the avoidance of hurt-from-within threats. The task of this drive is to cause the avoidance of sick others, "off" foods, disease vectors, and pathogen contamination (Curtis, 2013). Although both *fear* and *disgust* involve avoidance of environmental threats, the two systems have diverged in terms of psychological mechanisms over millions of years of evolution (Curtis, 2013; Curtis et al., 2011; Neuberg et al., 2011). For example, in humans, they can be located in somewhat different parts of the brain (Lawrence et al., 2004).

Affective Learning and Emotional Memory

Because drives are so closely tied to biological fitness, it would be advantageous for an animal to be able to recall specific lessons from successful goal achievement. This indeed seems to be the case; for example, a negative experience (e.g., nausea) with a particular type of food lowers the incentive to seek it out again in the future, while a positive experience (e.g., good taste sensation) increases motivation (Rozin & Vollmeke, 1986). In other words, end-states can come to be associated with the characteristics of events that co-occur with them; these characteristics make the goal more or less salient (Balleine & Dickinson, 1998; Berridge, 2003). This is affective learning, and we postulate that this form of learning arose around the time of the early vertebrates so as to store the information resulting from reaching goals associated with physiological end-states.

Also, once animals could value their experience using the dopaminergic system (based on how well an action helped them toward achievement of a goal), they applied this ability to their memories, and began to evaluate them as well. What psychologists call emotional memory is a neural representation of a positive or negative affect associated with specific stimuli. Neuroscientific studies indicate that emotional stimuli engage specific cognitive mechanisms to enhance memory (Hamann, 2001; Schacter, 1996). Emotional arousal acts during memory encoding to focus attention and elaboration and increase the likelihood of memory consolidation. Typically, such memories are not subject to conscious recollection but are reflected in attraction, avoidance, or autonomic nervous system activation. Such memories provide the ability to link rewards to places, times, and other actors, giving temporal and social depth to environmental knowledge (Poucet, 1993; Wang & Spelke, 2002).

Two dimensions of emotion appear to independently influence this type of memory encoding: arousal (from calm to excited) and valence (positive to negative; Kensinger & Corkin, 2004). Memories are more easily formed about, and at, times during which the animal is aroused; information that has not been associated with physiological excitement is more difficult to recall later (Cahill & McGaugh, 1995; Kensinger & Corkin, 2004; Sharot & Phelps, 2004). This is probably due to a narrowing of the types of cues that can spark attention and subsequent processing when an animal is not aroused (Easterbrook, 1959). Thus, emotionally arousing stimuli result in enhanced memory for details central to the appearance or meaning of an emotional stimulus and impaired memory for peripheral features (Burke et al., 1992).

Similarly, valence can have an independent effect in enhancing long-term memory: items that are not arousing but that have positive or negative valence can be better remembered than neutral items (Ochsner & Barrett, 2001). Valence is the memory of the reward or punishment resulting from a behavior—a vital piece of information needed to judge appropriate responses in the next instance of similar circumstances. Hence, positive or negative events are likely to be recalled more often and with greater clarity and detail than neutral events. In particular, the amygdala has been implicated in enhancing explicit memory for both pleasant and unpleasant emotional stimuli through modulation of encoding and consolidation processes (Cahill et al., 1996; Maren, 1999; McGaugh, 2004). For example, much of autobiographical memory is composed of highly emotional events (Conway et al., 1994). Associations between states of arousal and environmental features can also be stored as emotional memories—that is, associations learned from emotionally relevant experience (Cahill et al., 1996; Kensinger, 2009).

It thus seems that, with the advent of the midbrain evaluation system, there was a selective advantage to learning from events that bore a strong influence on biological fitness (survival and reproduction). In particular, arousal constitutes a physiological condition that heightens memory retention by exciting neurochemical activity affecting areas of the brain responsible for encoding and recall (MacLean, 1990). Events that have a considerable impact on fitness will be highly reinforced and lead to long-term abilities to recall the relevant response to the same situation when it arises again.

Interests

Another type of need for most animals (including humans) is to improve their own abilities at meeting all the needs outlined previously. What we call "interests" are a kind of default behavior for those with an abundance of energy and no other pressing needs. They do not have to be a response to a particular indicator, but can arise when there is a lack of problems or opportunities. Interests are similar to *exploration* in this respect (Biederman & Vessel, 2006; Burghardt, 2005). However, they differ from reflexive *exploration* in two ways. First, the advent of goal-directed behavior in vertebrates meant that learning could be associated with psychological rewards. However, in interested behavior, the production of these rewards (and the associated learning) becomes the desired end-state, meaning that what had been a means for modifying behavioral propensities becomes the function of the behavior. In effect, learning—a form of behavioral feedback—becomes an end in itself. This is why engaging in interests is "fun" (Biederman & Vessel, 2006).

We can see two classes of interested BPUs that are motivated and that lead to aptitudinal end-states in early vertebrates (see Table 2.1): *curiosity* and *nonsocial play*.

Curiosity. In complex, stochastic environments, animals can become out-of-date with respect to their knowledge of where environmental threats and opportunities reside. Ranging behavior (circling through one's territory or surroundings) can reduce uncertainty about the amount or location of resources, or the presence of dangers or escape routes—information that is stored in memory (Inglis, 2000). The function of the *curiosity* motive is to collect and codify information, thus reducing gaps in knowledge about some facet of the world (Loewenstein, 1994). *Curiosity* thus motivates both random and directed behavior in quest of knowledge. *Curiosity* results in brain structures being created or updated with specific facts about the environment and situational expectancies, often via activation of the amygdala to make long-term memories (Beswick, 1971; O'Keefe & Nadel, 1978).

This is demonstrated by the finding that when an animal is put in an unfamiliar environment, it engages in ranging behavior until it gets a good knowledge of the area within its domain (Nissen, 1930; Shillito, 1963; Wolfe, 1969; Wood-Gush & Vestergaard, 1991). Interest is shown in things that are new, complex, and unfamiliar. But as the degree of uncertainty about the environment is reduced by each new unit of information, additional units produce less important improvements in knowledge about local conditions. Additional effort expended on exploration is thus associated with decreasing marginal returns. Eventually, reduced energy stores will lead to the cessation of *curiosity*-based "info-vore" behavior (Silvia, 2006). *Curiosity* can be regarded as a motive that is engaged when animals have sufficient energy stores and no pressing emergencies (Nissen, 1930; Panksepp, 1998).

Curiosity can be seen as a cognitive elaboration of earlier forms of *exploration*, the initial, most primitive form of which was taxis. *Exploration*, in this view, is a locomotor response designed to determine characteristics of the spatial environment, while *curiosity* is a more sophisticated form of investigation designed to learn not just about objects or places, but about more abstract concepts and relationships among things purely imaginary as well as real (Pisula, 1998). *Curious* behavior should thus be clustered at times when a new environment is entered (e.g., after migration), or when environmental change has occurred (Toates, 1986).

In humans, particular perceptual features of a stimulus provoke *curious* investigation—specifically novelty, complexity, and uncertainty about its nature (Berlyne, 1960). *Curiosity* in humans has been linked to areas of the prefrontal cortex (Brodmann areas 8–11 and 45–47; Bekhtereva et al., 2000). It also correlates with scores on information-seeking scales (Reuter et al., 2004). Indeed, two dimensions of *curiosity* have been isolated by recent psychometric work: being motivated to seek knowledge and new experiences ("stretching"); and a general willingness to embrace the novel, uncertain, and unpredictable nature of everyday life ("embracing"; Kashdan et al., 2009). Thus *curiosity* appears to be an evolutionary extension of *exploration*, with increased cognitive resources being devoted to the focused pursuit of particular knowledge goals that will reduce uncertainty about everyday matters.

Nonsocial play. A second type of interested motivated BPU is *play* (Burghardt, 2005; Izard, 1977; Panksepp, 1998; Tomkins, 1962). *Play* drives behavior that increases aptitude—the knowledge and skill that can be put to work to improve reproductive and survival changes—both directly and indirectly (Burghardt, 2005). *Play* concerns the acquisition of embodied skills and knowledge of one's own physical competencies through the repeated practice of particular behavior sequences. *Play* is thus about training the brain to control the body, and particularly skills in interaction with the world, while *curiosity* is about updating the brain's databases to reflect recent (local) circumstances. Both have a future orientation—the information and skills they result in will produce evolutionary benefits only later in time.

Play not only results from having surplus physiological resources; it also creates new resources that can be used later (Burghardt, 2005; Fagen, 1991). *Play* builds up informational capital in one of three forms: personal, environmental, or social. First, an animal can simply practice manipulatory or locomotory behaviors to gain greater control over its own motor system. So personal *play* is generally called *locomotor play*. Typically, *locomotor play* involves juvenile animals (e.g., bovids) carrying out movements such as running, leaping, pirouetting, or heel kicking in ways that are similar to the physical actions of adults, but not in the context of satisfying an obvious goal. *Locomotor play* is probably the most primitive form of play behavior (Bekoff, 1984).

Second, *play* can involve an animal modifying the physical environment (i.e., niche construction; Odling-Smee et al., 2003); this is a form of learning to manipulate physical structures (Fagen, 1991). This form is typically called *object play*, which can be seen as a specialized form of investment behavior where complex, but biologically important, skills are acquired through practice. This kind of *play* is often not about making permanent modifications to the environment, but rather investigating novel objects. Its purpose is to develop abilities to manipulate the object in question (Sazima, 2008). For example, human hunters are known to "whittle," honing their abilities to make subsistence tools by carving bits of wood (part of the larger algorithmic process of making the tool itself) (Bock 2005).

Claims have been made for *object play* in species such as turtles (Burghardt et al., 1996), crocodiles (Glickman & Sroges, 1968), and octopi (Kuba et al., 2003; Mather & Anderson, 1999). Octopus *play* involves repeatedly manipulating non-food objects (like lego toys) in complex, non-stereotyped ways for a significant amount of time, whether hungry or not, including several days after initial presentation of the artificial objects (which rules out *exploration* as an explanation; Kuba et al., 2006). Finding *play* in octopi is not completely unexpected as they have perhaps the most complex brains among nonvertebrate species (Mather, 2008). However, these studies have concerned provisioned animals living in zoos or laboratories, so it is difficult to know whether such behaviors form part of their natural repertoire. *Object play* is difficult to distinguish from object *exploration*, which is stereotypical and reduces uncertainty, but does not facilitate the acquisition of motor skills (Power, 2000).

The third type of *play*, *social play*— which involves simulating activities such as nurturing babies, courting, hunting, and fighting (without its related dangers)—is discussed in Chapter 4.

Generally, *play* has neither been well-defined nor well-studied, although Burghardt (2005) has attempted a codified definition. He suggests that *play* is behavior that is not fully functional, but rather spontaneous, voluntary, and pleasurable; that it differs from serious performance of the same behaviors either structurally or temporally; that it is repeated but not stereotyped (which would probably mean that it is instinctual rather than motivated); and that it occurs when the animal is in a relaxed state (e.g., well-fed, safe, and healthy). Some argue that *play* is primarily observed in mammals and birds because they have a long immaturity period, are dependent on parental care, and have high encephalization (Bekoff, 1984). Hence claims of even *object play* among species other than birds and mammals remain controversial (Burghardt, 2005). Nevertheless, we predict that *object play* will be found to exist among other vertebrates like fish and reptiles, because they all have a reward system that can be applied to persistent investigations and manipulations of the environment. We would extend a similar argument to the exhibition of *curiosity*: both would bear informed investigation in a wider range of species.

Obviously, interests share with all other forms of behavior the fact that learning occurs as a result of performing the behavior. What makes interest-produced behavior different from the other forms is that this is the primary function of the behavior, rather than a byproduct of behavior performed for other evolutionary reasons (such as improving status or getting food into the body).

Procedural Memory

The learning acquired through *playing* with objects is stored in the form of procedural memories—specific knowledge about how to conduct particular kinds of complex behavioral sequences (i.e., skills). Procedural memory (memory for "knowing how") is commonly distinguished from declarative memory (memory for "knowing that"), as one of the two major forms of memory (Cohen & Squire, 1980). At this gross level, procedural memory can be divided into three forms: simple associative learning or conditioning, nonassociative learning (habituation and sensitization), and skill acquisition (Schacter, 1996). As a result, some scholars argue that simple animals such as snails exhibit procedural memory (Gainutdinova et al., 2005). Here, however, we propose to restrict use of the term to skill acquisition; the other, simpler forms of memory are covered by other, equally specialized terms discussed earlier, such as classical and operant conditioning.

Thus, when a skill is being acquired, animals exert attention, but after repeated practice the skill becomes nearly automatic (Fitts, 1964). This allows the animal to concentrate on learning a new action while performing previously learned actions with little attention, gradually assembling longer sequences of well-practiced and consistently performed actions. In humans it appears that a neural code or representation for the learned skill is created in the brain (a procedural memory) which encodes the procedures or algorithms underlying the motor performance.

Memory for skills takes the form of hierarchically structured or chunked clusters of associations that allow the nuanced, contextualized performance of the complex behavior sequences required to interact with *play* objects (Byrne et al., 2001; Schank & Abelson, 1977). Such skills—playing tennis, for instance—are shaped by reinforcement learning through repeated practice and typically result in increased speed or accuracy through repetitions. Such practice results in the mental representation of a series of actions or perceptual processing functions that typically occurs unconsciously. This memory is then recalled to efficiently perform the previously learned skill using some variant of the prototypical sequence. Skill-based memory is therefore more complex than the simple associations between stimuli and responses characteristic of instincts.

Such hierarchically organized memories can be characteristic only of brains that enabled mental representations—presumably restricted to the complex cortical structures characteristic of vertebrates. In humans, skill-based memory is associated with the cerebellum and basal ganglia (Heindel et al., 1989). There appear to be distinct neurological networks for skill acquisition and consolidation; the latter improves with sleep while the former does not (Debas et al., 2010).

In this chapter, we have argued that motivated behavior represents a major advance because it enables more sophisticated kinds of responses to the situations in which animals find themselves. Early forms of motivated behavior were drives, which helped animals improve their physiological end-states, and interests, which helped them improve their aptitudes. Drives were enhanced by affective learning and interests by skill-based learning.

As we will see in subsequent chapters, goal-direction could also be used to achieve more complex kinds of end-states, where rewards were not so immediate, nor directed at (or sensed by), the body or the brain. Instead, they were targeted at changing the state of the environment.

CHAPTER 4

CHANGING THE WORLD
FOR THE BETTER

The next major stage in animal evolution involved new kinds of lifestyles with a move out of the oceans and onto the land. For life in this new niche reptiles evolved behavior production units (BPUs) which we call the ecological emotions, and then mammals made a further transition to a social way of life employing behavior driven by the social emotions.

Reptiles

About 320 million years ago the first animals moved full-time onto land: the reptiles. This change in habitat had a number of repercussions. The new environment provided new kinds of things to eat, so reptiles acquired new feeding strategies including herbivory and carnivory, their predecessors having been only insectivores and piscivores (Sahney et al., 2010). Reptiles rapidly radiated to inhabit a variety of niches on land, but, as we will see, still underwent selective pressure, primarily over access to the best territories. Their ability to enter new habitats was limited by their remaining cold-blooded, which required them to get the necessary heat energy to move through their environments from the environment itself—meaning they could not migrate to cold climates.

Ecological Emotions

While drives motivate animals to seek physiological benefits, and interests to acquire new aptitudes, further advantages can be gained by animals that are motivated to put themselves in a better situation with respect to the world (situational end-states—see the sixth and eighth row of Table 2.1). In this way, the animal can put itself in a better position for survival and reproduction. For example, a lizard that is motivated to defend territory through a strategy of dominating conspecifics gains access to a resource base that will provide it with somatic and (potentially) reproductive benefits in future. A human who acquires and maintains a pair-bond by donating resources to his mate becomes more likely to rear successful offspring (Kaplan, 1996).

However, in each case, the animal is behaving in a costly way with no immediate benefit in return. The evolutionary innovation at this point is to find a means to motivate and reward such behavior, making it worth the animal's while to make the effort. We propose that this is exactly the role of "emotions." The lizard indulging in angry displays and aggressive behavior—which is costly in the short term, but beneficial in the long term—could be said to be motivated by a need to defend its territory—the *hoard* emotion. The human is motivated to make sacrifices to maintain a pair-bond by the need to invest in *pair-bond love*.

An emotion, then, motivates a sequence of behaviors which changes the state of the world or the animal's relationship to it in a way likely to lead to future fitness benefits (Aunger & Curtis, 2008). Instead of working to improve their physiological states, as in the case of drives, they work to improve their situation in the world, which makes them better able to acquire evolutionary benefits.

The fact that emotions are goal-directed distinguishes them from another type of BPU which also leads animals to achieve situational end-states: instincts. Instincts are instigated by cues (simple stimuli), which means they cannot keep an animal on target if the environment unexpectedly changes. For example, nesting graylag geese continue trying to roll wayward eggs back to the nest even when they have been replaced with balls by experimenters (Lorenz, 1937).

The evolutionary tasks an animal has to solve depend in turn on the animal's niche. Each emotion can be associated with the task it attempts to solve, such as securing a mate, improving social status, or protecting an offspring from predation. Emotions are thus defined by a task that is pursued using motivated control, and when achieved, leaves an animal in a better situation (but not directly with evolutionary benefits).

We call this class of BPU "emotions" because many of them (but not all) resemble what are often described in everyday language as emotions. Note that we are here proposing a new and principled definition for what is one of the most contested classes of phenomena in psychology (Barrett, 2006; Cosmides & Tooby, 2000a; Darwin, 1872; Ekman, 1992; Fredrickson, 2001; Griffiths, 2004b; James, 1884; Lazarus, 1991; Mesquita & Frijda, 1992; Prinz, 2004). Contrary to common parlance, we do not define emotions by the feelings they may arouse, where most everyday emotion words such as "fear" and "anger" describe states of feeling. Nor do we equate motives with feelings such as pleasure or excitement. In our schema the arousal of motives and/or their satisfaction in humans is often, but not always, accompanied by specific affective states—for example, hunger followed by satiation, or anxiety followed by calm. Achievement of or failure to attain a goal can be but are not required to be associated with feelings of pleasure or satisfaction after goal acquisition in humans (McClelland, 1987; Sheldon et al., 2001; Winter, 1996). The subjective nature of feelings has led people (including some psychologists) to identify them with motivation, even though, from our perspective, they are not the instigators, nor the promoters, of action. They typically rise to consciousness, and so become felt, after the fact, rather than representing the impetus to engage in sustained goal-directed behavior of a particular type (Damasio, 1994). This post-facto nature suggests a link to psychological rewards after behavior, rather than spurs to action to meet needs. It is rather the meeting of a need that is commonly followed by a release of rewarding neurochemicals that produce a feeling of well-being (Rolls, 1999). This reinforcement helps an animal to learn how to meet its needs better in future. We hypothesize that feelings may be a late addition to the behavioral repertoire associated with reflective learning and conscious decision making (see Chapter 5).

The evolutionary beginnings of emotions, we argue, can be found in the fact that there is variation in access to resources. Scarce resources inspire competition. The first, and until recently most important, resource has been high-quality territory. Animals defend particular areas from conspecifics because those tracts provide valuable resources such as food, water, or mating sites. For example, fish compete for mates by defending copulation sites (Hollis et al., 1989). Some lizards exhibit territorial retinues (groups of lizards, for example, that move as a unit from territory to territory, following a dominant male, composed of the territory owner's "consort" and juveniles), as well as pride displays after successfully defending territory, and submissive displays (acquiescence of male to territory owner; MacLean, 1990). Expending energy on maintaining control over access to the resources associated with particular places provides only indirect evolutionary benefits. By defending territory, an animal achieves a situational end-state through motivated behavior (our definition of an emotion).

Hoard. This motivated BPU drives behavior that involves the accumulation of resources, either directly by growing, collecting and storing them, or more indirectly by negotiating the rights to territory or the fruits of group production. As noted earlier, many reptiles defend territories. Some birds also cache large numbers of seeds over the winter in specific locations (Clayton & Dickinson, 1999). *Hoarding* may also require the guarding of resources from pilfering by envious others (e.g., territorial defense; Gintis, 2007). Humans, at least since the agricultural revolution, have been able to produce ever-increasing food surpluses on plots of land (Marx, 1887). The ability to *hoard* enables species to have longer-range concerns and reduced risk of shortage.

Create. In specialized cases, species can manipulate the quality of their territory directly through behavior. Investing energy in improving the environment to make it more productive or to reduce threats can have fitness payoffs. This is the motive to improve habitat and maintain that improvement such that it is more conducive to survival and reproduction. We label this motive *create*. Obvious examples include *creating* safe, clean, dry shelters. So beavers build dams, and birds build nests. In humans, *creative* tactics also include planting, weeding, and irrigating; cleaning, tidying, and repairing habitats; and making artifacts such as bows and plows that aid the diversion of energy toward survival and reproduction. Indeed, humans have taken this ability to an extreme, with the cumulative *creation* of highly complex technologies of many kinds, including infrastructures such as electricity and sewerage systems, and the World Wide Web (Aunger, 2010). (Note that this motive is not necessarily related to the personality trait of creativity, although certain aspects of human creativity no doubt derive from expertise at these kinds of niche constructive activities.)

Learning and Memory: Cognitive Maps

All of this interest in territories should be associated with an ability to learn how to find one's way reliably within specific landscapes, and to store in memory where resources can be acquired or *hoarded* and where dangers lurk. An efficient means of doing this is to be able to store representations of the relationships between particular points in space using spatial cognition (Dolins & Mitchell, 2010). The development in learning and memory that supported the emergence of the ecological emotions was the cognitive map (Table 2.1).

Since the beginning of behavioral evolution (with *exploration*), animals have had an interest in reducing uncertainty about their surroundings. Some form of spatial representation is probably universal in animals, but the sophistication of such representations can vary considerably (Wang & Spelke, 2002). We argue that animals prior to reptiles made do with relatively simple representational mechanisms for storing information about their physical environment. In particular, earlier animals relied on either route-following or path integration to get around. (Route-following is getting to point C by following straight lines from one's current location to known point A, from point A to known point B, and point B to known point C, regardless of how roundabout this makes the path followed. Path integration—or dead reckoning—is the practice of returning directly to home after a period of meandering travel (e.g., during search for food), by constantly updating one's current position with respect to an origin, without necessarily recording details of the path already followed.) Because there is no need for a memory trace of the path, the animal may not be able to repeat its route. As the terms "bee-line" and "crow-fly" suggest, this is presumed to be a common mechanism among invertebrates and other relatively early-evolved species (Gallistel, 1990).

Navigation based on a cognitive map, on the other hand, implies an ability to select the most economical path (including the shortest path and shortcuts) in both familiar and unfamiliar settings. This method relies on features of the external environment such as landmarks and celestial guides, using geometric relations between them to create a network of interconnected places and using rules to estimate relationships between points (O'Keefe & Nadel, 1978; Tolman, 1948). Reliance on such maps allows for more sophisticated way-finding, resulting in broader-ranging behavior and provides means to cross unfamiliar territory to efficiently reach a specific target location.

If a cognitive map alone is used, then piloting and path following can take place without either the use of beacons or reference to external landmarks. There may not yet be convincing evidence that spatial knowledge reaches this degree of coherence in species other than primates (Etienne et al., 2004).

Nevertheless, it is known that the hippocampal formation in the brains of mammals and birds mediates spatial orientation behaviors consistent with a map-like representation, which allows the navigator to construct a new route across unfamiliar terrain. This suggests that at least one function of the ancestral medial pallium was spatial navigation. Further, there may be a structure homologous to the medial pallium in fish and reptiles that does spatial integration. Studies of the goldfish and certain reptile species have shown that the homologue of the medial pallium in these species can also play an important role in spatial orientation (Jacobs, 2003). There is some recent evidence of mapping abilities in tortoises (Wilkinson et al., 2009) and snakes (Pittman et al., 2014).

In any case, we argue that reptiles and fish probably have the mental equipment to do some form of map-based spatial navigation (Wilkinson & Huber, 2012). Cognitive maps also serve as a more robust means of representing and storing information acquired through *curious* recognizance activities about the local environment, which arose with somewhat earlier vertebrate species.

Mammals

Mammals, which emerged some 250 million years ago, constituted a new group of animals with novel evolutionary features, including homeothermy (the ability to regulate body temperature) and a placenta for provisioning offspring developing inside the parent's body. However, the feature most relevant to our story of the evolution of behavior is that mammals live in groups with offspring that are dependent on nutrition from maternal mammaries. Many of the new motives that arose from this point in our lineage onward were designed to ensure the smooth functioning of groups of animals that came to depend on one another for everyday benefits.

Social Emotions

The advent of mammals brought a new kind of emotion online: the social emotions. We have already established that emotions are motivated BPUs that lead an animal to a better situation in the world (situational end-states). For animals with a social way of life one of the most important aspects of their niche is other animals. These animals need to invest in creating social conditions for their own flourishing—this is the role of the social emotions. For example, female aggressiveness increases during lactation, presumably to protect offspring from conspecifics, which in rodents means deterring infanticidal behavior by adult kin, while in primates it probably protects infants from general harassment by others in the social group (Maestripieri, 1992).

Note that fish *shoaling* is a BPU that achieves situational end-states (fish in a shoal are better protected from predation and/or can feed more efficiently), but this behavior is cue-rather than goal-driven, and hence instinctive. The cue is simply to maintain the distance to the closest conspecific within a certain range (Parrish et al., 2002). Should the expected degree of contact with the nearest neighbor be lost, panic ensues, and contact is regained, while if contact is too close, the fish begins to swim a bit further away. By contrast, a human who decides to go out in the evening to seek social company in a bar is being guided by a mental representation of a goal, to reinforce their belonging to a social group. Their internal reward system makes successful attempts at convivial interaction pleasurable. Because such behavior is goal-seeking rather than cue-driven, it qualifies as emotional (driven by a BPU we dub *affiliation*, as described later).

It only becomes necessary to use rewards to motivate an animal to reach situational end-states when the route to those states is unpredictable (otherwise an instinct would work). Social life is particularly unpredictable. Achieving social goals requires that other animals be manipulated into behaving in a certain way, such as allowing access to resources, or granting the animal an improved reputation. Since other animals are independent agents, responses cannot be guaranteed and repeated attempts may be needed to achieve the desired end-state. The social emotions use goal-direction and reward to keep animals on track toward the end-state. (Of course not all social behavior is emotional; some social behaviors are produced by other kinds of BPUs. For example, a male animal might react to a female display of sexual receptivity with copulation. This is reflexive because it is cue-based, and serves physiological end-states (in the form of reproduction; Aunger & Curtis, 2008).)

For example, an internal indicator (such as a falling level of vasopressin) may tell animal A that he needs to increase status. Another indicator suggests that he needs a pair-bond. A recognizes that he can achieve both goals simultaneously by gaining access to the sexual resources of high-status animal C, who is currently pair-bonded to B. A therefore uses his cheapest option: he expresses anger at B. However, B does not signal that he relinquishes control over C, so A makes a new assessment (based on an indicator that status has not yet improved): that B will only acquiesce after an escalation in strategic investment, a physical contest. So A aggresses against B, such that B cannot maintain control over C. A collects C and, recognizing that the status goal has been achieved (i.e., the status indicator is reduced below its threshold value), expresses pride to fellow group members, thus displaying his ownership of C. B meanwhile displays shame at his loss of status and resource base. In effect, emotions involve mentally seeking a route through the social world to find an effective strategy that achieves the desired situational end-state. The strategies used are guided by the internal system of rewards, which motivates evolutionarily beneficial behavior.

Social behaviors are thus highly interdependent, where outcomes for each party depend on the particular strategy adopted by the other (i.e., strategies are asymmetric). As a result, more attention needs to be paid to determining which option is likely to be chosen by an interactant, and one's own choice will then crucially reflect this—that is, it will be strategic, and the payoff to each party depends on which combination of responses are made (von Neumann & Morgenstern, 1944). Engaging in social *emotions* can thus be seen as a form of strategic game playing.

When did true sociality arise? Vertebrates like fish exhibit a variety of quasi-social behaviors, such as shoaling and leader-follower behavior (Bshary, 2010; Laland & Reader, 1999). But these are behaviors that simply provide protection through aggregation or hints about where to find food. Many animals also engage in sexual reproduction, but this is the only—and typically brief—coordinated interaction during the animal's lifetime, so we do not call such species social either. True sociality, as we use the term, is defined by sequentially contingent, interdependent behavior such as coordinated group hunting. (Of course, some fish, reptile, and amphibian species do engage social behaviors as we would define them, including group hunting. But given the typically solitary nature of reptiles and amphibians, we assume that the ancestral state of the vertebrates was one of isolation; social traits in these groups—including aggregation for defense seen in most fish—are derived traits evolved to deal with specific needs, which is why these species exhibit only particular aspects of social life (Bshary et al., 2007).) In this strict sense, then, we argue that sociality does not constitute the way of life for species in the human lineage prior to mammals. For these reasons, we suggest that social emotions coevolved with the advent of this group. Social emotions thus arose together with mammals, the first clade in the human lineage to involve complex interdependencies with conspecifics (Aunger & Curtis, 2008).

True sociality introduced new kinds of opportunities for resource acquisition and environmental management via both competition and cooperation with fellow animals. Emotional BPUs allowed social organisms to accomplish goals unavailable to solitary individuals, such as collective enterprise or division of labor (Maynard Smith & Szathmary, 1995). Evolving mechanisms to take advantage of these opportunities would have been selectively advantageous. Competition, however, being asocial, is ancestral to cooperation. The social emotions would have sparked evolutionary arms races, with the most manipulative animals surviving and breeding most successfully (Sterelny, 2003). The social emotions motivate mammals to behave in ways that manipulate the behavior of others, so as to get themselves into advantageous positions vis-à-vis those others. The achievement of these situational end-states depends on the behavioral responses of these other animals, so emotional behavior is intrinsically strategic. Social emotions are thus designed by evolution to motivate social gambits to modify an animal's social niche to its own (or its kin's) advantage.

The Coevolution of Social Emotions and Social Organization

The number of social emotions exhibited by animals depend on the degree of complexity of their social niche. In the human lineage more emotions were added as social life became more complex, from mother-child relationships in early mammals, to clans in carnivores, to hierarchical groups in primates, to nuclear families, to ultrasocial groups (see Table 4.1). This is one reason a positive correlation has been found between social forms and degree of encephalization in mammals (Shultz & Dunbar, 2010).

Table 4.1: Social Motives as Responses to Novel Forms of Social Organization

Social organization	Motive	Origin	Cooperative mechanism
Mother + dependent child	*Nurture*	Early mammals	Kin selection
Clan (small group of related individuals)	*Affiliation*	Carnivores	Direct reciprocity (reciprocal altruism)
Larger, hierarchically organized groups	*Status*	Primates	Indirect reciprocity (reputation/gossip)
Nuclear family (Parental pair + dependent offspring)	*Attract, Pair-bond love*	Humans	Mutual genetic interest (in offspring)
Ultrasocial groups (very large groups of unrelated individuals)	*Justice*	Humans	Strong reciprocity (third-party punishment)

New social emotions came online as new tasks became relevant to the niche—for example, the need for paternal investment in offspring, and the need to compete with other family groups. (Note that in our account most emotions—being strictly motivated behavior—arose before the ability to do planning or to experience consciousness, the subject of the next chapter.)

Each new aspect of the social niche can be associated with a particular kind of evolutionary mechanism for cooperative or competitive behavior. In effect, new kinds of social relationships can be sustained over generations only if they are consistent with some sort of evolutionary "logic" that those engaged in such relationships have selective advantages. These advantages are typically demonstrated in evolutionary game theoretic models in which competition between agents exhibiting such relationships are shown to out-reproduce those who lack such relationships—a good indication of evolutionary advantage (Nowak, 2006, 2013). We now consider the origin of each of our postulated social emotions and kind of cooperative mechanisms that support them one by one.

Mother and dependent child. True sociality first evolved in early mammals, when offspring became dependent on maternal care for survival. Mammalian offspring are born live but highly dependent, requiring provisioning, protection, and education. Rearing offspring (parental care) is therefore another important aspect of the mammalian lifestyle.

Nurture. The motive to rear offspring and aid other kin we label *nurture.* Such care is most likely to be directed at immature relatives, but may target any member of the individual's kin group, with the degree of investment reflecting the likelihood of gene copies being present in that individual (i.e., the degree of relatedness; Hamilton, 1964). The nurture BPU is a motive that encourages maternal (and paternal) feeding, cleaning, and protective behavior, as well as providing opportunities for play learning and attempts at influencing the social world in favor of the dependent (nepotism; Geary & Flinn, 2001). Offspring can manipulate the nurture motive by panicking if contact with mother is lost and by attaching themselves to primary carers to maintain an optimum level of investment from their kin (Bowlby, 1979; Panksepp, 1998).

Clan organization. Group-living species have to manage relationships between kin clusters. Outside of the extended kin group, genetic commonalities becomes irrelevant, so in-group and out-group social relations based on cooperation and competition predominate. However, a number of species live in groups of over one hundred (e.g., baboons), which requires new forms of social interaction to operate effectively.

Affiliate. One of the most important aspects of the environment for such groups is other group members. To gain the benefits of group life social animals need to invest in behavior that increases their social capital. The first way they do this is through membership in various groups and subgroups. Baboons, for example, form friendship alliances (Smuts, 1985) and apes engage in "political" coalitions (de Waal, 1982). In humans, the *affiliate* motive causes participation in social activities, formation of alliances, conformity with group norms, displays of intentions to cooperate, and attempts to engender trust; it results in the sharing of resources, including knowledge, especially concerning the reputations of others with respect to their social cooperativeness (Baumeister & Leary, 1995; Cosmides & Tooby, 2005; Dunbar, 1998). It also leads to a search for elevating experiences where group connectedness is reinforced (Keltner & Haidt, 2003). Intra-group relations can be based on weak-kin *affiliation* or, in humans, on non-kin cooperative affiliation (task-based bonding; e.g., among group hunters or co-workers).

As well as cooperation, a new level of competition arose once animals clustered into groups. Inter-group competition due to a lack of overlap in genetic or economic interests can require major investment and provide a drain on resources. Inter-group competition for resources can lead to xenophobia, which can result in inter-group raids or warfare (Chagnon, 1983). In recent history, humans have developed a variety of cultural strategies for reducing the costs of such conflict, facilitating the formation of ever-larger groups (Pinker, 2012).

Social hierarchies. From an evolutionary standpoint, one of the most important features of primate social groups is that they are arranged hierarchically—that is, some individuals have privileged access to the resources produced by group living. One reason multilevel social hierarchies developed was that they are an evolutionarily stable strategy for regulating the costs of social contests for access to resources (Cummins, 2006).

Status. Many mammalian societies are organized by rank but not by status. Rank involves differential access to resources, but is due primarily to domination through physiological size and strength. However, primates can achieve high status through social means (Dahl, 2004; Willer, 2009). The formation of hierarchies within primate groups is likely to be an emergent property of individual behavioral rules. Winners of previous conflicts tend to escalate conflicts, whereas the losers of previous conflicts are less likely to do so. This constitutes a double reinforcement mechanism: winners reinforce their probability of winning and losers reinforce their probability of losing (as has been found in a social insect model; Bonabeau et al., 1999). The hierarchy is secure because it is self-reinforcing: additional conflicts tend to reinforce existing relative ranks. With mutual recognition of *status* differences, and the use of reputations to establish privileges of access, the social order need not be constantly challenged through competitive encounters. Memory of past encounters leads to display or play-fights rather than ongoing contests. When everyone knows, and accepts, everyone else's *status*, resources can be allocated without recourse to violence (Huberman et al., 2004).

In competitive disputes in apes, such as over food and mates, the costs of hostilities can be avoided by signaling relative rank rather than by fighting (de Waal, 1986; Ohman, 1986). Animals can signal their dominance—defined as priority of access to resources (Drews, 1993)—or their submission, which is recognition of the "right" of dominant individuals to this privileged access. We propose that the *status* emotion thus navigates higher apes to the highest status ground they can expect to be able to defend.

The *status* motive thus drives individuals to seek to enhance their relative social position within a group so as to have priority access to the resources they own and produce. *Status* does not in itself produce benefits, although it is associated with the (long-term) enjoyment of benefits (Lin, 1990). This is achieved by tactics such as making disproportionate or specialized contributions to one's social group; drawing attention to those contributions; flattering superiors; submitting to authority; displaying wealth, ability, and "taste"; and seeking recognition and title (Buss & Dedden, 1990; Henrich & Gil-White, 2001). Inappropriate or too naked attempts can lead to embarrassment and a quest to repair the damage to one's social reputation (Goffman, 1956; Tangney et al., 2007).

The *status* motive does not just drive competitive behavior; it can also drive coalition formation. Repeated affiliative efforts may be made by animal A, which may be accepted or repulsed by animal B. If accepted, B may still cheat on the implied coalition, which may result in revenge hostility from A, etc. Such repeated and conditional sequences of behaviors aimed at improving social rank are characteristic of motivated goal-pursuit behavior.

Family-based sociality. *Attract.* In any sexually reproducing species, there is competition for high-quality mates (Darwin, 1871). In humans, there is a need to form a long-term pair-bond to care for offspring. Therefore both sexes compete for suitable partners who will be around long-term or commit significant resources to the relationship. Men compete for younger, fertile women; women for men with greater resources and willingness to invest in offspring (Buss, 2004; Campbell, 2004). Attract causes investment in the means to secure such pair-bonds. It causes individuals to produce displays of sexual attractiveness through body adornment, painting, or modification; provocative clothing; or through activities that display mate quality, such as sports and dancing. It can further involve demonstration of one's ability to maintain physiological health by overcoming a self-imposed handicaps, such as scarification (Ludvico & Kurland, 1995) or risky gun-play by adolescent males (Wilson & Daly, 1985). Attract also causes individuals to seek pairings with the highest possible quality mates. Feelings of flirtatiousness and sexiness may accompany this motive (Geoffrey Miller, 2000).

Pair-bond love. While *attract* produces investment in self to help gain a pair-bond, *love*, in humans, drives investment in the special others that are family partners. Species requiring significant parental investment have the problem of parents securing long-term resource investments from each other. Through *pair-bond love*, individuals seek to build and defend a pair-bond such that offspring with a long period of dependence on parents can be brought up (Quinlan & Quinlan, 2007). Mothers, in particular, need to keep men around long enough so that they can share the burden of rearing offspring (Fox, 1984). Human females have developed means to achieve this goal—in particular, continuous estrus and enlarged breasts (Buss & Haselton, 2005; Hawkes, 2004; Sillen-Tullberg & Møller, 1993). *Love* causes both males and females to invest in the pair-bond with tactics that include making costly gifts, offering tokens of commitment, and the jealous driving away of rivals. Conflicts within this special relationship can inspire jealousy, which motivates mate-guarding behavior (Buss, 2000). Pair-bond *love* is the motived BPU that maintains the social end-state of a long-term mated relationship.

Ultrasociality. There was a final development in social life that is characteristically human: societies composed of large, complex groups of cooperating non-kin (i.e., "ultrasocial" groups; Richerson & Boyd, 1998). Aggregation into ultrasocial groups was made possible by the accumulation of significant resource surpluses, largely following from the agricultural revolution. This meant large groups of people cooperating despite being largely unrelated to one another—a unique form of social life with major evolutionary benefits, which could not have been stable without the coevolution of new forms of social regulation.

Justice. Since common genetic interests cannot be depended upon to maintain cooperation in large unrelated groups, other forms of policing of social relationships had to evolve. Primary among these is "strong reciprocity" and so-called third-party punishment, or the costly punishment of others, even when one has not been wronged oneself (Gintis, 2009). This is a strictly human phenomenon (Riedl et al., 2012).
We postulate that the *justice* motive evolved to cause humans to enjoy punishing those who behave antisocially, and even to enjoy punishing those who fail to punish such miscreants (de Quervain et al., 2004). Someone (or some set of people) within a group (i.e., a "leveling coalition") can take it upon themselves to ensure that resources

are properly distributed whenever they become overly clustered in the hands of some individual or subgroup (Boehm, 1999; de Waal, 1982, 1986). Because this "policing" is a public good and comes at an individual cost, there are considerable incentives to defect, letting others do the job rather than oneself (thereby enjoying the benefits of social cohesion without paying anything for it). Game theoretic results suggest such a system can be maintained only if those who do not engage in policing are themselves punished for violation of the norm to help maintain the egalitarian social ethos (Axelrod, 1986).

Justice is a motivated BPU that drives contingent strategies toward an end-state of "fairness" or social equity, hence qualifying as a social emotion in our proposed schema. Concern with a lack of equity is centered in the insula, like *disgust* (Hsu et al., 2008), suggesting that moral retribution against parasites on ultrasocial "bodies" or organizations may have built on the foundation of the motivational machinery of disgust, which was designed to protect individual bodies (Curtis, 2013).

Recent theoretical and experimental work demonstrates that ultrasocial life cannot be maintained without the kinds of punishment associated with *justice* (Fehr & Gachter, 2002; Price et al., 2002). Thus, ultrasociality, maintained through strong reciprocity, constitutes a novel form of evolved sociality that required new psychological and behavioral mechanisms. Others have suggested a further set of social emotions that they label the "self-conscious" emotions of shame, guilt, and embarrassment. These regulate one's own likelihood of transgressing social norms or appropriating unfair proportions of group resources, and provide incentives to repair social relationships damaged by overly selfish behavior (Tangney et al., 2007). Such emotions make it less likely that others will have to police social interactions in ultrasocial groups, since individuals police themselves through such psychological sanctions. Further, *justice*-based morality required contempt and/or indignation to induce the punishment of third-party defectors, charity toward third-party cooperators (i.e., toward those who haven't directly cooperated with you, but with others), and additional self-control in the form of shame and/or guilt to reduce tendencies to defect oneself (Jacquet et al., 2011; Tomasello, 2014). We have not included shame, guilt, embarrassment, contempt, or charity in our list of social emotions, because we propose they should be seen as strategic feelings associated with success or failure of the *justice* BPU.

Emotional Controversies

In this chapter, we have argued that new emotions arose over time as life became more complex in the lineage leading to humans. We have postulated only eight basic emotions. Two are ecological and arose in reptiles: *hoard* and *create*; six are social and arose in mammals: *nurture, affiliate, status, attract, pair-bond love,* and *justice.*

We have argued that emotions evolved via a set sequence of coevolutionary steps. The transition to new niches introduced opportunities for new kinds of behavior, which some animals in the human lineage took by evolving new kinds of BPUs, which in turn allowed them to further expand their niches. The earlier ecological emotions, arising in reptiles, are largely territorial and competitive. By contrast, mammalian developments in emotional life are essentially prosocial, designed to help manage family life through cooperative activities of various kinds.

Our evolutionary story is based on a definition of emotions as motivated systems designed by evolution to produce behavior aimed at improving an animal's situation with respect to the world. We are well aware that this is a novel definition and one that differs from other propositions in this highly controversial area. In general, emotions have been conceived as a system for achieving a number of highly disparate functions:

- interrupting behavior by focusing or redirecting attention (Sloman, 2001)
- limiting the search for behavioral options (Evans, 2002)
- valuing events or possible behavioral options (emotion as any form of affect; Dolan, 2002)
- finding the meaning of events (i.e., appraisal theory; M. Arnold, 1960; Lazarus, 1991; Scherer, 1999)
- helping people adjust to their local—that is, cultural—circumstances (i.e., social constructionism; Averill, 1980; Oatley, 1993)
- coordinating the physiological, expressive, subjective experiential, and behavioral aspects of responses within a person (Levenson, 1999)
- interpreting feelings (Damasio, 1994; James, 1884; Prinz, 2004)
- solving recurrent problems important to biological fitness (Delancey, 2002; Ekman, 1999; Nesse, 1990; Tooby & Cosmides, 1990)

In response to this range and diversity of perspectives, some see emotions as a cluster concept without a core set of features (Delancey, 2002; Sloman, 2001), while others despair of emotion ever becoming a useful scientific concept (Elster, 1999; Griffiths, 1997). Despite a hundred years of theorizing, a major problem remains: can a scientifically justifiable theory of emotions be found?

Our proposition is to place the concept within a larger framework, in which emotions have a specific role to play. From our perspective, emotions are just one kind of unit in a behavior production system (Aunger & Curtis, 2013). Within this system, emotions can be rigorously contrasted with other kinds of BPUs with respect to both function and mechanism.

Our definition of emotion, based on its evolutionary function (to achieve advantageous situational end-states) and means of control (motivated goal pursuit), is different from those in the literature in a number of ways. We do not see emotions as cognitive appraisals of the meaning of an individual's situation (Lazarus, 1991; Scherer et al., 2001), nor as intentional states that disrupt the flow of behavior (Kenny, 1963; Oatley, 1993). Nor do we see feelings caused by changes in physiological conditions as essential to the definition of emotions (Damasio, 1994; James, 1884). Certainly, successful achievement of a social goal results in a psychological reward, which reinforces the tendency to behave in the same way in future. As a result, we conceive of consciously perceived feelings of satisfaction, joy, or sadness as a part of the reward feedback system, and not definitive of emotion. Many consider joy and sadness as "basic" emotions because they have accompanying displays and feelings (Ekman, 1992; Frijda, 1986; Oatley & Johnson-Laird, 1987; Plutchik, 1980). However, in our view these are not emotions because they do not motivate particular behaviors that accomplish evolutionary tasks. Many also consider emotional "faces" to be an integral component of emotions (Ekman, 1999; Keltner & Haidt, 2001; Scherer, 1992; Tracy & Robins, 2004). Again we do not agree. Joy or sadness are rather signals about the quality of end-states achieved by previous behaviors (which an animal may want to display in certain circumstances via a recognizable signal). Since social emotions serve to manipulate the behavior of others, much of the behavior they motivate has communicative functions. However, particular faces are neither present in all emotions nor a required component of emotional behavior production.

Our definition of emotion does have commonalities with the "affect programme" school, which sees emotions as modular systems that coordinate animals' responses to recurrent situations that impact on fitness (Nesse, 1990; Panksepp, 1998; Plutchik, 1980). (A similar proposition has been put forward in the form of cross-species "emotion primitives." These are mental engines that produce behavior in a range of species when certain forms of stimulus are received; Anderson & Adolphs, 2014.) However, the affect program definition is still too wide-ranging—allowing almost any adaptive behavior to be emotional. The "social functionalist" approach (Hutcherson & Gross, 2011; Keltner et al., 2006), which sees the function of emotions as coordinating social interaction, is probably closest to our own view of the social emotions. However, social functionalism still mixes drives with emotions and does not articulate what, for us, is definitive of a social emotion—the motivation of a contextually determined sequence of behaviors that changes the state of the social world in a way likely to lead to fitness benefits. The approach set out here offers a precise definition of what is, and what is not, an emotion, and sets emotions within a context of other kinds of goal-directed behavior.

We emphasize that our approach defines emotions not by the feelings that often accompany them but by their behavioral purposes. Making this distinction explicit helps to clarify a long-standing conceptual confusion about affective states (Griffiths, 1997; Nesse, 1990). We consider feelings to be mental representations of body states that have changed as a consequence of emotionally inspired behavior (Damasio, 1994). Feelings are a conscious recognition that something has happened, and a "somatic marker" of how well progress toward a goal is faring based on peripheral nervous inputs from various bodily systems. Feelings allow us to reflect on the success of an emotional strategy, inspired by neuronal circuits responsible for tracking deviations from a homeostatic state. They are necessary because the execution of emotional strategies mostly takes place subconsciously and rather automatically. A feeling is the private, phenomenological experience of the perceived consequences of emotional behavior. According to our model, feelings may variously be associated with arousal, with satisfaction, and with the outcomes of motivated behavior. For example, a feeling of thirst or hunger may accompany a search for a drink or food, a feeling of satiation may result from consumption, and a feeling of contentment may accompany the conclusion of the behavioral episode, all of which are due to the *hunger* motive. There are thus many more feelings than there are emotions. The reverse is also true: particular feelings can be associated with a variety of emotions. For example, a feeling of anger can accompany action associated with the various BPUs of *hoard, status, love,* and *justice*. For these reasons, feelings are unreliable indicators of motives.

It is true that in this project we have sometimes employed a feeling word when naming BPUs (*hunger* is both a feeling and a BPU, as are *disgust* and *love*). This does not mean that we equate motives with feelings. The evolutionary import of feelings will be a matter for discussion in the next chapter, which concerns the next step in our human story, the evolution of planning and the dawn of consciousness.

Social Learning

The ability to achieve social end-states through complex strategic behavior was underpinned in mammals by social learning. Simple copying of strategies used by others must have been particularly useful for risky behaviors, or ones that depend on significant skill, when one can exploit information acquired by others through *their* hard experience (Rendell et al., 2011; Zentall & Galef, 2013). Developing biases to learn from those conspecifics most likely to have locally relevant information— such as those who look particularly robust physiologically (i.e., healthy) or who have achieved high status—should also have evolved (Boyd & Richerson, 1985). The neocortex, which arose in mammals (Butler, 2001; Northcutt & Kaas, 1995), is heavily activated by social problems and presumably provided these new behavioral control abilities (Adolphs, 2001). The neocortex is associated with the ability to learn vicariously from observing the behavior of conspecifics (Frith & Frith, 2012; Gariépy et al., 2014; Mitchell et al., 2005).

Since social emotions concern the manipulation of others' behavior to one's own situational advantage, it was vital to be able to rapidly learn from observing the behavior of others. The Von Economo neurons (so-called spindle cells) are of recent phylogenetic appearance, being present in ape brains, but in humans are especially large, numerous, and aggregated in clusters (Nimchinsky et al., 1999). This fact, together with their location (specific to layer five of the anterior cingulate cortex and frontoinsular cortex), suggests they are involved in social bonding, social emotions, and social reward. They may constitute a specific, recent adaptation for human social life, particularly the rapid assessment of complex social situations (Allman et al., 2005; Butti et al., 2013; Sherwood et al., 2009).

Interest: Social Play

Another development made possible by social life is *social play*. This is a variant of the *object play* BPU in which the object becomes a conspecific. Obviously, a conspecific cannot be effectively treated as an inert object, but will respond to overtures such that *play* becomes an interaction rather than mere action. For this reason, *social play* is considerably more sophisticated in control and execution than *object play*. In mammals, *social play* seems to be about "training for the unexpected" (Spinka et al., 2001).

Social play is motivated and goal-directed, aiming at the aptitudinal end-state of being better equipped to understand social interaction. It is not an emotion, by our definition, but rather a specific motivated BPU that leads to a specific kind of social learning (hence it is an interest).

When the *social play* BPU is engaged in a mammal it will search for opportunities to practice complex subsistence and social skills (Smith, 1982). *Social play* behavior can involve pretense (Allen & Bekoff, 1997; Lillard, 2001); it takes place in contexts in which actions have reduced consequences on biological fitness, so that any failure to perform the behavior correctly is mitigated (Fagen, 1991; Panksepp, 1998; Smith, 1982). Play is engaged in often by incompetent juveniles seeking to acquire skills or knowledge through the pretend practice of potentially dangerous behavior (Eibl-Eibesfeldt, 1997). In general, young animals play more than older ones, and species with longer periods of dependency play more than those without, which makes sense if play has a role in individual development (Bekoff & Byers, 2004). For example, "rough-and-tumble" play (Panksepp, 1998) is aggression without resources to be won, and practice hunting typically targets small, inconsequential, non-dangerous prey items. Similarly, play nurturing can involve "doll" objects that cannot be harmed by poor mothering (Pellegrini, 2003). Dogs playing "fetch" with sticks and children playing "soldier" in war games on computers are engaged in practice experiences that simulate important biological skills. Pretend aggression is a tactic used in *social play* that is primarily concerned with acquiring skills at competing for resources or social status (Panksepp, 1998).

Animals can apparently signal their intention to initiate play with specific actions. For example, canids (dogs, coyotes, and wolves) "bow" to each other prior to play-fights (crouching over and lowering their heads to their feet), which may signal to a partner that "I want to play" (Bekoff & Byers, 2004). Primates display the play "face," a relaxed, open-mouth expression that differentiates play-fighting from the tight-lipped expressions accompanying serious contests (Loizos, 1967).

Pretense is made possible by the more sophisticated nature of behavioral control available in mammals. Thus, animals may repeat important behaviors in harmless "test" situations to monitor their level of expertise at executing tasks (K. Thompson, 1998). Neurological studies show increased brain mass and neural connections (Siiter, 1999) and increased mental flexibility after such play activities (Siviy, 1998).

Social play behavior not only improves an animal's own social skills, but also those of its companions. For example, in "rough-and-tumble" play, animals learn how to engage in dominance contests without actual violence. This helps the individual but also the partner, teaching it about its strength relative to the other. Hence success in pretend battles can affect the real reputations of the players.

Play in early vertebrates is limited to *object play*, which is the least sophisticated in cognitive terms; marsupial mammals exhibit only one form of *social play*—predatory chasing—while placental mammals exhibit more complex forms of interactive social play, such as pretend dominance contests (Burghardt, 2005). Thus, play may be associated with a physiological or situational end-state, but its function is to enhance the organism's aptitudes, which can then be subsequently employed in the acquisition of evolutionary benefits (Fagen, 1991).

A number of scholars have suggested that there is a transition from *exploration* to play (Burghardt, 1984; Hutt, 1966; Power, 2000). In human children, purposeful play develops ontogenetically from undirected *exploration* (Hughes, 1983), a lifespan sequence that may replicate the evolutionary one. Here, we propose that curiosity, rather than play, is the evolutionary elaboration of *exploration* in humans. Curiosity is the source for much of the spontaneous creativity observed in endeavors such as science and the arts, whereas play is elaborated into sports and other recreational activities such as hobbies, which build on expertise in specific motor skills.

CHAPTER 5

IMAGINING THE FUTURE

Thus far we have seen six classes of behavior production units (BPUs) evolve in the human lineage: reflexes, instincts, and exploration at the reactive level; drives, emotions, and interests at the motivated level. One final Rubicon was left to be crossed. This was the evolution of executive control over behavior, which allowed some primates to plan and thereby meet objectives over the long term. This development allowed them access to new benefits, whether physiological, situational, or aptitudinal, that could not be obtained via short-term reactive responses nor by medium-term motivated goal pursuit. For example, apes carry tools around with them until they become necessary (Mulcahy & Call, 2006). Without this apparent ability to plan ahead, opportunities to take advantage of some food resources—accessible only through use of the tool, like nuts that need cracking—might be lost. Humans, of course, take this ability to an extreme by developing long-term (indeed, possibly lifelong) plans—such as saving money now to expend during the retirement years, or engaging in an elaborate sequence of actions that ultimately result in revenge against a group of rivals (as in Dumas's story of the Count of Monte Cristo). This is a kind of task that no animals in the human lineage before primates could accomplish, and brings evolutionary benefits via the achievement of end-states that could be reached only in this way.

As we saw, mammals use internal representations of end-states (i.e., goals) to guide behavior. However, these are singular and do not connect with one another. The ability to plan takes this ability to represent possible future states a significant step further. The ability to plan behavior depends on being able to hold and manipulate representations in working memory. Higher primates gained greater control over their behavior by evolving the ability to represent representations—that is, to "meta-represent" (Hughlings Jackson, 1958; Perner, 1991; Sterelny, 1998).

The essence of meta-representation is the ability to hold a complex set of representations within one's own mind and manipulate it while continuing to maintain a consistent body of knowledge about the world (Sperber, 2000). Representations can include chains of possible future events and even simulations of the likely behavior of other animals and their thought processes, which enables an animal to engage in more sophisticated prosocial and competitive strategies. It endows the meta-representing animal with the ability to conditionally navigate multiple obstacles and find or invent new beneficial end-states.

How was this quantum leap in behavior production ability achieved in brain tissue? Control over complex cognitions is associated with the prefrontal cortex (Jackson et al., 1999; Miller & Cohen, 2001; Schall, 2001). In particular, the prefrontal cortex has been linked to goal maintenance, being active when primates learn a task but uninvolved when the task becomes automatized (Miller & Cohen, 2001). It is also associated with the human ability to suppress or withhold behavior, another measure of control (Jackson et al., 1999; Kiefer et al., 1998). Further, patients with frontal lobotomies lack the ability to prioritize or to order events into planned activities (Hoffman, 1949). It has been shown that signals looping through neural circuits between the prefrontal cortex and the basal ganglia and can bootstrap increasingly complex representations, thus recursively performing increasingly abstract tasks (Pasupathy & Miller, 2005). A particular area of the human brain called the rostro-lateral prefrontal cortex, or Brodmann area 10—which is of recent evolutionary origin and which has increased in size between chimpanzees and humans (Semendeferi et al., 1997, 2001)—seems to be recruited when abstract, meta-representational tasks must be processed, regardless of task domain (reasoning, working memory, episodic retrieval, attention, or language), and specifically for tasks that involve relating multiple domains of experience to one another (Christoff & Gabrieli, 2000; Christoff et al., 2001).

The ability to meta-represent constitutes a qualitative leap in the production of behavior. A brain that works by reflex or goal-direction, with their associated forms of learning and memory, cannot nest representations into complex hierarchical structures through experience. Meta-representation is a true advance that required new cognitive equipment for control over behavior (Proust, 2013; Sperber, 2000). Just as the ability to have internal representations led to a new level of control over production in vertebrates through goal-direction (a state of the world "kept in mind" to guide behavior), so meta-representation represents a qualitative change in behavioral production. Meta-representation further leads to metacognitive abilities: some animals can use it to have knowledge of, and control over, their own cognitive processes, being able to actively monitor and regulate their behavior (Koechlin et al., 2003). This is an obvious elaboration of motivational stage abilities, and constitutes a major advance in the ability to produce patterned behavior over long periods of time. We therefore nominate executive control as another major step in the evolution of human behavior.

Primates

The animal group associated with meta-representational abilities in the human lineage is the primates (Whiten & Byrne, 1991). Primates differ from other mammals in having hands with opposable thumbs, stereoscopic vision, a prolonged period of offspring dependence, and hierarchical social groups. Their expanded neocortex is associated with mental abilities to deal with the complexity of their social life (Boyd & Silk, 2006; Humphrey, 1976).

Planning

We propose that the psychological novelty made possible by meta-representation is what we will call "planning." By *planning* we mean behavior designed to reach arbitrarily distant or abstract end-states, which we call "objectives" (Fincham et al., 2002; van den Heuvel et al., 2005). *Planning* requires the ability to generate representations of future action sequences and their likely outcomes (George Miller et al., 1960). This internal trial of foreseen behavior allows multiple hypotheses or plans to be generated and tested without physical effort or risk. In some cases this allows the plan to die instead of the animal, with obvious evolutionary benefits (Dennett, 1996). It should be noted that the representations manipulated in generating planned behavior do not necessarily require conscious thought. We will discuss this further when we come to humans.

The ability to *plan* is evident in apes, which make tools through a complex series of sequence-dependent behaviors (Byrne et al., 2001). They also carry tools around for significant periods of time when trained to expect future opportunities to use them (Mulcahy & Call, 2006), again suggesting that they are *planning*. Primates thus have the ability to hold a number of different possible sequences of future actions "in mind" and to select the sequence that is most likely to provide the highest returns. *Planning* thus allows an animal to explore and deal with complex contingencies (Hughes et al., 1994; Osvath & Gärdenfors, 2005; Rolls, 2005). By maximizing likely returns over longer time horizons, *planning* allows animals to explore a larger problem space and achieve higher levels of fitness as a consequence of pursuing strategies that wouldn't be possible to an animal without the same levels of control over its behavior.

Planning builds on the previous ability to pursue goals or end-states by being able to represent them, and hence to manipulate them. They became part of the process of behavior production itself rather than simply the consequence of enacting a BPU. In effect, end-states were themselves represented inside other representations, to be constructed, learned, and freely chosen (Cosmides & Tooby, 2000b; Stanovich, 2004). For this reason, *planning* is a BPU that can be used to achieve end-states of any kind, serving physiological or situational ends, such as satisfying hunger or increasing one's status, but can also be used to enhance one's aptitudes—or any multiple of these.

So, for example, in humans, *planning* can be applied to a variety of aptitudinal objectives, including scientific discovery (e.g., lab-based simulations of simplified realities), or the production of art-forms (e.g., fictional narratives simulating what might happen if . . .). Indeed, planned behavior can be used to pursue objectives that may achieve end-states evolution would not select (e.g., maladaptive end-states such as childlessness due to the use of contraceptive technologies). Thus, although *planning* evolved because it allowed the pursuit of long-term objectives that were adaptive, the outcomes it produces do not always or necessarily produce benefits to inclusive fitness in modern environments (Curtis, 2013). However, the initial spur to the evolution of the *planning* BPU was likely the need to be able to negotiate toward a beneficial objective through multiple episodes, rather than having to treat each episode independently, as emotions do. So, for example, while the ecological emotion *create* could lead an animal to fashion a tool to use to break open a marrow bone, only *planning* would allow a spear to be fashioned so as to carry it on a hunt, or arrow points to be manufactured to trade for other valuable items. *Planning* enabled animals to foresee their own futures, through imagination.

Note that this implies planning ability is much less "modular" in nature than earlier brain adaptations. In fact, planning probably depends on a very complex network of neural tissue. A complex network associated with what is generally termed executive control has recently been identified, involving the dorsolateral prefrontal, anterior cingulate, and parietal cortices (Niendam et al., 2012).

Abstract Concept Learning

New types of learning modalities enhanced the abilities of the *planning* BPU. It became possible to store not just representations of objects and states but also representations *about* them. Objects and events could be now ordered into abstract categories. This allowed the idea of the thing such as an "arrow" or a "chair" to be stored and manipulated rather than the individual instances. Psychologists generally call these representations "concepts." These are categories that constitute a representation of some class of the typical entities or situations encountered (Zentall et al., 2008). Being able to categorize promotes cognitive economy by sparing the individual from having to learn every instance of each concept. Instead, individuals generate broad classifications of items so that they can transfer appropriate responses to novel instances that fulfill the basic criteria defining that category. Using concepts as tokens that are mentally manipulated in simulated possible futures is a powerful means of improving predictive ability. Social species that are dependent on remembering many kinds of social relationships—such as primates—could benefit particularly from this ability. Primates are able to categorize individuals by their abstract qualities such as trustworthiness, foraging skills, or courageousness. Capuchin monkeys can even generalize to abstract relationships (i.e., ones not dependent on physical similarity), indicating, for example, whether two stimuli have the same or a different number of objects belonging to them (Truppa et al., 2011).

Is the ability to generate concepts limited to higher primates, as our schema suggests it must be? While many animals can generalize, it has been argued that the ability to do abstract concept learning is restricted to primates, cetaceans, and a few species of birds (Katz et al., 2007) However, honeybees are said to be able to tell the difference between high and low (Avargues-Weber et al., 2011), suggesting that the ability to learn abstract concepts is more widespread. The disagreement may be due to the tests used. It has been argued that tests such as the simultaneous same-different task, the relational match-to-sample task, and the delayed match-to-sample task don't properly discriminate between the detection of similarity in a stimulus set and complex manipulations of feature clusters, which would indicate abstract concept learning (Giurfa, 2013; Penn et al., 2008). In the absence of definitive information or tests that can adequately distinguish such abilities in different species, we suggest that complex concept learning, at least, should be present only in animals with the ability to *plan*.

Declarative Memory

Declarative memory is the ability to store information about facts, including specific events. *Planning* is possible only for an animal that can do this. Declarative memory comes in two varieties, both of which are required for *planning*. First, we postulate, was episodic memory, which came onstream with the ability to mentally represent complex combinations of "what," "where," and "when" about an imagined event (Eichenbaum et al., 2012; Tulving, 1985). Memories of episodes are organized primarily by time, so that an animal can recall events in sequence (Dusek & Eichenbaum, 1997; Eichenbaum and Fortin, 2003)—a primary requirement for *planning* effectively.

Episodic memories are "one-shot" consolidations that tie together many elements in a linked memory. One form is the so-called flashbulb memory of a particularly emotional event such as the death of a president, or a terrorist attack (Conway et al., 1994). Such abilities are not limited to primates. Seed-caching birds can do this for a specific kind of behavior—their foraging strategy of depositing large numbers of seeds underground (Clayton & Dickinson, 1999). However, finding similar abilities for behaviors not associated with food or sex has been difficult, and similar results have not been found in rats or monkeys (Hampton & Schwartz, 2004), suggesting that this may be a specially evolved adaptation to support that most central of activities—feeding—rather than a general propensity.

(It has been argued that we should extend (proto)episodic memory abilities to most mammals and birds based on the association in humans of this ability with brain areas that have analogs in these other species (Allen & Fortin, 2013). However, this argument ignores the fact that the tell-tale behaviors don't appear in these species—except in a few anecdotal accounts (Ferkin et al., 2008) and in birds, which are not in our lineage—and that having analogous brain areas does not imply analogous functionality, especially as episodic memory requires integration of separate information streams: a sophisticated ability.)

Semantic memories are the second type of declarative memory (Tulving, 1985). Semantic memories store general knowledge about conditions in the world—"facts" that can be reported verbally, such as that plastic is artificially made or that blue eyes are rare (Pulvermüller, 2013). They may be derived from prelinguistic conceptual memory, but are different in being more complex. Semantic memories are not just a labeled expression of a single concept, but involve multiple related concepts—for example, knowledge that can be expressed in a sentence such as "A cat has hair, four legs, and meows." Ape language experiments suggest that apes have a form of semantic memory, since they can manipulate graphical symbols meaningfully (Savage-Rumbaugh, 1987). Unlike episodic memory, the knowledge stored semantically does not always come from personal experience, and is acquired through gradual training, sometimes with difficulty, rather than effortlessly through a single "aha" experience.

Both forms of declarative memory are also referred to as "explicit" memory because they allow particular bits of information to bubble into consciousness and to be reported (e.g., via language). However, consciousness is not a necessary feature; we argue that this is a later development, as it is not clear that all primates are consciously aware of the contents of these memories.

The two types of declarative memory are related to one another. Episodic memories can depend heavily on semantic knowledge about the components of events—for example, if the memory concerns a man being bitten by a dog, then semantic knowledge about dogs (such as that they can be vicious) will be recalled to help "fill in" the episode. It is also argued that over time episodic memories lose their specificity, gradually degrading into semantic ones via a process that involves losing time and place referents for the constituent elements of the memory, which become more generalized knowledge of facts rather than events (for example, all dogs are vicious; Baddeley, 1984). This can occur with age or simply many recalls of the relevant information (Rubin & Schulkind, 1997). This overlap in functionality and content is mirrored by a degree of overlap in the neural areas excited during episodic and semantic memory tasks (Rajah & McIntosh, 2005).

In humans, the neural basis of declarative memory appears to reside in bidirectional connections between the neocortex (where executive control lies), the parahippocampal region, and the hippocampus (which serves as the gateway for long-term memory storage; Eichenbaum, 2000; Eichenbaum et al., 2012). This suite of locations is consistent with these being high-level forms of memory, as we suggest.

Humans

Homo sapiens bring entirely new kinds of novelties to the table: symbolic thought, complex syntactic language, cultural rituals, and a phenomenological sense of consciousness, among other things. These abilities enabled our species to spread across the planet and to reconstruct the landscape as it goes—even to the point of influencing the planet's atmosphere. We are also the only species to live in very large groups of unrelated individuals ("ultrasociality"; Richerson & Boyd, 1998). These capabilities are linked to a massive increase in the size of the human brain (relative to body size) and further enlargement of the prefrontal cortex compared to other primates (Sherwood et al., 2009).

Explicit Planning

Despite the sophisticated nature of complex cognition in some primates, including humans, much of it goes on "implicitly," occurring below conscious awareness (Bargh & Chartrand, 1999; Reber, 1996; Wilson, 2004). The ability to manipulate mental representations does not imply that one is consciously aware of one's own mental states. For example, primates can engage in deception of conspecifics without necessarily congratulating themselves on their cleverness (Whiten & Byrne, 1991). Even in humans, much of what we imagine to be behavior based on explicit reasoning is simply a post-facto conscious representation of decisions already taken at a lower level (Libet et al., 2000; Stich, 2001; Wegner, 2002). Complex representations can be evoked and manipulated without being accessible to introspection even in humans (Bargh & Chartrand, 1999; Dijksterhuis & Nordgren, 2006).

We therefore propose that executive abilities evolved in two stages. In primates, the *planning* ability was implicit, or below awareness, while sometime on the way to modern humans came the additional capacity to be able to make explicitly represented, conscious plans. The latter stage involved self-consciousness, theory of mind, symbolic reasoning, and language (Deacon, 1997; Pulvermüller, 2005; Wellman et al., 1990; Wood & Grafman, 2003). As a result, there should be two systems for *planning*:

implicit and explicit (Camerer et al., 2005; Rolls, 2005). Explicit *planning* is our candidate for the most recent category of behavior production unit in our lineage. It represents the last major development in control thus far.

Implicit cognition is presumably inaccessible to consciousness due to its subsymbolic, distributed representation in the brain, while explicit knowledge is captured (in computational models, at least) by symbolic, localized representations in which each processing unit is more easily interpretable and has a clearer conceptual meaning (Clark & Karmiloff-Smith, 1993; Sun et al., 2005). Brain imaging suggests the implicit evaluation system is primarily located in the orbitofrontal and cingulate cortex; the explicit system is located in the lateral prefrontal and parietal cortex (Rolls, 2005).

We postulate that the ability to explicitly engage in *planning* arose when the brain learned to focus on itself. This step constitutes a turn inward, with a switch from representations that refer to the outside world in favor of self-referentiality, or what can be called "reflexivity." Reflexive meta-representation is the ability to make reference to mental states as objects; it is the state of having thoughts about thoughts (Perner, 1991; Wood & Grafman, 2003). The ability to reflexively meta-represent paved the way for a series of adaptations that followed in quick succession in our lineage (probably since our last common ancestor with other primates, and hence within the last few million years). These adaptations include consciousness, self-awareness, theory of mind, reasoning, and language, all of which require some kind of reflexive representation and so can be explained as consequences of the presentation of representations to the mind as objects (Deacon, 1997; Leslie, 1987; Llinas, 2002; Metzinger, 2003; Wood & Grafman, 2003).

In particular, the ability to pursue long-term objectives required seeing goals as a means rather than an (ultimate) end, thus creating the chains of goals that can characterize plans. This ability derived from meta-representation: goals could themselves be represented within a larger frame. Given the ability to meta-represent, goals could also be treated hierarchically, such that one goal could be elevated among others (i.e., become an overarching objective to which other goals would be subservient). Thanks also to meta-representation, multiple routes to that objective could be envisaged and evaluated, each plan involving different sequences of behaviors or sets of goals to be achieved. With time and experience, behavior sequences could be labeled (using linguistic facilities) and chunked in memory. Feelings, or representations based on inputs from sensory systems (Damasio, 1994), could also be attached to behaviors (past or imagined), allowing one to reflect on experience, and value them independently of the reward system. This is the evolutionary function we propose for feelings—not as characteristic of emotion, but as representations of the stages (initiation, pursuit, and outcome) in the operation of some emotional BPUs, as set out in the previous chapter on emotions.

Through *planning*, humans can achieve complex long-term objectives such as training to get a driver's license, getting fit, or saving for retirement. These objectives are achieved through idiosyncratic plans, constructed as a series of steps. For example, saving for retirement can involve setting up a pension fund, investing in a portfolio of stocks, and constantly adjusting investments throughout one's adult life. Saving for retirement is not a species-typical evolved goal, but rather a set of plans to achieve an objective that may or may not help meet a number of evolved needs. Indeed, some plans, such as collecting trinkets, are not related to meeting evolutionarily important needs at all, and in a technologically novel environment, some plans, such as working long hours or employing contraception, may even work against the individual's inclusive fitness. Achieving these complex objectives can require an ability to ignore current motives. For example, achieving the long-term objective of physical fitness may require ignoring current motives such as *hunger*. We thus distinguish objectives that are recent, individual, composite, idiosyncratic, and that require *planning* to reach, from universal, ancient, and necessary kinds of goals—that motivational systems evolved to achieve. Individual plans are not evolutionary in nature but constructed on-the-fly via cognitive processes.

The reflexive or "explicit" representation system probably evolved to allow the construction of one-off plans and cost-benefit decision making based on long-deferred rewards (Rolls, 2005). The assessment of options can be based on an exponential decay function applied to the value of future rewards (Glimcher et al., 2007). This requires several end-states to be held in working memory simultaneously to perform the trade-off calculation, perhaps using the numerical calculation faculty for comparison.

Consciousness

Treating representations as objects by a conscious subject appears to be a separate cognitive step in the human phylogeny. At some point in recent evolutionary history, at least some of the processes underlying executive control became conscious. We know this from introspection. Making any claims about the origins or functions of consciousness is highly contentious (Blackmore, 2011). However, we postulate that the ability to explicitly engage in planning arose when meta-representation learned to focus on itself. This stage of control can thus be considered a wrinkle on the basic meta-representational ability; it is special form of meta-representation: representation *about* representation (which philosophers call "intentionality"; Dennett, 1978).

Consciousness—and attention, on which it depends—is informationally constrained, having limited access to memory and information processing capacities. For example, devising complex plans consciously is effortful and subject to constraints on working memory (Miller, 1956); it can lead to less optimal decisions than reliance on unconscious or implicit cognitive processes, which have access to a broader range of mental resources (Dijksterhuis & Nordgren, 2006; Wilson, 2004).

We therefore suggest that explicit or conscious control is weak and inefficient relative to earlier-evolved forms of control (Haidt, 2001; Mele, 1992). For example, it is likely that people may have the requisite knowledge and skills to achieve a long-term goal, but short-term motivations, especially those triggered by the current situation, can override this ambition (Ainslie, 1975; Loewenstein, 1996; Metcalfe & Mischel, 1999). For this reason, people can have difficulty executing long-term plans to their end.

Indeed, some argue that consciousness is not involved in behavior production at all because it is a consequence, not a cause of behavior. That is, consciousness is epiphenomenal because action is initiated by implicit processes before we become aware of our intention to act (Libet et al., 2000; Wegner, 2002), or is simply an emergent phenomenon arising from a complex network of neural connections (Thompson & Varela, 2001). From this perspective, action is a consequence of implicit cognition, whereas consciousness is post-facto awareness of a rationale for what has already happened. If true, this makes consciousness superfluous to the production of current behavior, but not to learning and planning future behavior. Consciousness then is a form of learning through which new variations on behavioral strategies are acquired. For example, a primary role for consciousness could be error correction in plans: normally, it can be difficult to assign responsibility for failure to achieve a goal to a particular step in a long sequence of goal-directed actions; however, explicit meta-representation of behavior sequences allows credit for failures to be assigned to particular steps, allowing the planning faculty to correct more efficiently (Rolls, 2005; Wilson, 2004).

We should note that it is not clear that *phenomenological* consciousness needs to have arisen from this evolutionary step in cognition: it is perfectly reasonable to assume that human beings could exhibit all the appropriate behavior without conscious awareness of doing so (the so-called zombie hypothesis; Chalmers, 1993). While subjectivity is a consequence of the division between represented and representer, the feeling of being a subjectivity—having a sense of being an agent in the world—is an added complication, the explanation of which remains a "hard problem" (Chalmers, 1995). Phenomenal consciousness is classically expressed in the notion that there is "something it is like to be" in that state (Nagel, 1974). Animals prior to this level of control have silent or opaque mental states: they can represent "it-is-raining" as a state of the world but do not "know" that they are thinking that it is raining; they can sense "pain-in-foot" but not recognize that "I feel pain in my foot" (Dennett, 1983). The non-phenomenological state is that of an animal seeing the world through a window without knowing a window frame is there (Metzinger, 2003).

The evolutionary innovation was being able to pull back and recognize the representational frames through which one is looking. This constitutes the breakthrough of "objectivity," or self-aware representation. We hypothesize that once it became possible to simulate other minds inside one's own, it was necessary to distinguish self from other, if only to keep clear whether one's own survival and reproduction was at stake in a given situation, or someone else's. Subjectivity or information related to self, acquired through experience, came to be felt and recognized as different from knowledge; feelings put a spotlight on one's own situational criteria when there were salient threats or opportunities afoot (Humphrey, 2006). Thus we suggest a "phenomenal" aspect came to be added very recently to *planning*.

There were further longer-term consequences to the evolution of meta-representation abilities. Domains of explicit *planning* in humans include scientific discovery (e.g., laboratory experiments are specialized kinds of contexts for behavior, which isolate the influence of a particular causal factor on the phenomenon in question), the production of art-forms (e.g., fictional narratives as virtual "simulations" for mentally simulated or acted-out behavior), and religious practices (e.g., rituals as a symbolic form of social play). These behaviors may be adaptive, because such patterns may have predictive and social value and hence can be traded for resources or status (e.g. scientific advances, stimulating music). Due to the global nature of behavioral control with meta-representation, explicit *planning* shows similarities across domains of science, art, and humor (Koestler, 1964). The "symbolic revolution" therefore made a number of things possible which are quintessentially human. We argue that these special features of human cognition can be derived directly from reflexivity, an awareness of representations as representations, and considered to be various forms of *planning*, the primary application of meta-representation to behavior production.

Reflective Learning

As noted earlier, a variety of innovations, primarily associated with the expansion of the neocortex in primates (such as the novel Brodmann area 10), have followed from the ability to meta-represent in both implicit and explicit fashion. The difference between the two systems is mirrored in their different specializations with respect to learning. If the relationships to be learned are simple (i.e., with a relatively small number of dimensions), then explicit learning can be more efficient; however, for problems involving more complex relationships and a larger number of dimensions, implicit learning seems to be preferred (Sun et al., 2005). Thus, implicit learning mechanisms appear able to handle more complex situations (Dijksterhuis & Nordgren, 2006; Lewicki et al., 1992). The explicit system, which involves consciousness, appears to be more concerned with after-the-fact reflection and long-range planning (Timmermans et al., 2012; Wilson, 2004).

Reflective thought may have little direct control over the production of current behavior, but is important in terms of its indirect effects on later behavior via "offline" information processing (Baumeister & Masicampo, 2010). This includes replaying past events (including counterfactually), recounting the amount of feedback from past performances, inferring implications of proposed events, and predicting what others might do and feel. Reflective learning can be self-generated, and loop through the brain without novel environmental inputs or actual behavior. By reflecting on a chain of proposed events, reflective thought can discover weak links in the reasoning underlying the plan and correct it with an alternative course of action (Gärdenfors, 2003; Rolls, 2007). Reflection may (but not always) also override automatic impulses, thus overcoming short-term inclinations and temptations so as to advance long-term goals (Libet, 2004; Wegner & Bargh, 1998).

Autobiographical Memory

Another consequence of meta-representation—and probably of consciousness itself—has been that the brain has become able to reflect on its own existence. The subjective experience of having control over our thoughts and actions consists of both awareness (an ability to reflect on one's own mental processes) and a sense of agency (a sense that automatic processes may be occurring and motivation to counteract them; Bargh & Chartrand, 1999; James, 1890). A history of such reflections, as well as the episodic memories associated with them, can be stored as a life narrative, or what has been called "autobiographical memory." Autobiographical memory adds a "who" to the "what," "where," and "when" of episodic memories, and then chains them together into a coherent narrative about the individual's life history (Williams et al., 2008). This requires complex representational abilities probably beyond the ability of any species except humans. In particular, this type of memory requires a concept of self (Conway, 2005; Rubin, 1986).

Such autobiographical memories are not always reliable; they can be artificially created (i.e., without experience of the "recalled" events) by careful manipulations (Loftus & Pickrell, 1995). Events consistent with the self-image are more likely to be stored and recalled whereas those incompatible with the self-image tend to be forgotten. Keeping a consistent self-concept probably helps long-term planning, as events consistent with life goals can be seen as progress toward plan completion (Conway et al., 2001). Arousal and affect can also influence the encoding and retrieval of auto-biographical memories. Such emotionally charged autobiographical memories are reactivated more often, remembered better, and have more attention devoted to them (D'Argembeau et al., 2003). Events recalled as being autobiographical are typically multimodal, involving all the senses of vision, hearing, smell, taste, touch, and bodily movement, making them particularly vivid in many cases.

As one would expect, the areas activated during autobiographical memory retrieval are the newer facets of the human brain: networks in the left frontal dorso-lateral cortex and bilaterally in the prefrontal cortex (Conway et al., 2001). This form of "high-level" memory, together with reflective thinking, enables the sophisticated long-term *planning* that underlies many of our most cherished abilities, such as build-ing complex technologies, writing novels, and designing scientific experiments.

Having now reached the most recent developments, we have come to the end of our evolutionary story about how behavioral control systems have developed. What remains is to outline some of the implications this story can have for our understand-ing of ourselves.

SECTION 3

PHILOSOPHICAL PERSPECTIVES

In the first section of this book, we presented a theoretical framework for understanding how behavior is produced. In the second, we told an evolutionary narrative about how human behavior production evolved from simpler forms. These two sections represent the primary content of the book. In this third section, we offer two different perspectives on this content. Both chapters in this section are primarily philosophical in nature, suggesting ways in which our narrative can be made more theoretically solid and interesting—not just an historical account of random events. In Chapter 6, we argue that the behavior production units we have described can be considered the fundamental building blocks of psychology—what philosophers call the "natural kinds" of a science. In Chapter 7, we suggest that the evolutionary advances identified in the narrative of Section 2 share a fundamental characteristic: they can be considered examples of what philosophers of biology call "major evolutionary transitions." What this means we detail in that chapter.

CHAPTER 6

NATURAL KINDS OF BEHAVIOR

There is hardly a more powerful tool in science than what philosophers call "natural kinds" (Wagner & Wagner, 2003). Fruitful scientific investigation requires that entities, phenomena, and processes be placed in meaningful classes so as to be able to explain, generalize, and predict (Allen & Bekoff, 1997; Dupré, 2000; Griffiths, 1997; LaPorte, 2004; Quine, 1969). Modern chemistry, for example, derives its explanatory power from the recognition that substances are composed of a small number of different but unchangeable kinds of atoms. Its predecessor, alchemy, failed as a science because it assumed that a mysterious substance, the philosopher's stone, could transmute metals. As a result, alchemy could not correctly identify elements or predict their immutability. Similarly, evolutionary biology could not explain the inheritance of information until genes, the correct units of inheritance, were described (Wagner & Wagner, 2003). Atoms and genes are basic building blocks of their respective sciences, their natural kinds (Wagner, 1996). Natural kinds are forms "given by nature," not categories artificially constructed by the human mind (Boyd, 1991; Millikan, 1984). They are structures generated by processes that have distinctive intrinsic natures described by the causal factors at work in their production and maintenance. Instances of a natural kind can be meaningfully grouped together because they share something fundamentally real, which can be discovered through objective investigation (Boyd, 1991; Millikan, 1984). Science based on natural kinds thus allows us to map and measure what matters in the world, giving us understanding and, hence, power over it (Sterelny, 1990). However, the behavioral sciences have still to uncover, identify, and agree upon their fundamental units. In this chapter, we argue that the behavior processing units (BPUs) we have proposed in previous chapters are the natural kinds that the science of psychology is seeking.

Psychology is the science of mental processes and behavior (Editors, 2006; Myers, 2006). However, the behavioral sciences have still not identified or agreed upon a set of component natural kinds. Scholars have argued that the brain is designed to perform functions such as computation (Mountcastle, 1998), learning (Dayan & Abbott, 2001), detection of discrepancies, (Barlow, 1994) reasoning (Johnson-Laird, 2006), and predicting the future (Hawkins & Blakeslee, 2004). However, from an evolutionary perspective, the primary function of the brain is to produce adaptive behavior (Churchland & Sejnowski, 1992; Freeman, 1999; Hebb, 1949; Newell, 1990; Skinner, 1938). Attention, learning, reasoning, and prediction are of no use unless they facilitate the production of behaviors that help an animal stay alive a bit longer or reproduce itself. Animals are the only major kingdom of life to have adopted behavior as their primary means of adaptation (Lorenz, 1965; Tinbergen, 1951), and they alone have brains. Further, those animals that live in more complex niches tend to have more complex brains to deal with them (which makes it possible for them to behave in ways that allow them to live in such environments; Godfrey-Smith, 1996). Since brains serve to produce behavior, the natural kinds of psychology must be the entities or regular structures within the brain that produce behavior. In this chapter, we therefore argue that the BPUs we have uncovered, classed, and described in the previous chapters constitute the natural choice for natural kinds in psychology.

Defining Kinds of Behavior

What, then, is a "natural kind" in the context of psychology? The original conception of natural kinds, due to Aristotle and pursued by the English philosophers Locke and Mill, viewed them as sets of things characterized by a necessary and sufficient suite of characteristics. These characteristics are shared by all members of the kind because they are subject to universally applicable laws. For example, water, gold, and stars have the same composition and always do the same kinds of things, wherever and whenever they are. This commonality is due to a shared essence that guarantees the identity of the natural kind and serves as its principal defining element, regardless of what those instances actually look like (Kripke, 1972; Putnam, 1975).

This Aristotelian concept is now seen as being applicable to physical and chemical kinds, but not to biological or social kinds, which are more restricted in scope, both physically and temporally (Boyd, 1991, 1999a; Griffiths, 1999; Millikan, 1999). For example, any example of water will have exactly the same chemical constituents and structure (H_2O), but all members of the human species do not have exactly the same composition and structure (e.g., some are male, others female). Conversely, there may be an organism on the planet Venus with exactly the same composition and structure of a human, which would not qualify as human because it does not have the same history (Ghiselin, 1974; Hull, 1978). The objects of theory in the biological and social sciences are thus historical in ways that the objects of physical and chemical sciences are not. As a result, biological and social kinds are "fuzzier" and are subject to qualified laws (Hacking, 2002; Millikan, 1999, in press; Rieppel, 2005b).

The homeostatic property cluster (HPC) concept of natural kinds (Boyd, 1991, 1999b) is now widely taken to be the best foundation for biological and social kinds (Charland, 2002; Griffiths, 1999; Kornblith, 2002; Millikan, 1999; Rieppel, 2005a). HPC kinds are "homeostatic" because some force causes deviations in the qualities of members to return toward a central tendency (Boyd, 1991, 1999b). HPC kinds are the result of the same causal force acting on all of its members. While the Aristotelian, essentialist position assumes that the members of a kind are similar due to a shared essence or intrinsic property, HPC theory allows a broad range of properties and mechanisms jointly to constitute the kind (Mallon, 2003). For example, species are subject to natural selection pressures from environmental factors that cause members of that species to have similar qualities (e.g., morphological regularities). A member of an HPC kind does not have to share every feature of its kind with all of its brethren; instead, individual members need only have enough of the important properties in the defining cluster to qualify as belonging (Boyd, 1991, 1999b). This weaker concept of membership seems appropriate for objects that do not share an essence, as in Aristotelian natural kinds, but rather similar causes.

HPC kinds for which the homeostatic mechanism is common descent constitute a class which, following others, we will call "evolutionary kinds" (Charland, 2002; Griffiths, 1997, 2004a; Rieppel, 2005a). In this case, the reason that members of the kind have a number of features in common is their shared history of subjection to natural selection pressures. Evolutionary kinds thus have lawlike properties but are limited in the range to which the kind extends, due to their historical specificity (Boyd, 1991; Griffiths, 2004a; Rieppel, 2005a).

The members of evolutionary kinds produce effects that biologists recognize as phenotypes. These effects have been selected for the function they performed in the past; those that conferred higher fitness on the organism carrying them tended to be retained, while those with lower value tended to disappear. Eyes are a quintessential example (Fernald, 1997; Gehring & Ikeo, 1999). All eyes share a common function—that of converting photons to signals that can be registered by nervous tissue. However, some structures perform this function better than others. The current types of eyes within a given lineage, such as mammals, take the form they do as a consequence of a past history of selection for this function and are thus an evolutionary natural kind.

Classes of Behavioral Kinds

As with any evolutionary kind, the regular structures we are concerned with—BPUs—are produced, and can be distinguished, by their history and function. That is, members of a natural kind related to behavior must be functionally specific, and second, they must be restricted to a class of organisms that have a shared evolutionary history (what biological systematists call a "clade," due to being on the same branch of a phylogenetic tree (Hennig, 1966). In Chapter 2, we identified two ways of classifying behavior—first, by the degree of sophistication in the way brains evolved to control behavior in the human lineage (reactive, motivated, and then executive), and second, by the end-states the behavior is designed to produce (physiological, situational, and aptitudinal). These criteria correspond to the two qualities that define an evolutionary kind: shared history (within a phylogeny) and function. If we put the dimension of control together with the functional differences we have identified—that is, treat the levels of control as criteria orthogonal to the sorts of end-states achieved—the resulting two-dimensional matrix defines classes of behavior production systems. These BPUs regularly and consistently produce recognizable categories of adaptive behavior. Now we would like to argue that these BPUs constitute the fundamental natural kind associated with behavior.

We present our two-dimensional matrix in Table 6.1, which is a summary of the classes of BPUs proposed in the preceding chapters. We have identified seven categories: reflexes, instincts, *exploration*, drives, emotions, interests, and *planning*. Each class is either a distinct BPU (in italics) or a class of BPUs (e.g., emotions). We remind readers that we chose a set of names for the categories that do not necessarily coincide with lay or even established definitions, but have defined them anew (see glossary at the end of the book). We have had to do this because almost every term in the psychology of behavior—"instincts" "drives," "goals," "motivations," and "emotions"—come with a long history of association with now-defunct theories (Austin & Vancouver, 1996; Griffiths, 1997). This is, of course, part of the underlying problem with which we are grappling: psychology does not yet agree upon what its natural kinds *are*, let alone what to *call* them.

Reading across the table, all of the classes of BPUs at the same level have the same history with respect to the control mechanisms they employ. The first level is simple,

Table 6.1: Classes of behavior production units

Control Level	End-State		
	Physiological	Situational	Aptitudinal
Reactive	reflexes	instincts	*exploration*
Motivated	drives	emotions	interests
Executive	*planning*		

immediate, algorithmic, reactive response to stimuli. However, after the invention of goal-direction it became possible to reach beneficial end-states through motivated behavior (the second row of the table). Finally, with the invention of executive control, through being able to represent long-term objectives, higher primates became able to reach multiple end-states or any combination of them. Reading down the table classifies BPUs by their evolutionary function, in terms of the types of beneficial end-states that they help an animal get itself into (physiological, situational, aptitudinal).

Formulating our classes of behavior in this simple way allows us to identify relationships between them. To illustrate, reading down the table shows classes of behavior with shared functions. Instincts and emotions, for example, share the characteristic of leaving animals in situational end-states (as can *planning*), but differ from each other in their degree of control. We believe this is a powerful and parsimonious way of classifying behavior that should have utility in reducing the confusion surrounding claims about the psychological qualities of animal behavior in comparative psychology (e.g., whether seed-caching by birds is a form of planned behavior; Raby et al., 2007; Suddendorf & Busby, 2003; see our discussion of this issue in Chapter 8).

For example, keeping oneself free of parasites and pathogens is an important physiological end-state. To achieve this end, the roundworm (*Caenorhabditis elegans*) can detect the presence of a parasite in its vicinity and will recoil from it; fish avoid grazing in areas heavily contaminated by feces; rats and macaques avoid eating food containing feces. Reptiles and mammals scratch at ectoparasites, and many types of animal self-medicate (Curtis, 2013). We assume from various kinds of evidence—the relative paucity of neurons available, the lack of the requisite dopaminergic system in their nervous systems, the regimented sameness of their behavior patterns, and the inability to cope with unusual environmental conditions—that most of these behaviors are reflexively produced. On the other hand, humans avoid parasites by putting food in a refrigerator to prevent bacterial proliferation spoiling it. This seems to be motivated behavior because it can require getting around obstacles that might spring up on the way to the fridge, or be achieved while multitasking other activities in the kitchen. Humans also use vaccines to protect whole populations from infectious disease. This requires study of the epidemiology and pathogenesis of the disease, biochemical experimentation, and extensive field trials of potential compounds. This complex sequence of behaviors, taking years in many cases, with concerted efforts from groups of individuals, can only be accounted for by *planning*. It is therefore the complexity, diversity, and plasticity of the constituent behavior sequences, as well as direct examinations of the mental requirements, that determine the likely level of control operating in particular examples of behavior.

Similarly, reading across Table 6.1 shows classes of behavior production systems that share a common way of producing behavior, which, if we are right, must be related developments in evolutionary history. In the chapters preceding this we told our version of that evolutionary history, with reactive behavior evolving first (likely with the default BPU, *exploration*), simultaneously with reflexes, and then followed by instincts (because they are more complicated sets of reflexes). Then, with the advent of goal-direction, we again used relative degree of complexity of the behavior— evidence from contemporary species at different positions in the phylogeny leading to humans—as information to help deduce which capabilities appeared when, and in which clade of animals. Support for these suppositions should also come from greater knowledge of what extant species in the various clades can actually do (i.e., their behavioral repertoires), and growing knowledge about the chemical and genetic underpinnings of these various abilities.

Our classes of BPUs (e.g., reflex, emotion) are linked by function and history, but not necessarily structurally. This makes them similar to the biological kind of *organs* (e.g., heart, lung), which share functional characteristics but are morphologically and physically distinct. Individual BPUs, our fundamental natural kind, are the equivalent of atoms or cells in these other sciences: they are the basic physical building blocks of psychology, with an isolatable physical structure (which could be distributed or localized or some combination of both) and an isolatable genetic basis; they are the way an individual brain physically produces behavior with some kind of evolutionary benefit. The parallels with the kinds of other sciences are reassuring because they suggest that we have tapped into significant properties of the multiple levels of natural kinds more generally.

Individual Kinds

Within the classes of BPUs set out in Table 6.1 we have postulated "individual" kinds designed to address particular evolutionary tasks animals face in their ecological niche. For example, *startle* is a reflex that helps people quickly redirect their attention in an appropriate direction. *Separation panic* is an instinct that ensures infants remain in the social situation appropriate for their own flourishing (i.e., under parental care) (Panksepp 1998). *Disgust* is a drive that makes people avoid parasite vectors and construct parasite-free habitats, which helps to keep the body in a low-parasite state (Curtis, 2013). *Pair-bond love* is an emotion because it is goal-driven activity that improves an individual's state with respect to potential childrearing.

We suggest that natural selection devised BPUs able to respond appropriately to situations of evolutionary significance that were recurrent in an animal's phylogenetic history (Tooby & Cosmides, 1992). These mechanisms for generating behavior must be present in all the members of the species that have faced similar ecological problems throughout their phylogenetic history. These mechanisms must be BPUs (i.e., natural kinds), because one can extrapolate from their presence in one member of a species to another (Boyd, 1991; Millikan in press). By the same token, individual kinds will vary from species to species, as the niches of different species cannot overlap completely (Mayr, 1963).

The number of individual kinds that can be defined in this way may be large, but not very large, because the number of important evolutionary tasks is restricted to the dimensions of an animal's niche that distinguish it from other species in the same ecology (Hutchinson, 1957). (In fact, there are very many tactics by which one might achieve specific kinds of needs in humans, especially with regard to the social world, where there are a variety of ways to attract a mate, for example, or achieve higher status. However, we suspect that mechanisms specific to each tactic or strategy for achieving a need are highly situational, hence not repeatable, and therefore cannot be selected for directly, in terms of producing a separate adaptation for each means of achieving a need.)

A major exception to the argument that individual-level production mechanisms are BPUs are *planned* behaviors. Although the brain-based systems that implement such behaviors are themselves evolved, we do not believe there are units within the neocortex dedicated to the achievement of particular objectives. The *plans* that executive kinds produce are therefore not evolved but constructed individually to solve perceived problems on-the-fly. Thus, *planning* is both a class and an individual BPU: there is only one BPU, most likely in the isomorphic prefrontal cortex, capable of meta-representation and the pursuit of objectives.

Comparison to other Schemes

We have used deduction from the necessary characteristics of evolutionary kinds to define natural kinds for producing behavior at three levels. Our process of noticing regular patterns in empirical observations and deducing reasons for these consistent with fundamental theory (evolution by natural selection) follows a common pattern in science. For example, the structure of atoms was predicted by Bohr before it was ever observed (Bohr, 1913); the structure of genes was deduced from patterns observed in X-ray crystallographic plates (Watson & Crick, 1953); and the means by which genes express themselves was inferred from modeling prior to observation (Gamow, 1954). It is therefore reasonable to argue that deduction should also play a major role in the identification of natural psychological kinds.

We are not the first to hypothesize the existence of psychological kinds. Debates concerning potential natural kinds in psychology have centered around whether cognition (Pylyshyn, 1984), consciousness (Hardcastle, 1995), knowledge (Kornblith, 2002), concepts (Machery, 2005), psychiatric disorders (Kincaid & Sullivan, 2013; Zacher, 2000), particular emotions or the category of emotion itself (Barrett, 2006; Charland, 2002; Griffiths, 1997, 2004a, 2004b), or so-called human kinds—including things like human-specific diseases (alcoholism, hypertension) and institutions (government, marriage, etc.; Cooper, 2004; Hacking, 2002; Haslam, 1998; Khalidi, 2013)—are the proper candidates for this honorable role. None of these proposals—except that for emotion—have met with much acceptance, probably because no clear way has been found to distinguish different members of the kind within these basic categories.

We are also not the first to postulate the existence of natural kinds related to behavior. One influential predecessor in this endeavor has been ethology. In the twentieth century, this major disciplinary effort was devoted to the discovery of animal behavioral kinds with methods adopted from the natural sciences (Lorenz, 1950). However, ethology produced no widely accepted taxonomy of behavioral kinds, even though numerous attempts were made to construct schemes applicable to any species—that is, a "standardized" description or "ontology" of animal behavior (e.g., Catton et al., 2003; Golani, 1976; Schleidt et al., 1984) and the Standard Animal Behavior Ontology Project (<http://sourceforge.net/projects/sabo/>). The latter system consists of a hierarchy of categories, for example:

entity ➔ particular ➔ occurrence ➔ event ➔ achievement ➔ biological function ➔ grooming

We hope the scheme provided here can provide new direction to this general project.

We believe this approach has a number of major advantages over previous efforts to define classes of behavior. First, it is uniquely constrained by both functional and historical considerations to tell a plausible story about how the various kinds of production first evolved, from one level to the next, with support from known developments in nervous systems, learning and memory, and task repertoires. By basing the approach in evolutionary theory, we can make explicit claims about the order, timing, and means by which each kind of cause of behavior arose. Second, our account combines production types and output types (end-states) into a comprehensive and interdependent model of the causes of behavior; previous models have been limited to one or the other of these two dimensions. Third, we have provided new criteria for rigorously distinguishing among the various kinds of behavior production systems. These criteria result in new claims about the functions of instincts and emotions, for example.

Fourth, this proposal is consistent with the notion of hierarchical arrangement, and natural kinds tend to appear in nested hierarchies: in chemistry, substances are made up of molecules, which are made up of atoms; similarly, in biology, organisms contain organs, which contain tissues made of cells. Thus functional units exist at multiple levels of organization (Bolker, 2000; Dawkins, 1976; Hartwell et al., 1999; Raff, 1996; Wagner, 1996). Here, we have seen how there are types (e.g., reactive) and classes of behavioral kinds (e.g., *reflexes*), as well as individual ones that cluster into these classes (e.g., pupil dilation reflex, breathing reflex), presumably because they share neural substrates. In this way, our scheme is consistent with other kinds of kinds.

Fifth, the present account makes specific predictions that can be tested against other approaches. For example, we can compare predictions made from our approach about the nature of individual BPUs with those derived from a major alternative: folk psychology. Although we use nonstandard means to classify behavior into kinds, our typology does approximately map onto intuitive or "folk" categorizations of behavior in many cases. Hence, *hunger* is a drive, not because it causes a particular set of physiological states or feelings, but because it leads to evolutionarily significant returns through flexibly controlled, motivated consumption. Similarly, the emotion of *pair-bond love* leads an animal to work; it risks physical harm to defend rights of access to, or control of, a mate (a situational end-state). Loving behaviors can take many forms, and may endure until a particular strategic relationship is achieved. These two conditions define *pair-bond love* as an emotion.

However, a counterintuitive deduction from our approach is that behaviors commonly called "disgust" and "fear" should be considered drives rather than emotions. Fleeing from predation is an effort to avoid one's bodily resources becoming the predator's resources. Similarly, behaviors such as walking around excreta or rotten meat, or shunning someone who appears to be ill, involve a "negative appetite" for avoiding resources crossing the body boundary (in this case wanting to avoid being eaten from inside by pathogens). Our suggestion is that prey and parasite behaviors don't involve the same complex meta-representation as social interactions, and so are not emotional in nature. Emotional *fear* we reserve for behaviors that avoid conspecifics as threats to body or resources; emotional *disgust* is restricted to those motivated and contingent (i.e., strategic) behaviors that serve to shun "social parasites" (Curtis & Biran, 2001). Thus the overlap between our categories of behavior and those given commonsensical names is not perfect.

By redefining reflexes, instincts, *exploration*, drives, emotions, interests, and *planning* according to their evolved functions rather than by their mechanics or by the subjective states they create, we hope to provide a principled vocabulary that can be shared by behavioral scientists in any discipline, and applied to any species in our lineage. Most of these terms have long histories in psychology, of course, and have been abandoned by many precisely because of their imprecision. However, we believe that these concepts will continue to have value once couched in a natural-kinds framework. Establishing the natural kinds for psychology in functional terms (i.e., BPUs), as well as the means by which these kinds evolved (through neural transitions), should provide a central organizing framework for advances in the field.

Acknowledgment

This chapter is adapted from an earlier article (Aunger & Curtis, 2008), and is included here with the kind permission of Springer Science + Business Media.

CHAPTER 7

NEURAL TRANSITIONS

It could be argued that the evolutionary narrative in Section 2 of this book is just an ad hoc collection of events which get us to where we are today with respect to human psychological capabilities—that there is nothing systematic about the story we have told, except that it winds up in the right spot, with a creature looking like a contemporary person, having an intuitively sensible set of psychological talents. Even worse, we've made our task particularly easy, since we know where the story winds up, and only have to create a plausible "plot" from known events in the past, going from the end backward to the beginning. Like any other history, it appears to be just "one damn thing after another," without meaning beyond the telling of the story itself.

In this chapter, we will argue that this is not the case at all; that in fact we have picked out a meaningful set of events—possibly the *only* set of events—that satisfy important criteria. These criteria are, further, those of an important contemporary evolutionary theory of fulfilling the characteristics of major evolutionary transitions.

The only theory specifically concerning macro-evolution—that is, evolutionary processes on the scale of the fate of species—that is under significant development currently is major transition theory (MTT; Maynard Smith & Szathmáry, 1995). As the name suggests, it explains how to identify "big" events in the past history of evolution. (How it does so is described in detail in the following section.) This is the theory relevant to explanations at the scale of this book, which looks at processes happening over thousands of years, if not millennia, rather than the day-to-day problems of individual organisms passing the natural selection test—the situation covered by standard Darwinian micro-evolutionary theory. It is therefore an interesting question whether MTT can be said to apply to the kinds of events we have described earlier in this book. Further, MTT is designed to explain increasing complexity in the evolutionary record, and we have argued that the steps outlined in our narrative are examples of increasing complexity in behavior production—gaining control over behavior via more sophisticated mechanisms. MTT should therefore be relevant, at least potentially. But can we find a meaningful way to apply MTT to our history? If so, then rather than appearing to be a somewhat haphazard collection of events during human evolution, the steps we have identified could be shown to be members of a set of theoretical entities—major evolutionary transitions—that would add weight to our claims of their importance. Human history in this new light becomes not just "one damn thing after another" but a set of theoretically interesting events that share a common feature: they are each examples of major transitions.

In this chapter, we will argue that MTT provides us with a theoretical basis for choosing events in the history of behavior production. We show that application of the criteria implied by the major transition framework result in that particular suite of events that we have already identified. (Note that we could also have traced transitions in behavior production in other lineages than those that led to humans. However, since human behavior is our focus, we leave that task to other scholars.)

This argument is based on an important claim: that the concept of information inheritance in evolution can be meaningfully extended to include inheritance *within the lifespan* of individual animals. This is a potentially controversial claim, as the term "inheritance" in evolutionary biology thus far has been used exclusively in the context of intergenerational processes. (Even so-called epigenetic inheritance mechanisms remain intergenerational, just through mechanisms other than DNA.)

Suggesting that inheritance can apply within a generation—and to processes happening within an individual animal, no less—might therefore be seen as heretical. However, it is not as radical as it may seem at first glance. Maynard Smith & Szathmáry (1998) themselves extended their application of the concept of major transition to the mechanism of social learning, which is information inheritance *within* a generation, albeit between animals, when they argued that the transition from social to cultural group was a major transition (with the difference being the significant passing of non-genetic information via communication among members of cultural groups). In fact, the mechanisms of information transmission they identified range from the genetic to the technological (see the listing of major transitions in Table 7.1.) Acceptance of our argument here would extend the transition concept one step further, to within generational *and* intra-organismal inheritance.

In this chapter, we first outline the standard application of MTT to the history of revolutions in biological evolution on planet Earth, including recent additions to the list of transitions by colleagues of Maynard Smith and Szathmáry. We proceed to explain how the transition concept will be applied here to the novel context of individual (i.e., nonsocial) learning mechanisms associated with each of the steps of increasing complexity in human evolution identified in Section 2. The chapter concludes with some comparisons between what we call "neural transitions" and standard biological ones.

Table 7.1: Major Evolutionary Transitions

Transition	Source*	Novel Features				
		Level of Organisation	Heredity	Transmission	Storage	Inheritance System
Replicator to Cell	MSS 95	Cell	RNA?	molecules as groups	—	genetic
Gene to Chromosome	MSS 95	Chromosome	—	information in linked groups	coiled chromosomes	—
RNA to DNA + Protein	MSS 95	[double strand]	DNA	DNA replication	new genetic code	—
Prokaryote to Eukaryote	MSS 95	Eukaryote	—	coordinated reproduction of cellular material		—
Asexual clone to Sexual population	MSS 95	sexual population/ species	—	segregation/ recombination	species variation	—
Single-celled to Multicelled individual	MSS 95	multicellular organism	—	chemical intercellular signaling	differentiated gametes?	—
Individual to "Neural" individual	JL 06	neurally augmented individual	neurons	complex intercellular signaling	neural networks (memory)	psychological
Individual to Social group	MSS 95	social group	socially acquired information	social communication	social network	social

Table 7.1: (continued)

Transition	Source[*]		Novel Features				
		Level of Organisation	Heredity	Transmission	Storage	Inheritance System
Social group to Language	MSS 95	language group	—	symbolic communication	symbolic network	cultural
Language to Writing	MSS 98	Cities	artifactual information	persistent artifacts	form/message of artifact	technological
Writing to Information processing machines	MSS 98	global society	—	packet transmission	computer network	—

"—" means "no change"

[*] MSS 95 = Maynard Smith and Szathmáry (1995).

MSS 98 = Maynard Smith and Szathmáry (1998)

JL 06 = Jablonka and Lamb (2006)

Adapted from Journal of Theoretical Biology, 239 (2), Eva Jablonka and Marion J. Lamb, The evolution of information in the major transitions, pp 236–46, doi:10.1016/j.jtbi.2005.08.038 Copyright (2006), with permission from Elsevier.

Major Transitions

Explaining the organization and diversity of the living world is a major objective of evolutionary biology. In 1995 Maynard Smith and Eors Szathmáry introduced a powerful theoretical framework for understanding not just how evolution shaped natural phenomena: the premise of MTT is that the means by which information is stored, translated, and transmitted from one generation to the next has *itself* changed a number of times during the history of evolution (Godfrey-Smith, 2009). Examples include the switch from RNA to DNA molecules as the physical agent for genetic information storage, and from reliance on genetic information only to a period when information could also be transmitted between generations using language. Major transitions can also involve a change in the level of organization at which natural selection can work—for example, when cells became multicellular organisms, and organisms became social groups. Hence the premise is that the way that evolution works has itself evolved, with the result that some forms of life have achieved new levels of functional complexity.

Table 7.1 sets out the major transitions that have been identified by transition theorists. It describes the nature of the transition, who first identified it, and the novelties it introduced. These include information inheritance mechanisms, the level of organization of the resulting phenotype, the means by which replicated information is stored after transmission, and a general descriptor of the evolutionary system at work in each case.

The early evolutionary transitions involved new ways to inherit genetic information. For example, genetic information that was originally stored in single-stranded RNA came to be stored in double-stranded DNA molecules, with a slight change in code (a substitution of one peptide for another). Similarly, in another transition, cloning, a simple form of gene duplication was replaced in some groups of animals by sexual reproduction, with its more complex rule of a 50 percent probability that a maternal or paternal allele will be contributed to the offspring. In each case, the resulting mechanism permitted higher degrees of complexity in information inheritance (Maynard Smith & Szathmáry, 1995).

Later transitions have introduced means of "inheriting" information through mechanisms other than genes. For example, the transitions to social groups and linguistic communities depended on the transfer of nongenetic information between organisms through communication. In particular, social interactions came to be coordinated through the exchange of locally appropriate information (e.g., the use of calls to coordinate group hunting), and the transition to human language occurred when a much richer system of symbolic codes was developed. The two most recent transitions—writing and the invention of information processing machines

(Maynard Smith & Szathmáry, 1998)—both involve information inheritance working through nonbiological mechanisms. Writing involves the use of artifacts such as books to store symbolic information for later acquisition by others, and computers are artifacts that people use to store, manipulate, and transmit information (e.g., e-mailing spreadsheets to colleagues). All major transitions thus involve the evolution of new systems for the inheritance of information, using mechanisms ranging from the genetic to the technological.

For a major transition to occur, there must be a sustained period of directional selection that produces advantages for, and the time to consolidate, new levels of organization. This new kind of organization must also then work as a structure within which information transmission or inheritance occurs. Such a selection regime typically occurs only as a consequence of environmental change, like the movement of a species into a new niche (Elena & Lenski, 2003). The rate of change also has to be just right. Studies of long-term evolution in bacterial populations show that adaptive radiation (a fan of diverse new species on the 'tree of life') is more likely when there are moderate, rather than extremely fast or slow, rates of ecological disturbance (Chow et al., 2004; Kassen et al., 2004). Similarly, a computer simulation model shows that if organisms are allowed to select their niche, a permanent selective bias arises in favor of niche simplicity. However, if rates of environmental change are above a critical value, but slow enough to permit step-by-step adaptation to niches of gradually increasing complexity, well-adapted organisms living in complex niches will evolve (Walker, 1999).

To be relevant—and to be discovered in the evolutionary record—major transitions must also significantly alter the future course of biological evolution by influencing the way in which inherited information is translated into phenotypic traits (Calcott, 2005; Wagner, 2000). These phenotypic traits provide new, more complex kinds of targets on which selection can work. For example, the switch from RNA to DNA as a store of genetic information allowed DNA to specialize as a high-fidelity information store while proteins did the work of catalyzing chemical reactions and forming an organism's structure. Proteins, being more complex molecules than RNA, could perform a much larger range of phenotypic functions than RNA. Similarly, the evolution of sexual reproduction increased the variety of gene combinations available for making the next generation of offspring. Since different gene combinations are necessary to produce different phenotypes, the range of phenotypic functions those offspring could perform was also increased by the "sexual revolution" (Burt, 2000; Fisher, 1930; Weismann, 1889). In each case, then, the new system for converting genotypes into phenotypes permitted information to be translated into more diverse forms and hence to perform a greater variety of functions.

There is some controversy about what links the major transitions together as a group, with some arguing that no single characteristic links them all (McShea & Simpson, 2011). But this is largely due to a focus on consequences (e.g., a new level of organization, or individuality), none of which are true for all the identified transitions. What does serve as the central feature is some modification to the evolutionary mechanism (considered as having the characteristics of heritability, variation, and selection). So it is not novel consequences but *changes* to the evolutionary process itself that unify transitions as a class (Calcott, 2011), which in fact the original authors emphasized to a greater degree than those making use of the framework. Rosslenbroich (2009, 2014) makes a similar claim, arguing that the feature unifying the major transitions is that each serves to increase organismal "autonomy," defined as emancipation from direct responsiveness to environmental constraints, often in the form of greater sophistication over behavioral regulation. This correlates, he notes, with the evolution of increasingly complex nervous systems that can engage in progressively greater self-referential or "internal" processing. This obviously shares some commonality with our perspective, at least as a general proposition about the nature of major transitions, but Rosslenbroich's ideas do not extend to the identification of specific transitions.

Next, we show how behavioral systems share a number of important evolutionary features with genetic inheritance, then make the argument about what mechanisms of information inheritance can be associated with each step in our narrative about human behavioral control.

Comparing Genetic and Behavioral Systems

Behavioral systems exhibit striking parallels with genetic mechanisms of inheritance (see Table 7.2). Biological inheritance involves genes as a storehouse of information (or genotype), which is used by various processes in cells to produce phenotypes in the form of proteins. Behavioral "inheritance," on the other hand, involves memory and innate brain structures as storehouses of information, which are used by BPUs to produce phenotypes in the form of behavior. In effect, genetic information is "read off" genes to produce proteins; similarly, psychological information is "read off" neurons to produce behavior when neurons are excited into firing, which then stimulate motor commands to the body. In both cases, this is the "expression," not inheritance, of stored information, because the information is converted to a different form: proteins or bodily movements. A given BPU thus produces behavior (as its phenotypic product) from memories (as its genotype), much like a ribosome uses DNA to produce a protein.

Table 7.2: Comparing Genetic and Behavioral Systems

Aspect	Genetic System	Behavioral System
Genotype (information store)	genes	BPU (memory + innate brain structures)
Genotype modification (variation)	mutation/recombination	learning
Genotypic inheritance	gene replication	memory consolidation
Phenotype (product)	protein	behavior (bodily movements)
Phenotype production (information processing)	DNA translation/ transcription	behavior production
Generation	reproductive cycle	event cycle

Novel variants also arise in both systems. The genotype of the biological system can be modified by mutation and genetic recombination; memory (the genotype of the behavioral system) can be modified by learning. Selection occurs on both behavioral and morphological phenotypes as well. The parallels between genetic and behavioral systems thus encompass all major aspects of the evolutionary process.

Further, in both genetic and behavioral systems, specific events in evolutionary history can be identified that constitute the first appearance of a novel inheritance mechanism—the transition event itself—which then influences each cycle of the expression of information in a genotype-phenotype cycle (Wagner & Altenberg, 1996). The new genotype-phenotype mapping process is then repeatedly executed to produce each new generation of phenotypes. For example, the prokaryote-eukaryote transition occurred roughly two billion years ago, when a more complex type of cell found a way to develop and survive. But within the eukaryote lineage, each generation has continued to rely on the development of eukaryotic cells, presumably depending on the inheritance of a more complex store of genetic information, for many thousands of generations. Similarly, innovations in the means of producing behavior can become encapsulated in genetically inherited brain structures, which then work to produce many thousands of behaviors in the course of the lives of the organisms with those brains. An analog of the genotype-phenotype cycle thus exists during an animal's lifetime in the form of an event cycle. We believe these parallels suggest that it is appropriate to see the evolution of behavioral control in terms of major transitions.

We argue that each event of increasing behavioral control introduced a new mechanism by which information could be "inherited" through a behavior production process, via advances in how information is stored, translated, and transmitted by an organism from one point of time in its lifespan to another. The generalization of the major transition concept is thus to suggest that we can speak of behavioral rather than reproductive "generations" over which information inheritance can be said to occur.

All of these transitions occurred in the lineage of "neural individuals" (i.e., animals with nervous systems; Jablonka & Lamb, 2006), because only these organisms had the physiological means for storing information for later use. Because these transitions took place in neural tissue we call them "neural transitions." Of course, all neural transitions are also biological ones in that they involve natural selection on species with particular phenotypic traits. We suggest, however, that a distinction needs to be made between transitions that are fundamentally concerned with information inheritance through genes, and those in which the inheritance takes place through learning and memory. Like the other major transitions, ours involve evolutionary innovations in how information is inherited. However, unlike the standard transitions, ours involve innovations in the way information is inherited by a single individual, in neural tissue, rather than between organisms. In effect, new means arise for an individual to "communicate" information to itself at a later date.

Some interplay can be identified between the major transitions of relevance to psychology and those identified by evolutionary biologists. In particular, some occurred in the same clades of animals at roughly the same time, and so might be seen as mirrors of one another—or indeed the same transition viewed under different lights. Of particular interest here are the human transitions. For example, human language in biology, and meta-representation in psychology, are intimately linked. Language is itself a mechanism facilitating ontogenetic inheritance through cultural transmission. Thus, Maynard Smith & Szathmáry (1998) allowed that developments in information systems other than DNA could be significant enough to qualify as evolutionary transitions. We have taken heart from that argument to suggest a number of other ones.

The original list of transitions left a significant gap of nearly one billion years between two major transitions: the rise of the first multicellular organisms and the advent of sociality with mammals. In this book, we follow the lead of Jablonka & Lamb (2006) to propose that other transitions occurred during this period that have not yet been identified. At first, the ability for one cell to communicate to another allowed the development of multicellular organisms, one of the original transitions identified by Maynard Smith and Szathmáry. Later, this facility was extended to communication between individuals. This social transmission of information supported the coordination of activities among animals, facilitating the evolution of social groups and human language, two other transitions already identified. However, social communication has a prerequisite unrecognized by the authors of MTT: an animal must first be able to generate messages, and this required specialized cells that communicate with one another within an organism. (Maynard Smith and Szathmáry planned to add the origin of nervous systems to the list of major transitions in an update to their book; Szathmáry & Fernando, 2011.)

However, in parallel with these developments were others also involving neural tissue. First, in complex neural networks, some neurons could be taken "offline" to be devoted to the task of storing information for later use (i.e., perform memory functions). This permitted animals to learn from previous experience, and to apply the lessons learned to later, similar situations, thus increasing the likelihood of an appropriate response. For example, the ability to plan responses in advance, together with the ability to ignore other rewarding options, enabled humans to develop behavioral skills that required considerable investment before they paid off in evolutionary terms. Learning how to use a bow and arrow, for example, called for an apprenticeship and lots of practice before the first prey animal could be brought down and eaten.

The biological transition to social life led to a number of neural transitions. Indeed, we have argued that there was a coevolutionary relationship between developments into more complex forms of social life and new kinds of information inheritance through psychological systems (e.g., specific emotions were required to deal with the new tasks that arose, such as social hierarchies).

Our claim, then, is that the evolutionary story of brains and behavior we have told here can be seen as a description of a sequence of major transitions as well. The system that inherits information in our case is the animal itself, through the coordinated operation of brain, body, and environment. Inheritance works through the expression of information via behavior (i.e., behavior production), which causes a change in the environment, which is fed back to the animal through sensory systems, which modifies the animal's psychology through a learning process, the consequences of which can eventually be stored in the form of a memory. (This process is depicted in Figure 1.1.) Neural transitions thus involve coordinated changes in behavior production, learning, and memory (as well as potential changes in physiological abilities to produce new types of motor actions, such as sexual displays). This process of information inheritance thus works through a cycle of feedback between an animal and its environment, the intersection of which is behavior.

Inheriting Information during the Lifespan

As we have argued, then, each of the seven evolutionary steps in Section 2 of this book can be associated with specific changes in the way animals learn and store knowledge about the world and themselves—the characteristic that defines major evolutionary transitions. Here we describe exactly what these mechanisms of information inheritance are (see Table 7.3).

The first transition, to reflexive behavior, took place when multicellular organisms without internal differentiation became organisms with neural networks (the default for behavior being, of course, no behavior at all). Reflexes and *exploration* evolved simultaneously but independently with the ability to move the body. Reflexes are automatic responses to a cue from the environment or an internal bodily system. Reflexes tend to be automatized and well-tuned by genetic evolution, given the often significant fitness effects of failing to respond appropriately (e.g., to predation attempts). However, reflexes can be modified through experience, so that the right kinds of stimuli will serve as cues (i.e., tuning), or for the strength of response to be calibrated (habituation), which are quite limited forms of information storage. Reflexes can be considered the "baseline" behavior of these animals, arising when they first learned to control their movement. For example, a large, rapidly approaching object will cause an individual to duck, while a bad taste will cause a gagging reflex.

Exploration, the second transition, is a response to an internal trigger to move (perhaps in reaction to a physiological state of well-being). Thus *exploration* is initiation of a behavioral response via a different kind of information source than reflexes. *Exploration* is also about acquiring information for later use; such storage (i.e., as memory) is the primary purpose of such behavior. Information storage is a novel function, and so constitutes a neural transition. It is initiated by a default trigger that suggests that no other action is required at the moment. Instincts are environmentally determined, but unlike reflexes, can be a response to conditions in a prior environment at some

Table 7.3: Changes to Information Inheritance in the Neural Transitions

Major Transition	Novel Pathway of Information Inheritance
Reflexes	environmental condition at $t-1$
Exploration	internal trigger at $t-1$; long-term memory
Instincts	environmental condition at $t-n$
Drives	indicator at $t-1$ (which is a function of the environment at $t-n$)
Interests	internal trigger at $t-n$
Social emotions	social learning from conspecific (which is function of action-situation at $t-1$)
Planning	arbitrary stimulus at $t-n$

remove in time (i.e., t minus some arbitrary number of events, n). This is because instinctive behaviors can be chunked by evolution, with the entire sequence coming to be automatically executed once initiated by a cue. At this point, the last event in a chunked chain of behaviors has been "informed" by a cue appearing prior to the first event in the chain.

The transition from reflexes to instincts involved a clumping of reaction chains (Avital & Jablonka, 2000; Tinbergen, 1951) such that a behavior at one point in time could have been caused by a trigger happening some time earlier, not just prior to the response observed at that point. Thus, a kind of domino effect in causal terms could be achieved without high-level psychological control; instead, the fact that the environment could be depended upon to produce the right trigger at each point in the causal cascade (in consequence of what had happened before) enabled this chaining of reactive events.

Drives are determined by an internal state that reflects conditions in a prior environment (i.e., an indicator of some need). They are unlike instincts in being responsive to changing environmental conditions (i.e., goal-directed) rather than being automatically executed responses to current stimuli. This is because drives can use information about the environment acquired through previous experience to devise a route to a goal. Further, the reward system works as a "progress" tracking system to ensure that activities bring the animal closer to satisfaction of that goal. The transition here is to a system that can achieve environmental goals through motivated action.

Play is like *exploration* except in being able to proceed until a higher-priority behavior is required. *Play* builds skills (information stored in both the brain and peripheral nervous system) for use later. With this ability to store skills and knowledge through repeated practice, *play* constitutes a neural transition to a more sophisticated kind of aptitude development. It achieves these new capacities through the new behavioral phenotype of pretense. (This ability to achieve a broader range of possible end-states is the trademark of a major transition in behavior.)

Social emotions require that animals pay attention to signals coming from conspecifics to determine how to achieve a strategic goal, often through a sequence of interactions—that is, a succession of episodes of situational assessment and strategic social interaction until the goal is achieved. Such emotional actions are novel in being sensitive to the strategic reaction of a conspecific to the animal's own response in a previous interaction. This results in sequence dependence, such that the response to a conspecific at time $t + 2$ is influenced by what the conspecific did at time t.

The ability to engage in social learning to acquire new information is a new information transmission pathway linked to the emotions; the use of such information to reach situational end-states using motivational control constitutes a neural transition. This kind of strategic flexibility in behavior makes emotions a major transition in the complexity of behavior. Emotions are kinds of behavior produced using sophisticated means of bringing old information to bear in contemporary situations: information inherited from the animal's memory of past experiences with particular conspecifics, combined with what has immediately transpired in the current strategic back-and-forth to achieve a social goal. Thus, both long- and short-term memory are used to determine the next step in an interaction designed to reach a desired end-state.

The transition to *planning* occurred with the ability to see a goal as means rather than end, thus creating goal chains. Together with meta-representation, goal chains mean the animal can treat goals hierarchically, nested within one another. Thus, one goal can be elevated among others (i.e., become an objective), and multiple routes to that objective can be envisaged, each *plan* involving different sequences and/or sets of goals to be achieved.

A *plan* can cause behavior at an arbitrary remove in time and place from when it was formed, thanks to the ability to recall information stored by *planning* in long-term memory. Thus a decision made at time t influences what occurs at time $t + n$ (e.g., a career plan, made in college, to become a professor). With *planning*, information can be retrieved from a virtual future, having been projected into that future by the cognitive system, and evaluated by the reward system. This ability to live in a psychic time span extended beyond the present and recent past makes *planning* a neural transition. In this case, the novel behavioral phenotype is imagined or virtual experience: simulation within the nervous system of possible future situations, from which things can be learned, just as with enacted behavior (although probably at reduced salience).

Thus, in the case of each transition, new learning or memory abilities enabled the relevant creature to engage in new forms of information processing about the sequelae from behavior.

Two Types of Transitions

Although all major transitions involve changes in the way information is transmitted, the consequences of a transition can vary. This allows major transitions to be grouped into two classes, as Table 7.4 shows (Queller, 1997). In the first type, multiple copies of entities of a similar type come together to work as a group to perform new functions, as when genes formed chromosomes, or cells became multicellular organisms, or individuals clumped together in social groups. This class of transitions thus primarily results in the creation of a new level of organization (LOO). Examples of this type are single cells joining together to form multi-cellular organisms, or single individuals forming social groups.

Table 7.4: Types of Evolutionary Transition

Evolutionary Transition	Type*
Replicator to Cell	DOL
Gene to Chromosome	LOO
RNA to DNA + Protein	DOL
Prokaryote to Eukaryote	DOL
Asexual clone to Sexual population	DOL
Single-celled to Multicelled individual	LOO
Individual to "Neural" individual	DOL
Individual to Social group	LOO
Social group to Language	LOO
Language to Writing	DOL
Writing to Information processing machines	DOL

* LOO = level of organization: transition in which the new level of organization is made up of multiple similar units that were previously independent
DOL = division of labor: transition in which units combine to perform complementary functions

Data from David C. Queller, CoAperators since life began. Book review of The Major Transitions in Evolution, by J. Maynard Smith & E. Szathmáry, Quarterly Review of Biology, 72 (2), pp. 184–88, 1997, The University of Chicago Press.

In the second type of biological transition, units come together to play specific, complementary roles in a larger organization, often to accomplish an existing function. This second class of transitions involves a functional novelty resulting in a division of labor (DOL). Examples of this type are replicators and membranes jointly forming cells as units of replication (the first transition), males and females joining up to engage in reproduction (previously accomplished by the simpler mechanism of cloning), sexual reproduction (which involves specialization into gender roles), multicellular individuals developing multiple types of tissues (including neural tissue), and developing writing to also convey verbal messages along with language.

We suggest that the same two classes of transitions can be identified with respect to behavior: "organizational" neural transitions involve a new level of control over behavior, while "functional" ones enable organisms to reach new kinds of end-states through behavior without a major new form of control (see Table 7.5). One result of a new level of organization in neural tissue is that behavior can be controlled over longer periods of time. The first organizational transition, to reactive behavior, requires behavior production to respond to cues. The second organizational

Table 7.5: Types of Neural Transition

Neural Transition	Type*
No behavior to Reactive	LOO
Reflexes to *Exploration*	DOL
Exploration to Instincts	DOL
Reactive to Motivated	LOO
Drives to Emotions	DOL
Emotions to Interests	DOL
Motivated to *Planning*	LOO

transition, goal-direction, allows behavior production to ignore cues and continue with some direction to behavior. This directionality was made possible by the invention of an internal signaling system, the reward system. The third organizational transition, meta-representation and *planning*, allows goals to be chained together to achieve long-term objectives, which came to direct behavior through imagining various potential end-states. In each case, the length of time over which behavior can become patterned increases.

For each achievement of a new level of control, one or more transitions also occurred that enabled organisms to reach new kinds of functional end-states – which we suggest are like a new kind of division of labor within a level of organization or control over behavior. For example, motivated behaviors can bring physiological benefits (i.e., drives), change the state of the external world or situation (i.e., emotions), or influence an animal's ability to understand its world (i.e., interests), all within the same sort of time-frame. Thus, within each organizational transition (called LOOs for comparative purposes with the organic transitions) were several smaller (but still "major") functional transitions (called DOLs, again for ease of comparison with the biological original). These secondary, functional transitions do not require such significant physical differences in psychological mechanism as advances in control, and instead achieve a new sort of end-state over roughly the same amount of time.

Further, once each of the three LOO transitions in control had occurred, the cycle of smaller functional or DOL transitions went through the same sequence of steps— first the physiological and aptitudinal advances, then the situational one (although the final "cycle" was achieved in a single step by multifunctional *planning*.) Among these three classes of end-state, then, it seems that the BPUs producing physiological and aptitudinal end-states are about equally difficult to evolve, as they spring up at roughly the same time in all three cycles between organizational transitions, while BPUs achieving situational end-states always follow these other types. This is probably because situational end-states need not involve any changes to body states, whereas physiological and aptitudinal end-states do (to the body and brain, respectively). In this regard, situational end-states are more abstract, and so probably harder for sensory systems to recognize or measure. For both physiological and aptitudinal achievements, the body can produce signals to guide action, presumably from the peripheral nervous system. Behaviors like drives and *play* also produce dosage effects: thus, the more you exercise, the more tired you get; the more you eat, the more calories you get. This is not necessarily true of situational actions: great differences in rank or status, for example, can be achieved with relatively little work in some circumstances.

Implications of the Comparison

This focus on evolutionary advances can make it appear as if evolution produces a *scala naturae*, or ladder of progression toward the pinnacle of humanity. Clearly this is not the case: each extant species has its own history, which may have involved progressions of many kinds, not always from simple to complex. We are not suggesting that there is any teleological element to natural selection. However, by looking backward on the very long time scale between our single-celled and primate ancestors, we can identify a number of evolutionary transitions that have led to advances in the means by which behavior is controlled.

Note also that an interesting historical pattern is observable among the major behavioral transitions. Each transition took between 150 and 200 million years to occur (until the advent of humans, when the pace of change sped up somewhat). This steady rate of innovation suggests that each transition is a relatively independent event. Rather than relying on resources built up by earlier advances, each was a true innovation that required finding the solution to a roughly equally difficult problem to solve (i.e., search through problem space by natural selection pressures), which had to be instantiated in a new mechanism. This could explain why, for each step, the behavioral novelty is unlike any other, despite the recurrent patterns in other aspects of the transitions (e.g., end-state type sequences). The fact that they appear to be independent also works against a kind of *scala naturae* interpretation of this work.

If true, this comparison is more than just an analogy between biological and psychological innovations. It is an insight about an ontologically real process in which information—the primary "currency" of evolution (Bergstrom & Rosvall, 2011; Maynard Smith, 2000; Oyama, 2000)—works in new ways, enabling new forms of adaptation to environments. (The significant similarities between the traits of the evolutionary and neural transitions—such as the ability to categorize them into the same two classes, LOO and DOL—suggest that this is more than just analogy as well.) The comparison also explains why each of these historical steps occurred, identifying the evolutionary advantages the creatures that embodied these advances enjoyed in their day-to-day competition with other creatures, and hence why they were positively selected for these learning abilities. This perspective suggests that animals with more sophisticated ways of controlling their own behavior do better because they can select among a wider range of responses to given situations. In some kinds of niches, this is convenient, and leads to relatively greater success in survival and reproduction.

Further, inheriting information within one's lifetime allows individuals to accumulate knowledge and allows the social groups to which they belong to develop more complex cultures. This is a change in our phenotypes that have an impact on the world around us, and it is this selective advantage that caused these psychological advances to persist once they evolved: we were enabled to explore a much broader range of "behavior space," thus exploiting strategies not available to those without these abilities.

Thinking of advances in behavioral control as neural major transitions tells us why each of the steps we have described was necessary and important. It shows us how the steps are similar to each other in having the qualities of such transitions, and of being essentially about improving the ways information can be managed during an individual's lifetime so that new kinds of end-states can be reached, and the evolutionary benefits of such end-states enjoyed. Showing that the stepwise addition of new BPUs to human psychology were a kind of evolutionary transition explains how we have learned to acquire and manage more information, which has in turn allowed our behavior to have greater and greater impact upon the environment. The results of this process are all around us; for example, in our ecological domination of the planet.

SECTION 4

CONCLUDING
THOUGHTS

This final section, as its title suggests, collects together our reflective thoughts about the approach to explaining human behavior that we have been developing throughout this book. Chapter 8 discusses some interesting practical uses of our perspective to understanding human behavior production; Chapter 9 recapitulates aspects of our argument, with a few last thoughts about their implications.

CHAPTER 8

APPLICATIONS

Knowing how each development in the control of behavior production occurred has an intrinsic intellectual fascination, but also, we think, practical relevance. As Kurt Lewin (1951) said, "There is nothing as practical as a good theory." Theory provides a map and a means of navigation through the real world, guiding our understanding, allowing us to measure, test, and ultimately predict phenomena. Our ultimate purpose in carrying out this work has been to produce a theory of behavior that is predictive, and hence gives us power over behavior. (In our day jobs we work on behavior change in public health.) It seems to us that the approach we have outlined has a number of practical advantages. In neuroscience, it offers a principled way to identify, map, understand, and compare brain structures across BPUs and across species. In the broader behavioral sciences, it gives us the tools to think comparatively, such that we can answer questions about the degree of intelligence exhibited by various animals, for example. Providing an overarching theoretical schema for behavior production also allows different categories of behavioral scientists to talk to one another. Finally, we argue that this schema is helpful to applied behavioral scientists, such as ourselves, interested in resolving some of the conundrums about human maladaptive behavior which lead some of us to become obese, parasite-infected, or wasteful of planetary resources. In the rest of this chapter, we flesh out these claims.

Neuroscientific Uses

The first domain of academic implication concerns the brain sciences. Though huge strides have been made in understanding the architecture of the human brain, and that of some other animals, we are a long way from describing what each identified circuit that "lights up" in response to some stimulus actually does, and we are far from being able to produce comparative maps between species. We suggest that our approach could accelerate this enterprise in two ways.

First, it would be helpful to seek brain structure systematically from the perspective of the behavior that those brains evolved to produce. It has been regularities in the tasks that behavior has had to solve that has caused the evolution of regular structures in brains, and this is where we need to begin to identify brain structures. If our hypotheses about the existence and function of BPUs are correct, there should be a very good correspondence between the activation of these BPUs and regular structures and circuits in brains. If we use theory about the evolution of behavior to guide us, we should find that our brain maps become much sharper.

This is not what currently happens in neuroscience. The brain maps that currently emerge are fuzzier than they need be because the stimuli used to spark responses are not theoretically driven and the focus is not on behavior. So, for example, neuroimaging work on fear and disgust has mostly employed stimulus images that have been ranked for their affective feelings of disgust and fear (e.g., the IAPS set). This is misleading, since feelings are not the purpose of motivated BPUs, but an epiphenomenon, as we argued in Chapter 5. If, on the other hand, we begin with theory— that *disgust* is a BPU that evolved to protect us from parasites (Curtis, 2013)—then we would seek to engender parasite avoidance behavior in a scanner. Hence, for example, one of the IAPS images that is supposed to generate *fear*, a snarling dog, probably also serves to stimulate parasite avoidance behavior, because the dog is dribbling potentially infective fluids. Without clear and principled stimulus production, it will not be possible to isolate the neural correlates of the BPUs (indeed this may be why there is still controversy over the neural correlates of fear and disgust; Lawrence et al., 2004; Vossbeck-Elsebusch & Gerlach, 2012). An additional advantage is that imaging would be focused on behavior production and not on stimulus decoding (the "middle box" between perception and motor action). Hence, to study *disgust*, subjects should be scanned in action, behaving in ways that avoid parasites; for example, being asked to eat more or less apparently bacterially contaminated food items. The stimuli used in such experiments need to be strictly tuned to the evolutionary functions of the kinds of BPUs that are being mapped. We predict that using theory to define behavior-eliciting stimuli will provide much sharper results in brain imaging. We also suggest that more effort needs to go into experimental paradigms that involve the actual production of behavior (including developing portable/wearable scanning technologies).

Second, behavioral theory can be used to develop and test hypotheses about brain structure. For example, we have predicted how particular BPUs must be implemented in the brain based on the argument about the order in which different classes of BPU originated. Being among the oldest BPUs, reflexes should be found in the older parts of the human brain. Different reflexive BPUs (e.g., *startle* and *withdrawal*) will demonstrate similar structures—something like the classic 'reflex arc', or a simple chain of activated neurons – but as these chains evolved separately, they are unlikely to share much physical overlap. However, as individual reflexive BPUs do share a common ancestry across species, we should be able to recognize related structures in related species.

On the other hand, the *planning* BPU evolved recently, and in humans is associated with the prefrontal cortex (Adolphs, 2001; Christoff & Gabrieli, 2000; Miller et al., 2002). This type of BPU is flexible and multifunctional, and it is thus unlikely that there will be specific circuits associated with particular kinds of planned behavior. The prefrontal cortex should implement *planned* behavior using information in distributed networks spread widely through the prefrontal cortex, while involving older parts of the brain as well. Therefore, the *planning* BPU may not be implemented in exactly the same way in the brains of different individuals. The BPU for *planning* probably has a low level of genetic specificity, and is implemented using functionally and morphologically similar tissue, the isocortex (Fuster, 2003; Mountcastle, 1998). So there is a lower likelihood that *planning* will be associated with developmental programs or even structurally distinct ones. We therefore expect the BPU based in executive control to be less "locatable" and display more connectivity to memory and motivational BPUs than reflexes (e.g., using brain imaging).

In-between are the motivated BPUs. Although these are most likely modular, and so should have some aspects dedicated to specific purposes, they are also likely to overlap in their physical instantiation, with individual drives or emotions making use of components that serve as reactive circuits under other circumstances. Since evolution tends to tinker with pre-existing forms, motivated behavior should be built upon some of the components of reflexive behavior (but, we would predict, only when the function is the same; hence we have postulated that humans use both reflexive and motivated systems to avoid parasitization, for example, and we predict that the latter should share some of the neural structures of the former). Later-evolving circuits should invoke the use of components that evolved earlier. Further, motives share the quality of being goal-seeking rather than responsive to cues. Hence we would expect it to be possible to isolate and characterize the goal-seeking mechanisms common to motives in humans. It should also be possible to systematically investigate the degree to which such mechanisms are shared in other animals, and hence to reconstruct the evolutionary history of motives.

We have proposed that there are only a limited number of motives with specific adaptive functions (see the pictorial representation of their functional relationships in Figure 8.1; Aunger & Curtis, 2013). This hypothesis is highly testable. Distinct neural mechanisms should be traceable for each and there should be anatomical regularities that correspond to the behavioral regularities of history and function we propose for each. Hence the *fear, disgust, hunger,* and *lust* BPUs will be isolable and localized to older parts of the brain than more recently evolving *status* and *justice,* and will show

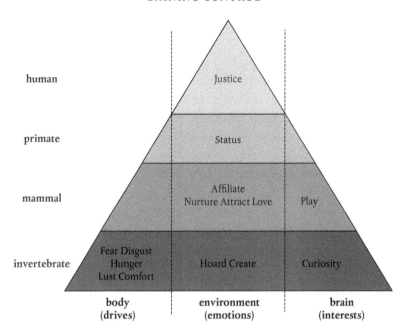

Fig. 8.1. The Human Motives

connections to the physiological systems they serve. The social emotions, however, have some evolutionary relationships between them, and will share some behavior production mechanisms. Motivated learning BPUs such as *social* and *nonsocial play* should be related but also isolable. All these should be tapped into by the *planning* tissue, perhaps via feelings.

The question of how to identify the set of human motives has long been debated in psychology (Cattell, 1957; James, 1884; Maslow, 1954; Murray, 1938; S. Reiss, 2008). We predict that the fourteen basic motives we have identified will be isolable in brain tissue, and will prove a better fit with imaging data than other schemas. This will best be done by attempting to elicit the theoretically predicted type of behavior in brains. A novel prediction from our approach is that the *hoard* BPU will be found to have a dedicated neural system (built perhaps on a more ancient instinctual capacity—of which an analog will be found in animals with close relations to our ancestors).

While BPUs in brains deliver behavioral propositions, BPUs operate in parallel. We have as yet far from a full understanding about when and how BPUs interact. Our schema proposes that there are evolutionary advantages for those at a higher level to be able to interrupt those at a lower level, and we would expect such neurological- and neurochemical-override mechanisms to be isolable. We know from evolutionary theory that animals make careful trade-offs between motives; for example, down-grading *disgust* when *hunger* or *lust* levels are high. We do not yet know how this is done. Once the distinct motives have been identified, we should be better equipped to understand how they trade off one against another. We have suggested that feelings are epiphenomena of some motives (but not all), such that they can be brought into conscious awareness for the purposes of planning and reflective learning. Neuroscience can clarify whether this is the case anatomically. If so, and if feelings circuits can be more strictly isolated, then we can identify whether it is true, as we predict, that feelings are confined to primates with planning ability, or if there are evolutionary precursors to feelings in older structures.

All of these constitute a rich and significant research agenda for neuroscience.

Comparative Psychology Uses

Controversies concerning the degree of mental sophistication underlying the behavior exhibited by animals continue to fill the literatures on comparative psychology and animal behavior. For example, claims have been made that dolphins have a "theory of mind" because they can recognize themselves in mirrors (Reiss & Marino, 2001); that chimpanzees (Arnold & Zuberbühler, 2006) and starlings (Gentner et al., 2006) can manipulate symbols syntactically; that cetaceans (Rendell & Whitehead, 2001) and primates (Whiten et al., 1999) have culture; that chimpanzees engage in deception (Hare et al., 2006) and object to unfair offers (Brosnan & de Waal, 2003); that dogs (Topál et al., 2006) and birds (Raby et al., 2007) do planning; and that rats laugh when they are tickled (Panksepp & Burgdor, 2003). Even lowly fish are being argued to lead a previously underappreciated mental life—including the ability to recognize other individuals, build up a mental map of their environment, use tools, memorize the order in which obstacles are encountered, feel pain, and exhibit awareness of their social status (Brown & Laland, 2003; Chandroo et al., 2004). It has been argued that some insects have just as broad a behavioral repertoire as some mammals, leading the authors to ask, "Are bigger brains better?" (Chittka & Niven, 2009). Debates thus continue as to which group of animals has the greatest mental powers; advocates variously suggesting apes (Savage-Rumbaugh et al., 2001), dogs (Hare & Tomasello, 2005), birds (Emery & Clayton, 2004), fish (Laland et al., 2003), and even flies (Dethier, 1964). A serious level of confusion reigns in comparative biology about the kinds of claims that can be made.

Certainly animals exhibit specific abilities that exceed our own. For example, food-caching birds have extraordinary memories for the placement and age of their caches (Clayton & Dickinson, 1999); dogs can perceive wavelengths beyond human ken;

shoaling fish exceed human abilities at rapid mass coordination; and birds and butterflies can navigate thousands of miles on their annual migrations. It is therefore now generally recognized that a species' mental skills and abilities are related to the kinds of problems its way of life requires (where way of life can be considered an interaction between an animal's morphology and niche; Hauser, 2000; Tooby & Cosmides, 1989). Thus every animal can be an "expert" in some kind of mental task by virtue of having evolved a special adaptation to a feature of its environment, allowing "lower" animals to outperform "higher" animals in some respects (Allen & Bekoff, 1997).

Arguing in this way—that mental powers are simply a reflection of niche-based problem solving—tends to be associated with purely functional descriptions of behavior. However, such functionalist explanations are likely to lead to errors in understanding of the sophistication of the mechanism assigned to production of a behavior because the same kind of functionality can be achieved by different means with greater or lesser complexity (Griffiths, 1997). For example, accomplishing the function of putting a cap on a container requires a complex sequence of behaviors. However, this sequence can be achieved through a chain of cue-driven automatic behaviors (e.g., cell-capping in honeybees; Arathi et al., 2000), or it can be achieved through highly a sophisticated process involving planning using multiple mental representations, as in bottle capping by employees in a soft drinks factory. The assumption that intelligence merely reflects ecology still leaves us with the fundamental problem of how to make comparisons between animals separated by phylogenetic distance. Therefore, considerations of ecology alone are not enough to disentangle the issues surrounding the interpretation of behavior mentioned earlier.

Further, ecological functionalism or engineering ignores the effects of history; it doesn't recognize that phylogenetic inertia will likely cause related animals to have similar traits. The features of extant animals are not just de novo consequences of circumstances; they are the result of long evolutionary histories. Comparative psychologists should thus be able to detect commonalities in mental toolkits across species, given their relative placement in the Tree of Life. But what criteria should they use to compare psychological mechanisms?

A variety of approaches have been taken to identifying how a behavior works or what it is for. We can classify these approaches according to which of four perspectives they favor (famously suggested by the ethologist Nico Tinbergen, 1963):

- **functional**: What is it good at doing? (i.e., its adaptive or survival value)
- **mechanistic**: What are its immediate causes?
- **developmental**: How does it grow/change during the animal's lifespan?
- **phylogenetic**: How did it evolve?

The most popular strategy recently has been to look for a behavior's adaptive function; this approach is characteristic of behavioral ecology and sociobiology (Krebs & Davies, 1978; Wilson, 1975). These disciplines apply population-level models of evolutionary processes (e.g., game theory, population genetics) to test adaptive hypotheses; they are less concerned with immediate causes of the behavior of individual animals, or its development, and the mechanisms responsible for generating optimal behavior are often simply assumed. For example, the genetic system is assumed able to search through "design space" (Dennett, 1996) to find the optimal solution (the "phenotypic gambit"; Grafen, 1982). Functionality is thus achieved without the constraint of prior forms; history is relevant only in the sense that it tells us when a species came to inhabit a particular niche.

However, considerations of ecology alone are not enough to disentangle the issues surrounding the interpretation of behavior mentioned earlier: purely functional descriptions are likely to lead to errors in assigning the mechanism of production because the same functionality can be achieved through alternative means (Griffiths, 1997). For example, a complex sequence of behaviors such as building a communal structure can be achieved using highly sophisticated mental equipment (e.g., via architectural planning in humans) or through a chain of cue-driven behavior (e.g., in termites; Bonabeau et al., 1998). Some knowledge of how mechanisms achieve functionality is required to assess whether two species' behaviors are homologous (Crowley & Allen, 2008).

Other disciplines concentrate on the second of Tinbergen's approaches, mechanism. This can be done at various points in the stream of behavior causation—by focusing either on genes or, more proximally, the nervous system. Advances are bound to be made in our understanding of the genetic underpinnings of behavior, which can be used to uncover homologous behaviors in related species (Bateson, 2003; Benzer, 1973). For example, homologous genes are associated in animals as distant as fruit flies and humans for the molecular mechanisms underlying circadian rhythms, learning and memory, and sleep (Greenspan & Dierick, 2004).

However, what a particular gene contributes to one of these behaviors is typically highly specific (e.g., producing a certain neurotransmitter that operates on synapses in a particular way), so that understanding its role offers only a partial picture of behavior causation. In particular, it often tells us only about the role of a particular molecule in brain structure, and very little about control or other proximate factors. Knowing that delayed sleep phase syndrome is associated with a variant of the *period* gene that regulates circadian rhythm in *Drosophila* (Ebisawa et al., 2001) hardly answers questions about the nature of cognitive control or mental sophistication.

Alternatively, neuroethology studies behavior causation by the nervous system. However, a lot of neuroethological work concentrates on how cellular interactions in the nervous system account for some species-typical behavior, so it tends to concentrate on invertebrates because exact wiring diagrams of how behavior is determined in their brains can be identified. This produces localized, scattershot studies of particular behaviors in particular species. Even neuroethology textbooks (Carew, 2000; Zupanc, 2004) consist mostly of case studies rather than general principles (e.g., bat echolocation, prey localization in barn owls, visual feature analysis in toads, mate calling in crickets, locust flight, crayfish escape, songbird learning, honeybee foraging, reflex conditioning in sea slugs). Whether such neural diagrams can be related to (and often scaled up to) those responsible for other behaviors or other species is unknown.

Thus, homologies in behaviors can currently be detected at small scale using neuroethology. Alternatively, through single gene studies, comparisons can be made at considerable phylogenetic distance, but only with respect to some aspect of a behavior. None of the approaches described thus far can properly address the confusions about how to interpret causal stories about behaviors in more distantly related species such as fish and humans—the type of problems with which this chapter started.

A number of scholars have advocated taking a phylogenetic approach to the understanding of behavior, in which inferences about the causes are restricted by where in an evolutionary tree a species appears (Ereshefsky, 2007; Griffiths, 1997; Tinbergen, 1951). However, these calls have not led to successful empirical programs that can effectively compare behaviors across species. As a result, widespread controversy continues to characterize comparative psychology. We believe this is primarily because a way has not been found to define homologies with respect to the psychological mechanisms underlying behavior. It is also the case that advocates of the abilities of particular species are not so forthcoming about what the species *cannot* do, which is often as important in determining what sort of mechanism is likely to be responsible for the claimed skill (Perry et al., 2013).

Here, we have adopted a particular strategy for defining psychological homologies, or traits similar due to a shared evolutionary history, rather than independent origin. This strategy makes reference to the primary evolutionary functions of mental mechanisms: control over behavior, and the ability to reach particular kinds of evolutionary end-states. Once classified in this way, two behaviors can be said to be homologous if they are produced by the same class of psychological mechanism—that is, they are produced by mechanisms with the same level of control, which achieve the same kind of end-state. Our definition of homology thus includes considerations of both common ancestry and kind of evolutionary functionality. For example, swimming and walking can be defined as homologous behaviors if they are produced by mechanisms of equal complexity in terms of control, because both kinds of behavior result in situational improvements in the state of the behaving organism (i.e., situational evolutionary benefits). Of course, we expect that in many cases these homologous mechanisms will also produce behaviors that are similar in many respects (although perhaps not in the exact sequence of motor actions). For example, specific episodes of swimming or walking can be considered homologous if they are automatic responses to stimuli and improve the animal's access to evolutionary benefits.

It is also the case that, in general, it is not behavior itself but the physiological and psychological mechanisms producing behavior that must be considered the focus of homology. It is, after all, these mechanisms that are the adaptations for behavior. Although selection works on the returns from behavior, it is the means by which that behavior is produced that are the phylogenetic result of selection pressures, the structures on which selection can act over the long term. Developing the ability to compare these mechanisms in different species requires tracing developments in the physiological "choices" (e.g., leg versus fin) and psychological level of control over behavior in a particular lineage. We have done the latter in this book for the Metazoan lineage leading to humans, defining seven different classes of psychological mechanisms that produce behavior in this group of animals, each of which we argue arose at a particular point in time (in the narrative of Chapters 2 to 5).

We have also made specific claims about the order in which the different BPUs have evolved. Primitive functions tend to arise earlier in development and to be more similar among species in a clade (Kirschner & Gerhart, 2006; West-Eberhard, 2003). Hence among animals in the human lineage, later-evolved BPUs should develop later in brain ontogeny, and diverge more greatly between species. We thus expect most animals will not exhibit higher cognitive skills, causing them to diverge from primates, and that these cognitive kinds will develop only relatively late in human ontogeny (i.e., with the frontal cortex, which develops last; Fuster, 2003), while earlier-evolved BPUs, such as instincts, will be found in earlier-developing parts of the human brain.

We therefore suggest that psychological mechanisms must be compared on evolutionary grounds. We should base the categorization of psychological mechanisms on the characteristics most important in evolutionary terms. We argue that the most important feature of behavior production is the brain's ability to control behavior so as to produce the highest overall level of fitness during the animal's lifetime. Better mechanisms can consider a wider range of responses to the current situation, or can better gauge the best options over the longer term, thus reaching a higher overall level of fitness for the animal. To put it another way, control mechanisms allow animals not to wind up with low levels of fitness because only a narrow range of options or a limited time horizon have been considered. A truly comparative biology of behavior therefore requires an understanding of the level of control over behavior (Bateson, 2003).

Our approach provides a priori expectations about the level of sophistication of a particular species' behavior, based on the kinds of mental operations it is able to perform, given its place in a phylogenetic tree. We argue that psychological mechanisms can be simultaneously classified by evolutionary history (as reflected in particular abilities to control behavior) and functionality. Importantly, however, this functionality is defined not ecologically but evolutionarily, with respect to the produced behavior's relationship to the provision of evolutionary (i.e., fitness) benefits. By relying on this kind of functionality, the problem of ecological relativism is avoided, so that our classification scheme enables behaviors to be compared regardless of ecological differences.

The classes of behavior of which a species is capable are thus determined by its phylogenetic history. Using the approach described here, hypotheses concerning the complexity of behavioral causes in a particular species can be confined to a function of its place in a phylogenetic tree. An empirical deduction from our approach is therefore that animals in any given clade will have only certain types of production unit available for their behavioral repertoire. Thus, chordates prior to vertebrates will be "instinctual creatures" (i.e., limited to instincts, reflexes, and *exploration*); mammals will also display drives, emotive, and interested behavior; and *planning* will be limited to primates. Further, once a new kind of behavior evolves, it tends to persist in that lineage. Hence, we can expect that human behavior is an amalgam of all that went before. In this way, we predict that human behavior will include everything from reflexes to *planning*.

Knowing these constraints on mental toolkits, we can now answer some of the questions with which we began this chapter, because any claim requiring that a behavior be of a kind not allowed to a species by its position in a phylogeny can be disqualified. For example, fish may be able to recognize conspecifics, but it is unlikely they will have "friends" in the sense of having specific individuals on which they depend for cooperative endeavors (contra Dugatkin & Wilson, 1992) because they are not truly social, and so do not have emotions. Similarly, rats may make laughing noises (Panksepp & Burgdor, 2003), but that does not mean that they have the representational capacity required to appreciate a joke. Neither can a scrub-jay *plan* where it will cache its seeds (Raby et al., 2007), at least in the sense of using meta-representations of its social and physical environment to do so.

These phylogenetic constraints and other considerations mentioned here represent a few examples of the advances in the study of behavior that we hope will materialize through future studies of the natural kinds we have introduced. This provides a priori expectations about the level of sophistication of a particular species' behavior, based on the kinds of mental operations it is able to perform given its place in our phylogenetic tree. We believe this perspective has major advantages in helping to interpret the nature of both human and nonhuman behavior, and thus should help to settle the various controversies that abound in the comparative psychology literature concerning the causes of behavior.

Another sort of difficulty is the isolation of psycho-behavioral mechanisms producing the functional benefits we have identified. We do not have a principled way of determining the level of abstraction at which BPUs work—that is, of distinguishing between the case of an animal with many *hoard* mechanisms (store-acorns; store-hazelnuts), versus just one (store-food). It seems reasonable to suppose that BPUs cannot be completely general, as general problem solvers in computational terms do not evolve—adaptations are created to deal with living through specific dangers and taking advantage of specific kinds of opportunities (Cosmides & Tooby, 1994; Wagner & Altenberg, 1996). Indeed, morphological and ecological constraints appear to restrict the kinds of psychological adaptations that can arise in different clades of animal (Holekamp et al., 2013). So we argue there must be *some* level of specificity in the mechanisms' evolution designs to solve ecological problems. We also know this to be the case for other kinds of adaptations—morphological, technological—so we have no reason not to expect the same here.

The level at which mechanisms work is to some degree irrelevant as long as the functional benefits are achieved through their execution. Further, the level at which mechanisms evolve probably depends on the history of niche-living and the particular computational features of the task. How specific are its perceptual inputs? How distinctive are the motor actions associated with achievement of the task? Thus determining the nature of evolved psychological mechanisms will depend on significant empirical work and is likely to vary from case to case.

What we *have* done is to claim that there is a specific set of functional units—just this set and no other. That is, there is a *hoard* drive but not a *sleep* drive, a *status* emotion but not a *do science* emotion or a *get angry* emotion. This is a significant claim in ontological terms, and worthy of further investigation.

We thus argue that comparative psychology can be illuminated by taking an evolutionary point of view. While it is possible to compare the behavior of any two species—crawfish and chickens, for example—using the tactics developed here, what we are often most concerned with (even as scientists in many cases) is understanding our own behavior. We hope the identification of major developments in the evolution of behavior—and the kinds of mechanisms for producing behavior that they fashioned—will inspire behavioral scientists and psychologists to use this framework when formulating hypotheses about the causes of behavior in different species.

Behavioral Science Uses

The third domain of implications of our classification of behavior concerns the study of behavior itself.

The behavioral scientist's job is to look for statistical regularities in behavior with respect to end-states. The stream of behavior can be split into chunked sequences that reach end-states providing evolutionary benefits (e.g., copulation, sleep, eating, predator defense, status improvement). Typically, the behavioral scientist will be looking for variation in the stream of behavior from one kind of end-state to another. Only through comparison with the behavior of the same animal or other animals in the species, resulting in the same category of beneficial end-state, can it be inferred that behavior has likely been reactive, motivated, or planned. A good indicator of the motivated nature of a stream of behavior is that it exhibits a point at which some evolutionary benefit within immediate reach has been ignored; an indicator of planned behavior, that some end-state achievable through motivated action has been ignored. Multiple routes that reach the same category of end-state (e.g., copulation, fruit consumption, territory acquisition) will be exhibited if behavior is motivated. *Plans* will exhibit patterns in the particular sequences in which beneficial end-states are reached. For example, *plans* that require high levels of skill to achieve will tend to require that multiple episodes of *playful* behavior occur before the objective is achieved (e.g., learning to serve in tennis). *Plans* can thus exhibit sequence dependence in motivated behaviors, where the achievement of each goal enables pursuit of the next.

From the perspective of our own profession, health promotion, knowing which level of control is responsible for a behavior is fundamental (and the reason that we undertook this project). Recognizing that changing a behavior requires overcoming motivation rather than reactive control, for example, increases the toolkit available for changing that behavior. Motivated behavior can be changed by providing incentives, knowledge, conditioned associations, or physiological sensations, whereas changing reactive behavior can be achieved only through the provision of evolved cues. Knowing which kind of end-state a behavior results in can also have implications for the means available to change it. Behaviors providing physiological rewards, even when unhealthy (e.g., drug taking, sugar consumption), are more difficult to overcome than situational behaviors such as not wearing seat belts, because immediate rewards have to be fought against.

For evolutionary biologists, it should be possible to identify the behavioral kinds that we have established in the brains of related species in the human lineage. For example, both rat and human brains should exhibit homologous structures to implement drives and emotions. This project is already underway, with a number of such homologies having been discovered (Panksepp, 1998; Streidter, 1998).

These represent a few examples of the significant potential advances in the study of behavior that we hope will materialize through future studies of the natural kinds we have introduced here.

Public Health Uses

Our attempt at theory building was ultimately inspired by a practical need. Our day jobs are in the world of behavior change, in which we encourage people to improve their hygiene, nutrition, or product-use behavior to improve their health. We were frustrated that the standard approach in developing countries was health *education*—on the assumption that imparting knowledge, even if culturally adapted, was the best way to change behavior. Our research, however, found that most people, even in remote rural areas of India, Vietnam, Burkina Faso, Uganda, or Zambia, with little formal schooling, knew that simple preventive measures like handwashing with soap were important and that they should exclusively breastfeed their children up to the age of six months, for example. They *knew*, but they did *act* on this knowledge. This provoked us to search for better ways of understanding the production of behavior, so as to be better at influencing it.

The schema outlined in this book forms the basis of a new, Darwinian approach to behavior change, which we call Evo-Eco, due its basis in evolutionary biology and ecological thinking (Aunger & Curtis, 2014). Instead of seeing behavior as driven by high-level cognition, as in the dominant theories from health psychology such as the Theory of Planned Behavior (Ajzen, 1991) and the Health Action Process approach (Schwarzer, 2008), or by "irrational" heuristics and biases (as in behavioral economics; Ariely, 2009), we see behavior as "evolutionarily rational." To design a behavior change program we seek out the BPUs that are likely to explain current behavior, and look for ways to engage BPUs that might be capable of causing the new, desired behavior. So, for example, we carried out formative research into handwashing behavior in rural India and found that it can be executed as a reactive, habitual response to a cue; that it can be motivated by *disgust, nurture, affiliation,* and *status*; and that it was rarely a planned response designed to achieve the long-term objective of better health (Curtis et al., 2009). We designed a program delivered in Indian villages to motivate hand hygiene via *disgust* (using a revolting pantomime character who made contaminated sweets with unwashed hands and tried offering them to children), and via *nurture/status* (an aspirational and nurturing mother—SuperAmma—who taught handwashing as good manners to her child so that he would grow up to be a doctor). We also used visual cues of program materials as reminders. The program led to a significant and long-lasting change in handwashing in a randomized controlled trial in rural India (Biran et al., 2014).

The "motives triangle" (Figure 8.1) has provided a rich source of (sometimes unexpected) insight about the drivers of behavior. For example, in exploring why mothers do not use oral rehydration salts (ORS) correctly to treat children with diarrhea in urban Zambia, we discovered the *hoard* BPU in operation. Despite ORS being offered free to mothers, they hated to make up a whole liter of solution, because they knew that it might go to waste if the child could not drink it all. Hence they were making up the solution using roughly half a packet to roughly half an unmeasured liter and so not providing the correct concentration. The implication is that ORS should be provided in smaller-size sachets, a conclusion that would not have been reached had only rational planning been investigated as a cause of behavior. We believe that more robustly theory-driven designs of behavior change programs are likely to be more effective than has been the case in the past.

Interdisciplinary Communication

If our approach has successfully isolated the natural kinds for the behavioral sciences (per the argument in Chapter 6), it offers real opportunities to improve interdisciplinary communication and collaboration. We have argued that psychology cannot advance as a science without terms that can attract agreement within and between the behavioral sciences. Our argument is that the best way to do this is to equate psychological constructs with biological natural kinds. Such kinds can form the foundation for interdisciplinary cooperation on the study of behavior. It is unfortunate, for example, that a term as basic to brain and behavior as "emotion" still has no agreed-upon definition. Our approach provides a short, crisp definition, not from introspection or empirical observation, but from the perspective of function and evolutionary history. For us, emotion is a class of BPUs in the brain that motivate behavior designed to improve an animal's situation with respect to its environment.

We have also argued that progress in psychological science is bedeviled by debates about terminology. True advance can arise only in any science once practitioners come to agreement as to the meanings of the analytical units they employ. Here we have used reasoning about the evolutionary purposes of different kinds of behavior to offer principled definitions of words concerning behavioral causation, such as motivation, motives, needs, and goals.

We also believe that our definitions of kinds of BPUs have advantages over previous uses of the terms we have adopted. For example, defining "instinct" by function and level of control sidesteps the history of controversy about the use of this word. Our definition does not require that instinctive behavior be species-typical, exhibited prior to experience, genetically programmed, or without the possibility of modification during an individual's development (Tinbergen, 1951). For example, one common definition has instincts as "innate predispositions" to perform particular behaviors when exposed to appropriate "releasing" stimuli (Logan, 1999; McDougall, 1908). However, this does not separate instincts from reflexes unless "releasing" cues can be rigorously distinguished from other kinds of cues (for which no criterion has been offered, to our knowledge). Further, it confounds instinct with innate behavior (Lorenz, 1937), which presents problems as there is no precise definition of "innate" (Mameli & Bateson, 2006). Another common definition suggests that instincts are complex combinations of behavior (Loeb, 1900; Tinbergen, 1951); for example, bird nest hygiene, or cell-capping in bees. However, some examples of what have commonly been considered instincts are single behaviors, such as snake avoidance in rhesus monkeys (Mineka et al., 1980). Further, reflexes can involve chains of behavior. For example, courtship behaviors in fish and birds involve each partner reacting to the stimulus of the other's prior bout of activity (Loeb, 1900). Common usage of the word "instinct" is thus too imprecise to categorize behaviors, and as a result it has fallen into disfavor (Bateson, 2000). Instead, we employ an adaptationist, or functional, criterion that avoids these problems: an instinct is a cue-generated behavior that provides fitness benefits indirectly through situational changes made by the actor.

We think that simply providing a well-defined vocabulary for psychology will enable psychologists to speak more profitably with one another. It will also enable those outside the discipline to rapidly pick up and understand the basic concepts so that they too can begin to interact effectively with psychology.

CHAPTER 9

IMPLICATIONS

In the preceding chapters, we have argued that the ability to behave has evolved through a sequence of major steps in which the causes of behavior have become increasingly sophisticated over time in species in the lineage leading to humans. We have sought to tell a plausible story about how one kind of behavior evolved out of earlier ones via realistic evolutionary processes. We have argued that in the evolutionary history of increasing complexity in behavior, steps can be identified that introduce novel ways of processing information during the lifespan of an individual organism.

We argued that, like other products of evolutionary processes, the kinds of structures that control behavior can be distinguished by their function and by their history. Taken together, history and function imply the existence of a number of classes of behavior production units (BPUs) in human brains. We argue that these innovations can be identified deductively by classing behavior first according to its level of behavioral control. We postulate three advances in control. First, early animals executed simple reactive behaviors in response to cues. Second, vertebrates evolved the ability to ignore immediate conditions to pursue goals through motivated behavior. Finally, primates added a new layer of executive control, which allowed them to achieve objectives through planned sequences of behavior.

Behavior can also be classified by the type of evolutionary benefit it bestows: it can deliver immediate benefits (e.g., food, gametes), the incorporation of which produce what we call "physiological" end-states. It can deliver improvements in the individual's position with respect to the world (e.g., resource access, social status), which we call "situational" end-states. It can also deliver improvements in the ability to secure future benefits (e.g., knowledge, skill), which we call "aptitudinal" end-states. There are thus three levels of behavioral control that can deliver three types of end-state. Within the first level of (reactive) control, we can distinguish three kinds of BPUs that produce each of the three kinds of end-states: a reflex achieves somatic and reproductive benefits; instincts put an animal into a better situation to get these benefits; and *exploration* helps the animal develop the aptitude for better achieving evolutionary goals in future. (Remember that we assign precise meanings to the italicized terms, despite the often contested history of previous usage.)

The next innovation was the development of the psychological reward system, which allowed animals to pursue goals. Goal-directed behavior at the second level of control (motivation) can be divided into drives, which motivate an animal to meet evolutionary needs immediately; emotions, which motivate animals to get into states that are advantageous but not immediately beneficial in evolutionary terms; and interests, which increase an animal's skills in dealing with its social and physical environment. Finally, a third-level innovation arose as more complex forms of thinking (executive control) led primates to engage in planning their future responses. *Planned* behavior (i.e., behavior produced by the *planning* BPU) can lead to two types of end-state (physiological or situational), and conscious, explicit *planning* (a late development within the third level of development) can achieve an objective that may or may not provide evolutionary benefits.

Thus, we suggest that a particular sequence of events can be identified, each leading to increasingly sophisticated behavior. This is a sequence of evolutionary advances, each one building on those previous to produce novel behavioral outcomes with clear evolutionary advantages for animals living in increasingly complex niches. We argue that these seven fundamental classes of BPUs—each type associated with one of the events earlier—account for any kind of human behavior in a parsimonious but empirically powerful way.

The issue of control is crucial to this story. The advances in the control of behavior that occurred during the course of human evolution are hierarchical in nature. At each level, control tends to take an input or output from a lower level, re-represent it, modulate it with other rules and information, and then execute a new form of behavior (Dretske, 2000; Proust, 2006). Each stage of control is thus derived from, but builds upon, pre-existing components that evolved earlier. Employing a control hierarchy makes sense, because as niches became more complex, it became increasingly difficult to manage independent production programs for every dimension of that niche. Once a new level of control has been achieved, it can be exercised on lower-level production programs. For example, defecation in humans, which involves search for an appropriate location to expel waste, is a development of excretion in Metazoans, a purely reflexive behavior. Higher levels of control can also guide the acquisition of behavioral performance by lower levels of control. For example, animals can reduce the level of control needed to produce a given behavior through the repeated reinforced practice of that behavior, as in habit formation (Everitt et al., 2001). Humans have to learn how to swim, for example, as opposed to rats, which swim instinctively when placed in water (although very young babies do have a reflex to paddle their arms and legs when their face touches water).

We suggest that this trend in increasing control has been accompanied by qualitative differences in the behavioral phenotypes produced by these types of BPU. Reactions consist of individual actions, and motivations produce relatively short sequences of actions (or episodes), composed of a number of habitual and automatic actions, often sequence-dependent, but controlled as a unit (e.g., getting dressed; Barker & Wright, 1954; Schank & Abelson, 1977). Executive control produces chains of actions that can be indefinitely long and which may last over a lifetime in the form of executed *plans*, which often accomplish multiple goals toward the achievement of an overall objective (Koechlin et al., 2003; Zacks & Tversky, 2001).

Of course there are many cases in which the same physiological mechanisms must be used for many different types of functions (e.g., eardrums must process the entire range of auditory stimuli, legs are used for running from predators as well as grasping mates). This argues against the ability of evolution to separately optimize bodily faculties for each and every ecological challenge, including (presumably) mental ones. Instead, evolution must often compromise, such that the same mechanism works via trade-offs across some range of input-output conditions. So why do we constantly assume there is a specialized module for each behavioral function? It is simply a default position in the absence of detailed investigation, making for a streamlined argument (as a first pass through complex material). While this default position may not always be right, it will often prove to be an adequate approximation to the solution that evolution has in fact managed, and should prove a fruitful starting point for closer investigations as to the nature of individual phenotypes.

We have also suggested that these steps can be seen as major transitions in the history of control over behavior production, and that they are analogous to the major transitions in evolutionary biology (Maynard Smith & Szathmáry,1995). Each *biological* transition is associated with a novel way for one generation to inherit information from the previous one. Similarly, we argue each major transition in *behavior* is associated with a novel organic mechanism or pathway through which information at a given time can influence behavior at a later time within the same organism. Each major neural transition produced a new mechanism for producing behavior, which we call BPUs. Neural transitions increase the kinds of targets for natural selection by creating new temporal patterns in behavior, due to the increase in the time horizon over which responses are calculated by BPUs (see Figure 9.1).

A consequence of having these different BPUs is that predicted behavior at any given point in time can be different depending on the level of control that is exerted. Reflexive behavior is almost instant; motives control behavior over periods of hours to days; *planning* controls behavior over the long term. This is because different kinds of valuations are being applied. We can say that a reactive response is choosing the

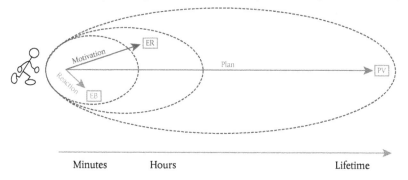

Fig. 9.1. Time Horizons of Control over Behavior

best option, given a very limited time horizon, based on the kinds of evolutionary benefits that have tended to result in similar circumstances during the evolutionary history of the species. However, should the species have motivational abilities, then it can apply a different valuation system: expected psychological rewards from a given current action (based on previous learning and experience), as judged over an episode of goal pursuit. Finally, if the species can *plan*, then it can calculate (at least implicitly) the present value to be attained by taking the next step in a projected course of action, culminating in achievement of an objective. The reason that these more sophisticated types of control have evolved is that taking in a wider variety of alternatives, which can become manifest over longer time periods, is likely to lead to higher total returns: with a wider set of options, more profitable courses of action become available.

Thanks to longer time horizons, increased control over behavior can achieve higher average rates of fitness benefits. If an animal's time horizon is short (due to limitations of memory or information processing), then its behavior is purely responsive to stimuli that just occurred; if its horizon is longer, then it can ignore a current stimulus to achieve a goal, thus performing a different sequence of behavior than if it had been purely responsive at each moment. With *planned* behavior, an organism can commit itself to follow a path that achieves a particular end-state at some arbitrary point in the future. Thus, reactive behaviors are individual actions (e.g., most reflexes) or automatically executed sequences of actions (e.g., some instincts as well as learned habits), while motivational control can produce behavioral "episodes" (Barker, 1963), composed of a number of habitual and automatic actions, and controlled as a unit (e.g., getting dressed). *Plans* reflect the controlled execution of sequences of episodes according to an overall objective (Schank & Abelson, 1977; Zacks & Tversky, 2001). *Planning* allowed primates to delay gratification to such an extent that there could be long interruptions in the pursuit of a planned objective, during which time other motivated sequences of behavior occur (e.g., ensuring that everyday needs get met while keeping the intended objective in the "back of one's mind").

For most of evolutionary history, behavior has been guided by processes operating outside the awareness of the behaving animal. Control over behavior has become conscious only recently. Many of these unconscious processes are still important in guiding human behavior. We are often mistaken as to the degree to which we consciously control our own actions; reasoning is often not causal causes, because reasons are post hoc rationalizations of deeper processes that can be only dimly viewed from "above." As a result, we frequently misattribute responsibility to a conscious level of control over behavior, when it is likely to have been automatically or subconsciously produced (even when it "feels" like we made a choice). This fact has interesting implications for debates about free will, the role of reason in everyday life, and legal responsibility, as moral and legal judgments often depend on whether the accused engaged in conscious deliberation (e.g., the distinction in the American legal system of intentional harm, leading to increased levels of punishment; Bargh & Morsella, 2010; Suhler & Churchland, 2009).

We thus believe that extending the time horizons over which behavior can be controlled is one important means by which new kinds of adaptive outcomes could be reached. But perhaps of equal importance was the ability to hold in memory a variety of potential courses of action and to make a discerning selection among them, based on a variety of criteria, such as expected utility, or with respect to specific qualities of likely future outcomes, such as financial recompense or sensory pleasure, as the need arose.

On the other hand, individual behaviors might not always be caused by particular BPUs but by combinations of them. Given the complexity of our brains, multiple motives are likely to feed into the causation of any given behavior. For example, playing sport can simultaneously involve a desire to increase skill (*play*), demonstrate prowess to the opposite sex (*attract*), and bond with fellow team members (*affiliation*)—although we argue that the primary evolved function of sport is *play*). In some cases, multiple, equally strong motives will pull an individual in different directions, like Buridan's ass, in which case some overriding concern will have to come into play to determine behavior. Thus, although we argue that BPUs evolved to become identifiable structures with particular functions, this does not require that they be independently activated and uniquely responsible for a given behavior. BPUs probably interact, with multiple BPUs being fed given inputs, and partaking in the decision to determine the organism's next activity. Often a behavior can serve multiple evolutionary functions, which poses an empirical challenge for our approach.

Nevertheless, we predict that certain kinds of functions cannot be combined in a single behavior; namely, those that leave animals in different kinds of end-states. Thus, a particular behavior cannot be both instinctual and driven, because that would involve one behavior winding up in two different kinds of end-states. Neither can behavior be simultaneously controlled at two different levels; thus it cannot be instinctual and emotional at the same time, because instinctual behavior is reactive whereas emotional behavior is motivated. These considerations make it particularly difficult to study, and explain, human behavior. Nevertheless, we hope that the conceptual tools we have provided here can help spawn new kinds of research that elucidate the causes of behavior in that most complex of species, *Homo sapiens*.

While this account necessarily remains only a plausible sketch at present, we have shown that it is consistent with a wide variety of evidence, ranging from comparative neuroanatomy and animal behavior to social psychology. We therefore believe that this story lends support to our contention that major transitions in animal behavior exist, and have occurred in an understandable, orderly sequence of increasing complexity, thanks to developments in systems of control over the way in which animals respond to their situations. We hope behavioral scientists will begin to use this framework when formulating hypotheses about the causes and functions of behavior, and begin to flesh out the outlines of the story presented here, so that we come to a better understanding of the causes of human behavior.

GLOSSARY OF TERMS

Concept	Definition	Examples
Action	Behavioral activity produced in response to a cue resulting from reactive-level control	Scratch, Suckle
Behavior	Self-propelled movement producing a functional interaction between an animal and its environment	Build shelter, Avoid predation, Hunt with others, Gossip
Behavior production unit (BPU)	An evolved psychological mechanism for producing an optimized response to a cue, situation, or goal	Eye blink producer, Submission-to-social-dominant producer, Planner
Cue	A signal of some evolutionarily salient state or variable (environmental or physiological)	Predator approaching, Low blood glucose
Drive	A class of BPUs and behaviors triggered by an indicator and designed to achieve a physiological end-state	Nutrient quest, Mate search
Emotion	A class of BPUs and behaviors triggered by an indicator and designed to achieve a situational end-state	Submission, Compete for status
Episode	A set of actions produced as a motivated response to a cue or situation	Display threat face → attack opponent → retreat
Evolutionary benefit	A resource tightly correlated with increases in biological fitness	Food, Copulation, Parental investment
Exploration	Behavior produced by a BPU triggered by default and designed to attain an aptitudinal end-state through reactive control	Environmental reconnaissance
Goal	A mental representation of an end-state	Satiety, Copulate with mate

(continued)

Concept	Definition	Examples
Indicator	A mental representation that indicates the degree of discrepancy between the current state of some variable (based on a cue) and its optimal state	Nutrient deficiency, Damaged social reputation
Instinct	A class of BPUs and behaviors triggered by a cue and designed to attain a situational end-state	Build nest
Interest	A class of BPUs and behaviors triggered by default and designed to achieve an aptitudinal end-state through motivated control	Object play, Pretend hunting
Motivation	A psychological state that arises when an indicator is greater than some threshold value	Low, High
Need	A task related to an evolutionarily significant aspect of an animal's ecological niche that requires goal-directed behavior to ameliorate	Invest in pair-bond, Maximize social status
Objective	An arbitrarily distant or abstract (i.e., non-evolved) goal	Have a job
Plan	An action sequence produced by the planning BPU	Search want ads → fill out application → mail application, etc.
Planning	A BPU designed to achieve objectives through executive-level control	—
Reflex	A class of BPUs and behaviors triggered by a cue and designed to attain a physiological end-state	Startle, Withdrawal
Reward	The value of feedback from behavior (may be expressed as deviation from expectation)	Somewhat negative, Significantly positive

REFERENCES

Abramson, C. I. (1994). *A Primer of Invertebrate Learning: The Behavioral Perspective*. Washington, DC: American Psychological Association.

Adolphs, R. (2001). The neurobiology of social cognition. *Current Opinion in Neurobiology*, 11, 231–39.

Adolphs, R. (2005). Could a robot have emotions? Theoretical perspectives from social cognitive neuroscience. In M. A. Arbib & J. M. Fellous (Eds.), *Who Needs Emotions? The brain meets the robot*. Oxford: Oxford University Press. 9–28.

Ainslie, G. (1975). Specious reward: A behavioral theory of impulsiveness and impulse control. *Psychological Bulletin*, 82, 463–96.

Ajzen, I. (1991). The theory of planned behavior. *Organizational Behavior and Human Decision Processes*, 50, 179–211.

Allen, C., & Bekoff, M. (1997). *Species of Mind: The Philosophy and Biology of Cognitive Ethology*. Cambridge, MA: MIT Press.

Allen, T. A., & Fortin, N. J. (2013). The evolution of episodic memory. *Proceedings of the National Academy of Sciences of the USA*, 110(Suppl. 2), 10379–86.

Allman, J. (1999). *Evolving Brains*. New York: Scientific American.

Allman, J. M, et al. (2005). Intuition and autism: A possible role for Von Economo neurons. *Trends in Cognitive Sciences*, 9, 367–73.

Amabile, T. M. (1996). *Creativity in Context*. Boulder, CO: Westview Press.

Anderson, D. J., & Adolphs, R. (2014). A framework for studying emotions across species. *Cell*, 157(1), 187–200.

Arathi, H. S., et al. (2000). Ethology of hygienic behaviour in the honey bee, *Apis mellifera. Hymenoptera: Apidae*: Behavioural repertoire of hygienic bees. *Ethology*, 106, 1–15.

Ariely, D. (2009). *Predictably Irrational*. New York: Harper Collins.

Arkin, R., et al. (2003). An ethological and emotional basis for human-robot interaction. *Robotics and Autonomous Systems*, 42(3–4), 191–201.

Arnold, M. B. (1960). *Emotion and Personality*. New York: Columbia University Press.

Arnold, K., & Zuberbühler, K. (2006). Language evolution: Semantic combinations in primate calls. *Nature*, 441, 303.

Aunger, R. (2010). What's special about human technology? *Cambridge Journal of Economics*, 34, 115–23.

Aunger, R., & Curtis, V. (2008). Kinds of behaviour. *Biology and Philosophy*, 23(3), 317–45.

Aunger, R., & Curtis, V. (2013). The anatomy of motivation: An evolutionary ecological approach. *Biological Theory*, 8, 49–63.

Aunger, R., & Curtis, V. (2014). The Evo-Eco approach to behaviour change. In D. W. Lawson & M. Gibson (Eds.), *Applied Evolutionary Anthropology*. London: Springer, pp. 271–95.

Austin, J. T., & Vancouver, J. B. (1996). Goal constructs in psychology: Structure, process, and content. *Psychological Bulletin*, 120, 338–75.

Avargues-Weber, A., et al. (2011). Conceptualization of above and below relationships by an insect. *Proceedings of the Royal Society B: Biological Sciences*, 278, 898–905.

Averill, J. R. (1980). A constructionist view of emotion. In R. Plutchik & H. Kellerman (Eds.), *Emotion: Theory, Research, and Experience* New York: Academic Press. 305–39.

Avital, E., & Jablonka, E. (2000). *Animal Traditions: Behavioural Inheritance in Evolution.* Cambridge: Cambridge University Press.

Axelrod, R. (1986). An evolutionary approach to norms. *American Political Science Review*, 80, 1095–1111.

Baddeley, A. D. (1984). Neuropsychological evidence and the semantic/episodic distinction. *Behavioral and Brain Sciences*, 7, 238–39.

Baldwin, J. M. (1896). A new factor in evolution. *The American Naturalist*, 30, 441–51.

Balleine, B. W., & Dickinson, A. (1998). Goal-directed instrumental action: Contingency and incentive learning and their cortical substrates. *Neuropharmacology*, 37, 407–19.

Bandura, A. (1986). *Social foundations of thought and action: A social cognitive theory.* Englewood Cliffs, NJ: Prentice Hall.

Bargh, J. A., & Chartrand, T. L. (1999). The unbearable automaticity of being. *American Psychologist*, 54, 462–79.

Bargh, J. A., & Morsella, E. (2010). Unconscious behavioral guidance systems. In C. Agnew et al. (Eds.), *Then a miracle occurs: Focusing on behavior in social psychological theory and research* New York: Oxford University Press. 89–118.

Barker, R. G. (1963). *The stream of behavior: Explorations of its structure and content.* New York: Appleton-Century-Crofts.

Barker, R. G., & Wright, H. F. (1954). *Midwest and its children: The psychological ecology of an American town.* Evanston, IL: Row, Peterson & Company.

Barlow, H. B. (1994). What is the computational goal of the neocortex? In C. Koch & J. L. Davis (Eds.), Large-scale Neuronal Theories of the Brain Boston, MA: MIT Press. 1–22.

Barrett, L. F. (2006). Emotions as natural kinds? *Perspectives on Psychological Science*, 1, 28–58.

Bateson, P. (2000). Taking the stink out of instinct. In H. Rose & S. Rose (Eds.), Alas Poor Darwin: Arguments against evolutionary psychology London: Cape. 157–73.

Bateson, P. (2003). The promise of behavioral biology. *Animal Behavior*, 65, 11–17.

Baumeister, R. F., & Leary, M. R. (1995). The need to belong: Desire for interpersonal attachments as a fundamental human motivation. *Psychological Bulletin*, 117, 497–529.

Baumeister, R. F., & Masicampo, E. J. (2010). Conscious thought is for facilitating social and cultural interactions: How mental simulations serve the animal–culture interface. *Psychological Review*, 117, 945–71.

Baxter, R., & Kimmel, H. D. (1963). Conditioning and extinction in the planarian. *American Journal of Psychology*, 76, 665–69.

Bekhtereva, N. P., et al. (2000). Study of the brain organization of creativity: II. Positron-emission tomography data. *Human Physiology*, 26, 516–22.

Bekoff, M. (1984). Social play behavior. *Bioscience*, 34, 228–33.

Bekoff, M., & Byers, J. A. (2004). *Animal play: Evolutionary, comparative and ecological perspectives.* Cambridge: Cambridge University Press.

Benzer, S. (1973). Genetic dissection of behavior. *Scientific American*, 229, 24–37.

Bergstrom, C. T., & Rosvall, M. (2011). The transmission sense of information. *Biology & Philosophy*, 26(2), 159–76.

Berlyne, D. E. (1960). *Conflict, arousal, and curiosity.* New York: McGraw-Hill.

Berridge, K. C. (2003). Comparing the emotion brain of humans to other animals. In R. J. Davidson et al. (Eds.), *Handbook of Affective Sciences* Oxford: Oxford University Press.

Berridge, K. C. (2004). Motivation concepts in behavioral neuroscience. *Physiology and Behavior*, 81(2), 179–209.

Berridge, K. C., & Robinson, T E. (1998). What is the role of dopamine in reward: Hedonic impact, reward learning, or incentive salience? *Brain Research Reviews*, 28(3), 309–69.

Beswick, D. G. (1971). Cognitive process theory of individual differences in curiosity. In H. I. Day et al. (Eds.), *Intrinsic Motivation: A new direction in education* Toronto: Holt, Rinehart and Winston, 156–70.

Biederman, I., & Vessel, E. A. (2006). Perceptual pleasure and the brain. *American Scientist*, 94, 249–55.

Bindra, D. (1978). How adaptive behaviour is produced: A perceptual-motivational alternative to response reinforcement. *Behavioral and Brain Sciences*, 1, 41–91.

Biran, A., et al. (2014). Effect of a behaviour-change intervention on handwashing with soap in India (SuperAmma): A cluster-randomised trial. *The Lancet Global Health*, 2(3), e145–e54.

Blackmore, S. (2011). *Consciousness: An introduction* (2nd ed.). Oxford: Oxford University Press.

Bock, J. (2005). What makes a competent adult forager? In Barry S. Hewlett and Michael E. Lamb (Eds) *Hunt- er-gatherer childhoods: Evolutionary, developmental, and cultural perspectives.*, New Jersey: Aldine Transaction, 109–28.

Boehm, C. (1999). *Hierarchy in the forest: The evolution of egalitarian behavior*. Cambridge, MA: Harvard University Press.

Bogin, B. (2009). Childhood, adolescence, and longevity: A multilevel model of the evolution of reserve capacity in human life history. *American Journal of Human Biology*, 21(4), 567–77.

Bohr, N. (1913). On the constitution of atoms and molecules. *Philosophical Magazine*, 26, 1–25.

Bolker, J. A. (2000). Modularity in development and why it matters to evo-devo. *American Zoologist*, 40, 770–76.

Bonabeau, E., et al. (1998). A model for the emergence of pillars, walls and royal chambers in termite nests. *Philosophical Transactions of the Royal Society B: Biological Sciences*, 353(1375). 1561–76.

Bonabeau, E., et al. (1999). *Swarm intelligence: From natural to artificial systems*. Oxford: Oxford University Press.

Bonasso, R. P., et al. (1997). Experiences with an architecture for intelligent, reactive agents. *Journal of Experimental and Theoretical Artificial Intelligence*, 9, 237–56.

Bowlby, J. (1979). *The making and breaking of affectional bonds*. London: Tavistock.

Boyd, Richard N. (1991). Realism, anti-foundationalism and the enthusiasm for natural kinds. *Philosophical Studies*, 61, 127–48.

Boyd, Richard N. (1999a). Kinds, complexity and multiple realization. *Philosophical Studies*, 95, 67–98.

Boyd, Richard N. (1999b). Homeostasis, species, and higher taxa. In R. A. Wilson (Ed.), *Species: New Interdisciplinary Essays* Cambridge, MA: MIT Press, 141–85.

Boyd, Robert, & Richerson, P. (1985). *The evolution of culture*. Chicago: University of Chicago Press.

Boyd, Robert, et al. (2011). The cultural niche: Why social learning is essential for human adaptation. *Proceedings of the National Academy of Sciences*, 108(Suppl. 2), 10918–25.

Boyd, Robert, & Silk, J. (2006). *How humans evolved* (4th ed.). New York: Norton.

Brembs, B., et al. (2002). Operant reward learning in Aplysia: Neuronal correlates and mechanisms. *Science*, 296, 1706–09.

Bressler, S. L., & Menon, V. (2010). Large-scale brain networks in cognition: Emerging methods and principles. *Trends in Cognitive Sciences*, 14(6), 277–90.

Brosnan, S., et al. (2003). Observational learning and predator inspection in guppies. *Ethology*, 109, 823–33.

Brosnan, S. F., & de Waal, F. B. M. (2003). Monkeys reject unequal pay. *Nature*, 425, 297–99.

Brown, C., & Laland, K.N. (2003). Social learning in fishes: A review. *Fish and Fisheries*, 4, 280–88.

Bshary, R. (2010). Decision making: Solving the battle of the fishes. *Current Biology*, 20, R70–R71.

Bshary, R., et al. (2007). Social cognition in non-primates. In R. I. M. Dunbar & L. S. Barrett (Eds.), *Evolutionary Psychology* Oxford: Oxford University Press. 83–101.

Burghardt, G. M. (1984). On the origins of play. In P. Smith (Ed.), *Play: In Animals and Humans* Oxford: Basil Blackwell. Burghardt, G. M. (2005). *The genesis of animal play.* Cambridge, MA: MIT Press.

Burghardt, G. M., et al. (1996). Problem of reptile play: Environmental enrichment and play behavior in a captive Nile soft-shelled turtle, *Trionyx triunguis. Zoo Biology*, 15, 223–38.

Burke, A., et al. (1992). Remembering emotional events. *Memory & Cognition*, 20, 277–90.

Burt, A. (2000). Perspective: Sex, recombination, and the efficacy of selection—was Weismann right? *Evolution*, 54, 337–51.

Buss, D. (2000). *The dangerous passion: Why jealousy is as necessary as love and sex.* New York: Free Press.

Buss, D. M. (2004). *Evolutionary psychology: The new science of the mind.* Boston: Pearson.

Buss, D. M., & Dedden, L. (1990). Derogation of competitors. *Journal of Social and Personal Relationships*, 7, 395–422.

Buss, D. M., & Haselton, M. G. (2005). The evolution of jealousy. *Trends in Cognitive Science*, 9, 506–07.

Butler, A. B. (2001). Brain evolution and comparative neuroanatomy. London: Macmillan Publishers), 1–8.

Butler, A. B., & Hodos, W. (2005). *Comparative vertebrate neuroanatomy: Evolution and adaptation* (2nd ed.). New York: Wiley-Liss.

Butler, P. J., & Jones, D R. (1997). Physiology of diving of birds and mammals. *Physiological Reviews*, 77, 837–99.

Butti, C., et al. (2013). Von Economo neurons: Clinical and evolutionary perspectives. *Cortex*, 49(1), 312–26.

Byrne, R. W., et al. (2001). Estimating the complexity of animal behaviour: How mountain gorillas eat thistles. *Behaviour*, 138, 525–57.

Cabanac, M. (1992). Pleasure—the common currency. *Journal of Theoretical Biology*, 155, 173–200.

Cahill, L., et al. (1996). Amygdala activity at encoding correlated with long-term free recall of emotional information. *Proceedings of the National Academy of Sciences of the USA*, 93, 8016–21.

Cahill, L., & McGaugh, J. L. (1995). A novel demonstration of enhanced memory associated with emotional arousal. *Consciousness and Cognition*, 4, 410–21.

Calcott, B. (2005). Selection, variation, and development in major evolutionary transitions. International Society for the History, Philosophy, and Social Studies of Biology. University of Guelph, Ontario, Canada.

Calcott, B. (2011). Alternative patterns of explanation for major transitions. In B. Calcott & K. Sterelny (Eds.), *The major transitions revisited.* Cambridge, MA: MIT Press, 35–51.

Camerer, C., et al. (2005). Neuroeconomics: How neuroscience can inform economics. *Journal of Economic Literature*, 43, 9–64.

Campbell, A. (2004). Female competition: Causes, constraints, content, and contexts. *Journal of Sex Research*, 41, 16–26.

Carew, T. J. (2000). *Behavioral neurobiology: The cellular organization of natural behavior.* Sunderland, MA: Sinauer Associates.

Carlson, N. (2013). *Physiology of behavior* (11th ed.). New York: Pearson.

Cattell, R. B. (1957). *Personality and motivation structure and measurement.* New York: World Book.

Catton, C., et al. (2003). SABO: A Standard Animal Behaviour Ontology (alpha version 0.1). <http://www.bioimage.org/publications.do%3E>

Chagnon, N. A. (1983). *Yanomamo: The fierce people*. New York: CBS College Publishing.

Chalmers, D. J. (1993). Self-ascription without qualia: A case-study. *Behavioral and Brain Sciences*, 16, 35–36.

Chalmers, D. J. (1995). Facing up to the problem of consciousness. *Journal of Consciousness Studies*, 2, 200–19.

Chandroo, K. P., et al. (2004). An evaluation of current perspectives on consciousness and pain in fishes. *Fish and Fisheries*, 5, 281–95.

Charland, L.C. (2002). The natural kind status of emotion. *British Journal for the Philosophy of Science*, 53, 511–37.

Chittka, L., & Niven, J. (2009). Are bigger brains better? *Journal of Current Biology*, 19, R995–R1008.

Chow, S. S., et al. (2004). Adaptive radiation from resource competition in digital organisms. *Science*, 305, 84–86.

Christoff, K., et al. (2001). Rostrolateral prefrontal cortex involvement in relational integration during reasoning. *Neuroimage*, 14, 1136–49.

Christoff, K., & Gabrieli, J. D. E. (2000). The frontopolar cortex and human cognition: Evidence for a rostrocaudal hierarchical organization within the human prefrontal cortex. *Psychobiology*, 28, 168–86.

Churchland, P., & Sejnowski, T. J. (1992). *The computational brain*. Boston, MA: MIT Press.

Clark, A., & Karmiloff-Smith, A. (1993). The cognizer's innards: A psychological and philosophical perspective on the development of thought. *Mind and Language*, 8, 487–519.

Clayton, N. S., & Dickinson, A. (1999). Scrub jays (Aphelocoma coerulescens) remember the relative time of caching as well as the location and content of their caches. *Journal of Comparative Psychology*, 113, 403–16.

Coates, M. I., et al. (2002). Fins to limbs: What the fossils say. *Evolution and Development*, 4, 390–401.

Cohen, N. J., & Squire, L. R. (1980). Preserved learning and retention of pattern-analyzing skill in amnesia: Dissociation of knowing how and knowing that. *Science*, 210, 207–10.

Cole, D. M., et al. (2012). Dopamine-dependent architecture of cortico-subcortical network connectivity. *Cerebral Cortex* 23 (7), 1509–16

Conway, M. A., et al. (1994). The formation of flash bulb memories. *Memory and Cognition*, 22, 326–43.

Conway, M. A. (2005). Memory and the self. *Journal of Memory and Language*, 53, 594–628.

Conway, M. A., et al. (2001). The neuroanatomy of autobiographical memory: A slow cortical potential study of autobiographical memory retrieval. *Journal of Memory and Language*, 45, 493–524.

Cooper, R. (2004). Why Hacking is wrong about human kinds. *British Journal for the Philosophy of Science*, 55, 73–85.

Cooper, R. P., & Shallice, T. (2006). Hierarchical schemas and goals in the control of sequential behavior. *Psychological Review*, 113, 887–916.

Cosmides, L., & Tooby, J. (1994). Origins of domain specificity: The evolution of functional organization. In L. A. Hirschfeld & S. A. Gelman (Eds.), *Mapping the mind: Domain specificity in cognition and culture*. New York: Cambridge University Press. 85–116.

Cosmides, L., & Tooby, J. (2000a). Consider the source: The evolution of adaptations for decoupling and metarepresentation. In D. Sperber (Ed.), *Metarepresentation: A Multidisciplinary Perspective* New York: Oxford University Press.

Cosmides, L., & Tooby, J. (2000b). Evolutionary psychology and the emotions. In M. Lewis & J. M. Haviland-Jones (Eds.), *Handbook of Emotions*. 2nd ed. New York: Guilford. 91–115.

Cosmides, L., & Tooby, J. (2005). Neurocognitive adaptations designed for social exchange. In D. M. Buss (Ed.), *The Handbook of Evolutionary Psychology* New York, NY: Wiley. 584–627.

Craig, W. (1908). The voices of Pigeons regarded as a means of social control. *American Journal of Sociology*, 41, 86–100.

Crowley, S., & Allen, C. (2008). Animal behavior: E pluribus unum? In M. Ruse (Ed.), *The Oxford handbook of the philosophy of biology*. Oxford: Oxford University Press. 327–48.

Cummins, D. (2006). Dominance, status, and social hierarchies. In D. M. Buss (Ed.), *The handbook of evolutionary psychology*. Hoboken, NJ: Wiley, 676–97.

Curtis, V. (2013). *Don't look, don't touch, don't eat: The science behind revulsion*. Chicago: University of Chicago Press.

Curtis, V. A., & Biran, A. (2001). Dirt, disgust and disease: Is hygiene in our genes? *Perspectives in Biology and Medicine*, 44(1), 17–31.

Curtis, V., et al. (2009). Planned, motivated and habitual hygiene behaviour: An eleven country review. *Health Education and Behavior*, 4, 655–67.

Curtis, V., et al. (2011). Disgust as an adaptive system for disease avoidance behaviour. *Philosophical Transactions of the Royal Society B: Biological Sciences*, 366(1563), 389–401.

Dahl, E. (2004). Social status versus formal rank of medical and other officers—an informal survey among passengers and seafarers on cruise ships. *International Maritime Health*, 55, 165–75.

Damasio, A. R. (1994). *Descartes' error: Emotion, reason, and the human brain*. New York: G. P. Putnam's Sons.

Damasio, A. R. (2003). *Looking for Spinoza*. New York: Harcourt.

Darwin, C. (1871). *The descent of man, and selection in relation to sex*. London: John Murray.

Darwin, C. (1965). *The expression of the emotions in man and animals*. Chicago: University of Chicago Press. (Original work published 1872)

Dawkins, R. (1976). Hierarchical organisation: A candidate principle for ethology. In P. Bateson & R. Hinde (Eds.), *Growing Points In Ethology* Cambridge: Cambridge University Press. 7–54.

Dayan, P., & Abbott, L. F. (2001). *Theoretical neuroscience: Computational and mathematical modeling of neural systems*. Boston, MA: MIT Press.

Deacon, T. (1997). *The symbolic species: The co-evolution of language and the brain*. New York: W. W. Norton.

Debas, K., et al. (2010). Brain plasticity related to the consolidation of motor sequence learning and motor adaptation. *PNAS*, 107(41), 17839–44.

Deci, E. L. (1971). Effects of externally mediated rewards on intrinsic motivation. *Journal of Personality and Social Psychology*, 18, 105–15.

Deci, E. L. (1975). *Intrinsic motivation*. New York: Plenum.

Deci, E. L., & Ryan, R. M. (1985). *Intrinsic motivation and self-determination in human behavior*. New York: Plenum.

Delancey, C. (2002). *Passionate engines: What emotions reveal about mind and artificial intelligence*. New York: Oxford University Press.

Dember, W. N., & Richman, C. L. (1989). *Spontaneous alternation behavior*. New York: Springer-Verlag.

Dennett, D. (1978). *Brainstorms: Philosophical essays on mind and psychology*. Cambridge: Bradford Books/MIT Press.

Dennett, D. (1996). *Kinds of minds: Toward an understanding of consciousness*. New York: Basic Books.

Dennett, D. C. (1983). Intentional systems in cognitive ethology: The Panglossian paradigm defended. *Behavioral and Brain Sciences*, 6, 343–90.

de Quervain, D. J., et al. (2004). The neural basis of altruistic punishment. *Science*, 305, 1254–58.

Dethier, V. G. (1964). Microscopic brains. *Science*, 143, 1138–45.

de Waal, F. B. M. (1982). *Chimpanzee politics: Power and sex among apes*. Baltimore: Johns Hopkins University Press.

de Waal, F. B. M. (1986). The integration of dominance and social bonding in Primates. *Quarterly Review of Biology*, 61, 459–79.

Dewey, J. (1896). The reflex arc concept in psychology. *Psychological Review*, 3(4), 357.

Dewey, J. (1922). *Human nature and conduct*. New York: Holt.

Dickinson, A. (1985). Actions and habits: The development of behavioral autonomy. *Philosophical Transactions of the Royal Society B: Biological Sciences*, 308, 67–78.

Dijksterhuis, A., & Nordgren, L. F. (2006). A theory of unconscious thought. *Perspectives in Psychological Science*, 1, 95–109.

Dolins, F. L., & Mitchell, R. W. (2010). *Spatial cognition, spatial perception: Mapping the self and space*. Cambridge: Cambridge University Press.

Dollard, J., & Miller, N. (1950). *Personality and psychotherapy: An analysis in terms of learning, thinking and culture*. New York: McGraw-Hill.

Dretske, F. (2000). *Perception, knowledge and belief*. Cambridge: Cambridge University Press.

Drews, C. (1993). The concept and definition of dominance in animal behaviour. *Behaviour*, 125, 283–313.

Dugatkin, L.A., & Wilson, D.S. (1992). The prerequisites for strategic behavior in bluegill sunfish, Lepomis macrochirus. *Animal Behaviour*, 44, 223–30.

Dunbar, R. (1998). *Grooming, gossip, and the evolution of language*. Cambridge, MA: Harvard University Press.

Dupré, J. A. (2000). Natural kinds. In W. H. Newton-Smith (Ed.), *A Companion to the Philosophy of Science* Oxford: Blackwell. 311–19.

Dusek, J. A., & Eichenbaum, H. (1997). The hippocampus and memory for orderly stimulus relations. *Proceedings of the National Academy of Sciences of the USA*, 94, 7109–14.

D'Argembeau, A., et al. (2003). Phenomenal characteristics of autobiographical memories for positive, negative, and neutral events. *Applied Cognitive Psychology*, 17, 281–94.

Easterbrook, J. A. (1959). The effect of emotion on cue utilization and the organization of behaviour. *Psychological Review*, 66, 183–201.

Ebisawa, T., et al. (2001). Association of structural polymorphisms in the human period3 gene with delayed sleep phase syndrome. *EMBO Reports*, 2, 342–46.

Editors (2006). *The American Heritage Dictionary of the English Language, F. Edition*. New York: Houghton Mifflin.

Eibl-Eibesfeldt, I. (1997). *Die Biologie des Menschlichen Verhaltens: Grundriss der Humanethology [The Biology of Human Behaviour: Outline of Human Ethology]*. Muenchen: Piper.

Eichenbaum, H. (2000). Declarative memory. *Nature Reviews Neuroscience*, 1, 41–50.

Eichenbaum, H., et al. (2012). Towards a functional organization of episodic memory in the medial temporal lobe. *Neuroscience & Biobehavioral Reviews*, 36(7), 1597–608.

Eichenbaum, H., & Fortin, N. (2003). Episodic memory and the hippocampus: It's about time. *Current Directions in Psychological Research*, 12, 53–57.

Ekman, P. (1992). An argument for basic emotions. *Cognition and Emotion*, 6, 169–200.

Ekman, P. (1999). Basic emotion. In T. Dalgleish & M. Power (Eds.), *Handbook of Cognition and Emotion* Sussex: Wiley. 45–60.

Elena, S. F., & Lenski, R. E. (2003). Evolution experiments with microorganisms: The dynamics and genetic bases of adaptation. *Nature Reviews Genetics*, 4, 457–69.

Elster, J. (1999). *Alchemies of the mind: Rationality and the emotions*. Cambridge: Cambridge University Press.

Emery, N. J., & Clayton, N. S. (2004). The mentality of crows: Convergent evolution of intelligence in corvids and apes. *Science*, 306, 1903–07.

Ereshefsky, M. (2007). Psychological categories as homologies: Lessons from ethology. *Biology and Philosophy*, 22, 659–74.

Etienne, A. S., et al. (2004). Resetting the path integrator: A basic condition for route-based navigation. *Journal of Experimental Biology*, 207, 1491–508.

Evans, D. (2002). The search hypothesis of emotion. *British Journal for the Philosophy of Science*, 53, 497–509.

Everitt, B. J., et al. (1999). Associative processes in addiction and reward: The role of amygdala-ventral striatal subsystems. *Annals of the New York Academy of Sciences*, 877, 412–38.

Everitt, B. J., et al. (2001). The neuropsychological basis of addictive behaviour. *Brain Research Reviews*, 36, 129–38.

Fagen, R. (1991). *Animal play behavior.* Oxford: Oxford University Press.

Fehr, E., & Gachter, S. (2002). Altruistic punishment in humans. *Nature*, 415, 137–40.

Ferkin, M. H., et al. (2008). Meadow voles, *M. pennsylvanicus*, have the capacity to recall the 'what,' 'where,' and 'when' of a single past event. *Animal Cognition*, 11(1), 147–59.

Fernald, R. D. (1997). The evolution of eyes. *Brain, Behavior and Evolution*, 50(4), 253–59.

Fincham, J. M., et al. (2002). Neural mechanisms of planning: A computational analysis using event-related fMRI. *Proceedings of the National Academy of Sciences of the USA*, 99, 3346–51.

Fishbein, M., & Ajzen, I. (1975). *Belief, attitude, intention, and behavior: An introduction to theory and research.* Reading, MA: Addison-Wesley.

Fisher, R. A. (1930). *The genetical theory of natural selection.* Oxford: Clarendon Press.

Fitts, P. M. (1964). Perceptual-motor skill learning. In A. W. Melton (Ed.), *Categories of Human Learning* New York: Academic Press. 234–85.

Fox, R. (1984). *Kinship and marriage: An anthropological perspective.* Cambridge: Cambridge University Press.

Franken, R. (2001). *Human motivation* (5th ed.). Pacific Grove, CA: Brooks/Cole.

Frederich, S., et al. (2002). Time discounting and time preference: A critical review. *Journal of Economic Literature*, 40, 351–401.

Fredrickson, B. L. (2001). The role of positive emotion in psychology: The broaden-and-build theory of positive emotions. *American Psychologist*, 56, 218–26.

Freeman, W. J. (1999). *How the brain makes up its mind.* London: Weidenfeld and Nicholson.

Freeman, W. J. (2000). Emotion is essential to all intentional behaviors. In M. D. Lewis & I. Granic (Eds.), *Emotion, Development, and Self-Organization: Dynamic Systems Approaches to Emotional Development* Cambridge: Cambridge University Press. 209–35.

Frijda, N. (1986). *The emotions.* Cambridge, UK: Cambridge University Press.

Friston, K. (2010). The free-energy principle: A unified brain theory? *Nature Reviews Neuroscience*, 11, 127–38.

Frith, C. D., & Frith, U. (2012). Mechanisms of social cognition. *Annual Review of Psychology*, 63, 287–313.

Fuster, J. (2003). *Cortex and mind: Unifying cognition.* Oxford: Oxford University Press.

Gainutdinova, T. H., et al. (2005). Reconsolidation of a context long-term memory in the terrestrial snail requires protein synthesis. *Learning and Memory*, 12, 620–25.

Galliot, B., et al. (2009). Origins of neurogenesis, a cnidarian view. *Developmental Biology*, 332, 2–24.

Gallistel, C. R. (1990). *The organization of learning.* Cambridge, MA: MIT Press.

Gamow, G. (1954). Possible relation between deoxyribonucleic acid and protein structures. *Nature*, 173, 318.

Gärdenfors, P. (2003). *How Homo became sapiens: On the evolution of thinking.* Oxford: Oxford University Press.

Gardner, H. (1986). *The mind's new science: A history of the cognitive revolution.* New York: Basic Books.

Gariépy, J. F., et al. (2014). Social learning in humans and other animals. *Frontiers in Neuroscience,* 8.

Gat, E. (1998). On three layer architectures. In D. Kortenkamp et al. (Eds.), *Artificial intelligence and mobile robots: Case studies of successful robot systems* Menlo Park, CA: AAAI Press. 195–210.

Geary, D. C., & Flinn, M. V. (2001). Evolution of human parental behavior and the human family. *Parenting: Science and Practice,* 1, 5–61.

Gehring, W. J., & Ikeo, K. (1999). Pax 6: Mastering eye morphogenesis and eye evolution. *Trends in Genetics,* 15, 371–77.

Gentner, T. Q., et al. (2006). Recursive syntactic pattern learning by songbirds. *Nature,* 440, 1204–1207.

Ghiselin, M. T. (1974). A radical solution to the species problem. *Systematic Zoology,* 23, 536–44.

Ginsburg, S., & Jablonka, E. (2007a). The transition to experiencing: I. Limited learning and limited experiencing. *Biological Theory,* 2, 218–30.

Ginsburg, S., & Jablonka, E. (2007b). The transition to experiencing: II. The evolution of associative learning based on feelings. *Biological Theory,* 2, 231–43.

Ginsburg, S., & Jablonka, E. (2009). Epigenetic learning in non-neural organisms. *Journal of Bioscience,* 34, 633–46.

Gintis, H. (2007). The evolution of private property. *Journal of Economic Behavior and Organization,* 64, 1–16.

Gintis, H. (2009). *The bounds of reason: Game theory and the unification of the behavioral sciences.* Princeton, NJ: Princeton University Press.

Giurfa, M. (2013). Cognition with few neurons: Higher-order learning in insects. *Trends in Neurosciences,* 36 (5), 285–94.

Northcutt, R. G. (2002). Understanding vertebrate brain evolution. *Integrative and Comparative Biology,* 42, 743–56.

Glickman, S. E., & Sroges, R. W. (1968). Curiosity in zoo animals. *Behaviour,* 26, 151–88.

Glimcher, P. W., et al. (2007). Neuroeconomic studies of impulsivity: Now or just as soon as possible? *American Economic Review,* 97, 142–47.

Godfrey-Smith, P. (1996). *Complexity and the function of mind in nature.* Cambridge: Cambridge University Press.

Godfrey-Smith, P. (2009). *Darwinian populations and natural selection.* Oxford: Oxford University Press.

Goffman, E. (1956). Embarrassment and social organization. *American Journal of Sociology,* 62, 264–71.

Golani, I. (1976). Homeostatic motor processes in mammalian interactions: A choreography of display. In P. P. G. Bateson & P. H. Klopfer (Eds.), New York: Plenum, 69–134.

Gould, S. J., & Vrba, E S. (1982). Exaptation—a missing term in the science of form. *Paleobiology,* 8, 4–15.

Grafen, A. (1982). How not to measure inclusive fitness. *Nature,* 298(5873), 425–6.

Greenspan, R. J., & Dierick, H. A. (2004). 'Am not I a fly like thee?' From genes in fruit flies to behavior in humans. *Human Molecular Genetics,* 13, R267–73.

Gregory, P. T., et al. (1999). Conflicts and interactions among reproduction, thermoregulation and feeding in viviparous reptiles: Are gravid snakes anorexic? *Journal of Zoology,* 248, 231–41.

Griffiths, P. (1997). *What emotions really are: The problem of psychological categories.* Chicago: University of Chicago Press.

Griffiths, P. E. (1999). Squaring the circle: Natural kinds with historical essences. In R. A. Wilson (Ed.), Cambridge, MA: MIT Press, 209–28.

Griffiths, P. E. (2004a). Emotions as natural and normative kinds. *Philosophy of Science*, 71, 901–11.

Griffiths, P. E. (2004b). Is emotion a natural kind? In R. C. Solomon (Ed.), *Thinking About Feeling: Contemporary Philosophers on Emotions* New York: Oxford University Press, 233–49.

Hacking, I. (2002). Making up people. In I. Hacking (Ed.), *Historical Ontology* Cambridge, MA: Harvard University Press, 99–114.

Haidt, J. (2001). The emotional dog and its rational tail: A social intuitionist approach to moral judgment. *Psychological Review*, 108, 814–34.

Hamann, S. B. (2001). Cognitive and neural mechanisms of emotional memory. *Trends in Cognitive Sciences*, 5, 394–400.

Hamilton, W. D. (1964). The genetical evolution of social behaviour I and II. *Journal of Theoretical Biology*, 7, 1–52.

Hampton, R. R., & Schwartz, B. L. (2004). Episodic memory in nonhumans: What, and where, is when? *Current Opinion in Neurobiology*, 14, 192–97.

Haralson, S. J., & Haralson, J. B. (1988). Habituation in the sea anemone (*Anthopleura elegantissima*): Spatial discrimination. *International Journal of Comparative Psychology*, 1, 245–53.

Hardcastle, V. G. (1995). *Locating consciousness*. Amsterdam & Philadelphia: John Benjamins.

Hare, B., et al. (2006). Chimpanzees deceive a human by hiding. *Cognition and Emotion*, 101, 495–514.

Hare, B., & Tomasello, M. (2005). Human-like social skills in dogs? *Trends in Cognitive Sciences*, 9, 439–44.

Harnish, R. (2001). *Minds, brains, computers: An historical introduction to the foundations of cognitive science*. London: Blackwell.

Hartwell, L. H., et al. (1999). From molecular to modular cell biology. *Nature*, 402, C47–C52.

Haslam, N. (1998). Natural kinds, human kinds, and essentialism. *Social Research*, 65, 291–314.

Hauser, M. (2000). *Wild minds: What animals really think*. New York: Henry Holt.

Hawkes, K. (2004). Mating, parenting and the evolution of human pair bonds. In B. Chapais & C. Berman (Eds.), *Kinship and Behavior in Primates* Oxford: Oxford University Press, 443–73.

Hawkins, J., & Blakeslee, S. (2004). *On intelligence: How a new understanding of the brain will lead to the creation of truly intelligent machines*. New York: Henry Holt & Company.

Hebb, D. O. (1949). *The organization of behavior*. New York: John Wiley and Sons.

Heindel, W. C., et al. (1989). Neuropsychological evidence for multiple implicit memory systems: A comparison of Alzheimer's, Huntington's, and Parkinson's disease patients. *Journal of Neuroscience*, 9, 582–87.

Hennig, W. (1966). *Phylogenetic systematics*. Urbana: University of Illinois Press.

Henrich, J., & Gil-White, F. (2001). The evolution of prestige: Freely conferred deference as a mechanism for enhancing the benefits of cultural transmission. *Evolution and Human Behavior*, 22, 165–96.

Hinde, R. A. (1970). *Animal behaviour: A synthesis of ethology and comparative psychology* (2nd ed.). New York: McGraw-Hill.

Hoffman, J. L. (1949). Clinical observations concerning schizophrenic patients treated by prefrontal leukotomy. *New England Journal of Medicine*, 241, 233–36.

Holekamp, K. E, et al. (2013). Developmental constraints on behavioural flexibility. *Philosophical Transactions of the Royal Society B: Biological Sciences*, 368(1618), 20120350.

Hollis, K. L., et al. (1989). The biological function of Pavlovian conditioning: A mechanism for mating success in the blue gourami, *Trichogaster trichopterus. Journal of Comparative Psychology*, 103, 115–21.

Hsu, M., et al. (2008). The right and the good: Distributive justice and neural encoding of equity and efficiency. *Science*, 320, 1092.

Huber, R., et al. (2011). Drug-sensitive reward in crayfish: An invertebrate model system for the study of SEEKING, reward, addiction, and withdrawal. *Neuroscience & Biobehavioral Reviews*, 35(9), 1847–53.

Huberman, B. A., et al. (2004). Status as a valued resource. *Social Psychology Quarterly*, 67(1), 103–14.

Hughes, M. (1983). Exploration and play in young children. In J. Archer & L. I. A. Birke (Eds.), *Exploration in Animals and Humans* Berkshire, England: Van Nostrand Reinhold. 230–44.

Hughes, C., et al. (1994). Evidence for executive dysfunction in autism. *Neuropsychologia*, 32, 477–92.

Hughlings Jackson, J. (1958). *Selected writings of John Hughlings Jackson* (Vols. 1 & 2). London: Staples Press.

Hull, C. L. (1943). *Principles of behavior: An introduction to behavior theory*. New York: Appleton-Century Co.

Hull, D. (1978). A matter of individuality. *Philosophy of Science*, 45, 335–60.

Humphrey, N. (1976). The social function of intellect. In P. P. G Bateson & R. A. Hinde (Eds.), *Growing Points in Ethology* Cambridge: Cambridge University Press, 303–17.

Humphrey, N. (2006). *Seeing red: A study in consciousness*. Cambridge, MA: Harvard University Press.

Hutcherson, C. A., & Gross, J. J. (2011). The moral emotions: A social–functionalist account of anger, disgust, and contempt. *Journal of Personality and Social Psychology*, 100(4), 719–37.

Hutchinson, G. E. (1957). Concluding remarks. *Cold Spring Harbor Symposia on Quantitative Biology*, 22, 415–27.

Hutt, C. (1966). Exploration and play in children. *Symposia of the Zoological Society of London*, 18, 61–81.

Inglis, I. R. (2000). Review: The central role of uncertainty reduction in determining behaviour. *Behaviour*, 137, 1567–99.

Izard, C. E. (1977). *Human emotions*. New York: Plenum Press.

Jablonka, E., & Lamb, Marion J. (2006). The evolution of information in the major transitions. *Journal of Theoretical Biology*, 239, 236–46.

Jackson, S. R., et al. (1999). The selection and suppression of action: ERP correlates of executive control in humans. *Neuroreport*, 10, 861–65.

Jacobs, L. F. (2003). The evolution of the cognitive map. *Brain, Behavior and Evolution*, 62, 128–39.

Jacobson, A. L., et al. (1967). Classical conditioning, pseudoconditioning, or sensitization in the planarian. *Journal of Comparative and Physiological Psychology*, 64, 73–79.

Jacquet, J., et al. (2011). Shame and honour drive cooperation. *Biology Letters*, 7(6), 899–901.

James, W. (1884). What is an emotion? *Mind*, 19, 188–204.

James, W. (1890). *The principles of psychology*. Boston: Henry Holt.

Johnson, M. C., & Wuensch, K. L. (1994). An investigation of habituation in the jellyfish *Aurelia aurita*. *Behavioral and Neural Biology*, 61, 54–59.

Johnson-Laird, P. N. (2006). *How we reason*. Oxford: Oxford University Press.

Kahneman, D. (2011). *Thinking, fast and slow*. New York: Macmillan.

Kandel, E. R., et al. (2014). The molecular and systems biology of memory. *Cell*, 157(1), 163–86.

Kandel, E. R., et al. (2000). *Principles of neural science*. New York: McGraw-Hill.

Kaplan, H. (1996). A theory of fertility and parental investment in traditional and modern human societies. *American Journal of Physical Anthropology*, 101(S23), 91–135.

Kashdan, T. B., et al. (2009). The curiosity and exploration inventory. II: Development, factor structure, and psychometrics. *Journal of Research in Personality*, 43, 987–98.

Kassen, R., et al. (2004). Ecological constraints in a model adaptive radiation. *Nature*, 431, 984–88.

Katz, J. S., et al. (2007). Issues in the comparative cognition of abstract-concept learning. *Comparative Cognition & Behavior Reviews*, 2, 79–92.

Kelley, J. L., & Magurran, A. E. (2003). Learned predator recognition and antipredator responses in fish. *Fish and Fisheries*, 4, 216–26.

Kelso, J.A. S. (1995). *Dynamic patterns: The self-organisation of brain and behavior.* Cambridge, MA: MIT Press.

Keltner, D., & Haidt, J. (2001). Social functions of emotions. In T. J. Mayne & G. A. Bonanno (Eds.), *Emotions* New York: Guilford, 192–213.

Keltner, D., & Haidt, J. (2003). Approaching awe, a moral, spiritual, and aesthetic emotion. *Cognition and Emotion*, 17, 297–314.

Keltner, D., et al. (2006). Social functionalism and the evolution of emotions. In M. Schaller et al. (Eds.), *Evolution and Social Psychology* Madison, CT: Psychosocial Press, 115–42.

Kenny, A. (1963). *Action, emotion and will.* London: Routledge and Kegan Paul.

Kensinger, E. A. (2009). Remembering the details: Effects of emotion. *Emotion Review*, 1, 99–113.

Kensinger, E. A., & Corkin, S. (2004). Two routes to emotional memory: Distinct neural processes for valence and arousal. *Proceedings of the National Academy of Sciences of the USA*, 101, 3310–15.

Khalidi, M. A. (2013). *Natural categories and human kinds: Classification in the natural and social sciences.* Cambridge: Cambridge University Press.

Kiefer, M., et al. (1998). The time course of brain activations during response inhibition: Evidence from event-related potentials in a go/no go task. *Neuroreport*, 9, 765–70.

Kielhofner, G. (2007). *Model of human occupation: Theory and application* (4th ed.). Philadelphia: Lippincott Williams & Wilkins.

Kincaid, H., & Sullivan, J. A. (Eds.) (2013). *Classifying psychopathology: Mental kinds and natural kinds.* Boston, MA: MIT Press.

Kirschner, M. W., & Gerhart, J. C. (2006). *The plausibility of life.* New Haven: Yale University Press.

Kleinginna Jr., P., & Kleinginna, A. (1981). A categorized list of motivation definitions, with suggestions for a consensual definition. *Motivation and Emotion*, 5, 263–91.

Koechlin, E., et al. (2003). The architecture of cognitive control in the human prefrontal cortex. *Science*, 302, 1181–85.

Koestler, A. (1964). *The act of creation.* London: Hutchinsons.

Kornblith, H. (2002). *Knowledge and its place in nature.* Oxford: Clarendon Press.

Krebs, J. R., & Davies, N B. (1978). *Behaviour ecology: An evolutionary approach.* Sunderland, MA: Sinauer Associates.

Kripke, S. A. (1972). *Naming and necessity.* Cambridge, MA: Harvard University Press.

Kuba, M., et al. (2003). Looking at play in *Octopus vulgaris. Berliner Paläobiol. Abh.*, 3, 163–69.

Kuba, M., et al. (2006). When do octopuses play? Effects of repeated testing, object type, age, and food deprivation on object play in Octopus vulgaris. *Journal of Comparative Psychology*, 120, 184–90.

Kumar, P., et al. (2014). Differential effects of acute stress on anticipatory and consummatory phases of reward processing. *Neuroscience*, 266, 1–12.

Kupfermann, I. (1974). Feeding behavior in Aplysia: A simple system for the study of motivation. *Behavioral Biology*, 10, 1–26.

LaPorte, J. (2004). *Natural kinds and conceptual change.* Cambridge: Cambridge University Press.

Laland, K. N., et al. (2003). Learning in fishes: From three-second memory to culture. *Fish and Fisheries*, 4, 199–202.

Laland, K. N., & Reader, S. M. (1999). Foraging innovation in the guppy. *Animal Behaviour*, 57, 331–40.

Lawrence, A. D., et al. (2004). Dissociating fear and disgust: Implications for the structure of emotions. 149–71.

Lazarus, R. (1991). *Emotion and adaptation*. New York: Oxford University Press.

LeDoux, J. E. (2000). Emotion circuits in the brain. *Annual Review of Neuroscience*, 23, 155–84.

Lepper, M. R., et al. (1973). Undermining children's intrinsic interest with extrinsic rewards: A test of the 'overjustification' hypothesis. *Journal of Personality and Social Psychology*, 28, 129–37.

Lepper, M. R., & Henderlong, J. (2000). Turning 'play' into 'work' and 'work' into 'play': 25 years of research on intrinsic versus extrinsic motivation. In C. Sansone & J. M. Harackiewicz (Eds.), *Intrinsic and Extrinsic Motivation: The Search for optimal motivation and performance* San Diego, CA: Academic. 257–307.

Leslie, A. M. (1987). Pretense and representation: The origins of 'theory of mind'. *Psychological Review*, 94, 412–26.

Levenson, R. W. (1999). The intrapersonal functions of emotion. *Cognition and Emotion*, 13, 481–504.

Lewicki, P., et al. (1992). Nonconscious acquisition of information. *American Psychologist*, 47, 796–801.

Lewin, K. (1951). *Field theory in social science*. New York: Harper and Row.

Libet, B. (2004). *Mind time: The temporal factor in consciousness*. Cambridge, MA: Harvard University Press.

Libet, B., et al. (2000). *The volitional brain: Towards a neuroscience of free will*. Oxford: Imprint Academic.

Lillard, A. (2001). Pretend play as twin earth: A social-cognitive analysis. *Developmental Review*, 21, 495–531.

Lin, N. (1990). Social resources and social mobility: A structural theory of status attainment. In R. L. Breiger (Ed.), *Social Mobility and Social Structure* Cambridge: Cambridge University Press, 247–71.

Llinas, R. (2002). *I of the vortex: From neurons to self*. Cambridge, MA: MIT Press.

Loeb, J. (1900). *Comparative physiology of the brain and comparative psychology*. New York: G. P. Putnam's Sons.

Loewenstein, G. (1994). The psychology of curiosity: A review and reinterpretation. *Psychological Bulletin*, 116, 75–98.

Loewenstein, G. (1996). Out of control: Visceral influences on behavior. *Organizational Behavior and Human Decision Processes*, 65, 272–92.

Loftus, E. F., & Pickrell, J. E. (1995). The formation of false memories. *Psychiatric Annals*, 25, 720–25.

Logan, F. A. (1999). Basic principles of learning. <http://www.unm.edu/~quadl%3E>

Loizos, C. (1967). Play behaviour in higher primates: A review. In D. Morris (Ed.), London: Weidenfeld and Nicholson. 176–218.

Lorenz, K. (1937). Uber die Bildung des Instinktbegriffs. *Naturwissenschaften*, 25, 289–331.

Lorenz, K. (1950). The comparative method in studying innate behaviour patterns. In J. F. Danielli & R. Brown (Eds.), Cambridge: Cambridge University Press.

Lorenz, K. (1965). *Evolution and the modification of behavior*. Chicago: University of Chicago Press.

Lourdais, O., et al. (2002). Costs of anorexia during pregnancy in a viviparous snake (*Vipera aspis*). *Journal of Experimental Zoology*, 292, 487–93.

Ludvico, L. R., & Kurland, J. A. (1995). Symbolic or not-so-symbolic wounds: The behavioral ecology of human scarification. *Ethology and Sociobiology*, 16, 155–72.

Machery, E. (2005). Concepts are not a natural kind. *Philosophy of Science*, 72, 444–67.

MacLean, P. D. (1990). *The triune brain in evolution: Role in paleocerebral functions*. New York: Plenum Press.

Maestripieri, D. (1992). Functional aspects of maternal aggression in mammals. *Canadian Journal of Zoology*, 70(6), 1069–77.

Mallatt, J. (1996). Ventilation and the origin of jawed vertebrates: A new mouth. *Zoological Journal of the Linnean Society*, 117, 329–404.

Mallon, R. (2003). Social construction, social roles, and stability. In F. Schmitt (Ed.), *Socializing Metaphysics* New York: Rowman and Littlefield. 327–53.

Mameli, M., & Bateson, P. (2006). Innateness and the sciences. *Biology and Philosophy*, 21, 155–88.

Maren, S. (1999). Long-term potentiation in the amygdala: A mechanism for emotional learning and memory. *Trends in the Neurosciences*, 22, 561–67.

Marx, K. (1887). *Capital*. Moscow: Progress Publishers.

Maslow, A. H. (1943). A theory of human motivation. *Psychological Review*, 50, 370–96.

Maslow, A. H. (1954). *Motivation and personality*. New York: Harper.

Mather, J. A. (2008). To boldly go where no mollusc has gone before: Personality, play, thinking, and consciousness in cephalopods. *American Malacological Bulletin*, 24, 51–58.

Mather, J. A., & Anderson, R. C. (1999). Exploration, play and habituation in *Octopus dofleini*. *Journal of Comparative Psychology*, 113, 333–38.

Maynard Smith, J. (2000). The concept of information in biology. *Philosophy of Science*, 67(2), 177–94.

Maynard Smith, J., & Szathmáry, E. (1995). *The major transitions in evolution*. Oxford: Oxford University Press.

Maynard Smith, J., & Szathmáry, E. (1998). *The origins of life*. Oxford: Oxford University Press.

Mayr, E. (1963). *Animal species and evolution*. Cambridge, MA: Harvard University Press.

McClelland, D. C. (1987). *Human motivation*. Cambridge: Cambridge University Press.

McClure, S. M., et al. (2004). Separate neural systems value immediate and delayed monetary rewards. *Science*, 306, 503–07.

McClure, S. M., et al. (2007). Time discounting for primary rewards. *Journal of Neuroscience*, 27, 5796–804.

McDougall, W. (1908). *An introduction to social psychology*. London: Methuen.

McFarland, D. (1998). *Animal behaviour: Psychobiology, ethology and evolution* (3rd ed.). New York: Prentice Hall.

McGaugh, J. L. (2004). The amygdala modulates the consolidation of memories of emotionally arousing experiences. *Annual Review of Neuroscience*, 27, 1–28.

McShea, D. W., & Simpson, C. (2011). The miscellaneous transitions in evolution. In B. Calcott & K. Sterelny (Eds.), *The major transitions in evolution revisited*. Cambridge, MA: MIT Press, 19–34.

Melanson, K. J., et al. (1999). Blood glucose and meal patterns in time-blinded males, after aspartame, carbohydrate, and fat consumption, in relation to sweetness perception. *British Journal of Nutrition*, 82, 437–46.

Mele, A. R. (1992). *Irrationality: An essay on akrasia, self-deception, and self-control*. Oxford: Oxford University Press.

Menon, V. (2011). Large-scale brain networks and psychopathology: A unifying triple network model. *Trends in Cognitive Sciences*, 15(10), 483–506.

Mesquita, B., & Frijda, N H. (1992). Cultural variation in emotions: A review. *Psychological Bulletin*, 112, 179–204.

Mesulam, M. M. (1998). From sensation to cognition. *Brain*, 121, 1013–52.

Metcalfe, J., & Mischel, W. (1999). A hot/cool-system analysis of delay of gratification: Dynamics and willpower. *Psychological Review*, 106, 3–19.

Metzinger, T. (2003). *Being no one: The self-model theory of subjectivity*. Cambridge, MA: MIT Press.

Miller, E. K., & Cohen, J. D. (2001). An integrative theory of prefrontal cortex function. *Annual Review of Neuroscience*, 24, 167–202.

Miller, E. K., et al. (2002). The prefrontal cortex: Categories, concepts, and cognition. *Philosophical Transactions: Biological Sciences*, 357, 1123–36.

Miller, Geoffrey. (2000). *The mating mind: How sexual choice shaped the evolution of human nature*. London: Heineman.

Miller, George A. (1956). The magical number seven, plus or minus two: Some limits on our capacity for processing information. *Psychological Review*, 63, 81–97.

Miller, George A., et al. (1960). *Plans and the structure of behavior*. New York: Holt Rinehart and Winston.

Millikan, R. G. (1984). *Language, thought and other biological categories*. Cambridge, MA: MIT Press.

Millikan, R. G. (1999). Historical kinds and the "special sciences." *Philosophical Studies*, 95, 45–65.

Millikan, R. G. (in press). Thoughts of real kinds. In J. Prinz (Ed.), *The Oxford Handbook of Philosophy of Psychology* Oxford: Oxford University Press.

Mineka, S., et al. (1980). Fear of snakes in wild- and laboratory-reared rhesus monkeys (*Macaca mulatta*). *Animal Learning & Behavior*, 8, 653–63.

Mineta, K., et al. (2003). Origin and evolutionary process of the CNS elucidated by comparative genomics analysis of planarian ESTs. *PNAS*, 100, 7666–71.

Minsky, M. (2006). *The emotion machine: Commonsense thinking, artificial intelligence, and the future of the human mind*. New York: Simon and Schuster.

Mitchell, J. P., et al. (2005). The link between social cognition and self-referential thought in the medial prefrontal cortex. *Journal of Cognitive Neuroscience*, 17, 1306–15.

Montague, P. R., & Berns, G. S. (2002). Neural economics and the biological substrates of valuation. *Neuron*, 36, 265–84.

Mountcastle, V. (1957). Modality and topographic properties of single neurons of cat's somatic sensory cortex. *Journal of Neurophysiology*, 20, 408–34.

Mountcastle, V. B. (1998). *Perceptual neuroscience: The cerebral cortex*. Cambridge, MA: Harvard University Press.

Mulcahy, N. J., & Call, J. (2006). Apes save tools for future use. *Science*, 312, 1038–40.

Murray, H. A. (1938). *Explorations in personality*. New York: Oxford University Press.

Myers, D. G. (2006). *Psychology* (8th ed.). New York: Worth.

Nagel, T. (1974). What is it like to be a bat? *Philosophical Review*, 4, 435–50.

Nairne, J. S., et al. (2007). Adaptive memory: Survival processing enhances retention. *Journal of Experimental Psychology: Animal Behaviour Processes*, 33, 263–73.

Nargeot, R., et al. (1999). Dopaminergic synapses mediate neuronal changes in an analogue of operant conditioning. *Journal of Neurophysiology*, 81, 1983–87.

Nesse, R. M. (1990). Evolutionary explanations of emotion. *Human Nature*, 1(3), 261–89.

Neuberg, S. L., et al. (2011). Human threat management systems: Self-protection and disease avoidance. *Neuroscience & Biobehavioral Reviews*, 35(4), 1042–51.

Newell, A. (1990). *Unified theories of cognition*. Cambridge, MA: Harvard University Press.

Niendam, T. A., et al. (2012). Meta-analytic evidence for a superordinate cognitive control network subserving diverse executive functions. *Cognitive, Affective & Behavioral Neuroscience*, 12(2), 241–68.

Nimchinsky, E. A., et al. (1999). A neuronal morphologic type unique to humans and great apes. *Proceedings of the National Academy of Sciences of the USA*, 96, 5268–73.

Nissen, H. W. (1930). A study of exploratory behavior in the white rat by means of the obstruction method. *Journal of Genetic Psychology*, 37, 361–76.

Norman, D., & Shallice, T. (1986). Attention to action: Willed and automatic control of behavior. In R. Davidson et al. (Eds.), *Consciousness and Self-regulation: Advances in Research and Theory*, vol. 4. New York, NY: Plenum, 1–18.

Northcutt, R. G., & Kaas, J. H. (1995). The emergence and evolution of mammalian neocortex. *Trends in the Neurosciences*, 18, 373–79.

Nowak, M. A. (2006). Five rules for the evolution of cooperation. *Science*, 314(5805). 1560–63.

Nowak, M. A. (2013). *Evolution, games, and God*. Boston, MA: Harvard University Press.

Oatley, K. J. (1993). Social construction in emotion. In M. Lewis & J. Haviland (Eds.), *Handbook of Emotions* New York: Guilford Press, 342–52.

Oatley, K. J., & Johnson-Laird, P. N. (1987). Towards a cognitive theory of emotions. *Emotion and Cognition*, 1, 29–50.

Ochsner, K. N., & Barrett, L. F. (2001). A multiprocess perspective on the neuroscience of emotion. In T. J. Mayne & G. A. Bonnano (Eds.), *Emotions* New York: Guilford, 38–81.

Odling-Smee, F. J., et al. (2003). *Niche construction: The neglected process in evolution*. Princeton: Princeton University Press.

O'Doherty, J., et al. (2001). Representation of pleasant and aversive taste in the human brain. *Journal of Neurophysiology*, 85, 1315–21.

Ohman, A. (1986). Face the beast and fear the face: Animal and social fears as prototypes for evolutionary analysis of emotions. *Psychophysiology*, 23, 123–45.

Ohman, A., & Mineka, S. (2003). The malicious serpent: Snakes as a prototypical stimulus for an evolved module of fear. *Current Directions in Psychological Science*, 12, 5–9.

O'Keefe, J. & Nadel, L. (1978). *The hippocampus as a cognitive map*. Oxford: Oxford University Press.

Olds, J., & Milner, P. M. (1954). Positive reinforcement produced by electrical stimulation of the septal area and other regions of the rat brain. *Journal of Comparative and Physiological Psychology*, 47, 419–27.

Ortony, A., et al. (2004). Affect and proto-affect in effective functioning. In J. M. Fellous & M. A. Arbib (Eds.), *Who Needs Emotions? The Brain Meets the Robot* Oxford: Oxford University Press, 173–202.

Osvath, M., & Gärdenfors, P. (2005). Oldowan culture and the evolution of anticipatory cognition. *Lund University Cognitive Science*, 122.

Ouellette, J., & Wood, W. (1998). Habit and intention in everyday life: The multiple processes by which past behavior predicts future behavior. *Psychological Bulletin*, 124, 54–74.

Oyama, S. (2000). *The ontogeny of information: Developmental systems and evolution*. Durham, NC: Duke University Press.

Panksepp, J. (1998). *Affective neuroscience: The foundations of human and animal emotions*. New York: Oxford University Press.

Panksepp, J., & Burgdor, J. (2003). 'Laughing' rats and the evolutionary antecedents of human joy? *Physiology & Behavior*, 79, 533–47.

Papini, M. R. (2011). *Comparative psychology: Evolution and development of behavior*. New York: Psychology Press.

Parrish, J. K., et al. (2002). Self-organized fish schools: An examination of emergent properties. *Biological Bulletin*, 202, 296–305.

Pasupathy, A., & Miller, E. K. (2005). Different time courses of learning-related activity in the prefrontal cortex and striatum. *Nature*, 433, 873–76.

Pavlov, I. P. (1927). *Conditioned reflexes: An investigation of the physiological activity of the cerebral cortex* (G. Anrep, Transl. and Ed.). London.

Pellegrini, A. D. (2003). Perceptions and functions of play and real fighting in early adolescence. *Child Development*, 74, 1522–33.

Penn, D. C., et al. (2008). Darwin's mistake: Explaining the discontinuity between human and nonhuman minds. *Behavioral and Brain Sciences* 31 (2), 109–78.

Perner, J. (1991). *Understanding the representational mind*. Cambridge, MA: MIT Press.

Perry, C. J., et al. (2013). Invertebrate learning and cognition: Relating phenomena to neural substrate. *Wiley Interdisciplinary Reviews: Cognitive Science*, 4(5), 561–82.

Pinker, S. (2012). *The better angels of our nature: A history of violence and humanity*. London: Penguin.

Pisula, W. (1998). Integrative levels in comparative psychology—the example of exploratory behavior. *European Psychologist*, 3, 62–69.

Pittman, S. E., et al. (2014). Homing of invasive Burmese pythons in South Florida: Evidence for map and compass senses in snakes. *Biology Letters*, 10(3).

Plutchik, R. (1980). *Emotion: A psychoevolutionary synthesis*. New York: Harper & Row.

Poucet, B. (1993). Spatial cognitive maps in animals: New hypotheses on their structure and neural mechanisms. *Psychological Review*, 100, 163–82.

Power, T. G. (2000). *Play and exploration in children and animals*. Mahwah, NJ: Erlbaum.

Prescott, T. J. (2007). Forced moves or good tricks in design space? Landmarks in the evolution of neural mechanisms for action selection. *Adaptive Behavior*, 15(9), 9–31.

Price, M. E., et al. (2002). Punitive sentiment as an anti-free rider psychological device. *Evolution and Human Behavior*, 23, 203–31.

Prinz, J. (2004). *Gut reactions: A perceptual theory of emotion*. Oxford: Oxford University Press.

Proust, J. (2006). Metacognition and animal rationality. In S. Hurley & M. Nudds (Eds.), *Rational Animals?* Oxford: Oxford University Press, 247–74.

Proust, J. (2013). *The philosophy of metacognition: Mental agency and self-awareness* Oxford: Oxford University Press.

Pulvermüller, F. (2005). Brain mechanisms linking language and action. *Nature Reviews Neuroscience*, 6, 576–82.

Pulvermüller, F. (2013). How neurons make meaning: Brain mechanisms for embodied and abstract-symbolic semantics. *Trends in Cognitive Sciences*, 17(9), 458–70.

Purves, D., et al. (2011). *Neuroscience* (5th ed.). London: Sinauer Associates.

Putnam, H. (1975). The meaning of 'meaning'. In H. Putnam (Ed.), *Mind, Language, and Reality* Cambridge: Cambridge University Press, 215–71.

Pylyshyn, Z. W. (1984). *Computation and cognition: Toward a foundation for cognitive science*. Cambridge, MA: MIT Press.

Queller, D. C. (1997). CoAperators since life began. Book review of *The Major Transitions in Evolution*, by J. Maynard Smith & E. Szathmáry. *Quarterly Review of Biology*, 72, 184–88.

Quine, W. V. (1969). Natural kinds. In N. Rescher (Ed.), *Essays in Honor of Carl. G. Hempel* Dordrecht: Reidel, 5–23.

Quinlan, R. J., & Quinlan, M. B. (2007). Evolutionary ecology of human pair-bonds: Cross-cultural tests of alternative hypotheses. *Cross-Cultural Research*, 41, 149–69.

Raby, C. R., et al. (2007). Planning for the future by western scrub-jays. *Nature*, 445, 919–21.

Raff, R. A. (1996). *The shape of life*. Chicago: Chicago University Press.

Rajah, M .N., & McIntosh, A. R. (2005). Overlap in the functional neural systems involved in semantic and episodic memory retrieval. *Journal of Cognitive Neuroscience*, 17, 470–82.

Reason, J. (1990). *Human error*. New York, NY: Cambridge University Press.

Reber, A. (1996). *Implicit learning and tacit knowledge: An essay on the cognitive unconscious*. Oxford: Oxford University Press.

Redgrave, P., et al. (1999). The basal ganglia: A vertebrate solution to the selection problem? *Neuroscience*, 89, 1009–23.

Redish, A. D. (2013). *The mind within the brain: How we make decisions and how those decisions go wrong*. Oxford: Oxford University Press.

Reichert, H., & Simeone, A. (2001). Developmental genetic evidence for a monophyletic origin of the bilaterian brain. *Philosophical Transactions of the Royal Society B: Biological Sciences*, 356(1414), 1533–44.

Reiss, S. (2008). *The normal personality: A new way of thinking about people*. Cambridge: Cambridge University Press.

Reiss, D., & Marino, L. (2001). Mirror self-recognition in the bottlenose dolphin: A case of cognitive convergence. *PNAS*, 98, 5937–42.

Rendell, L., et al. (2011). Cognitive culture: Theoretical and empirical insights into social learning strategies. *Trends in Cognitive Sciences*, 15(2), 68–76.

Rendell, L E., & Whitehead, H. (2001). Culture in whales and dolphins. *Behavioral and Brain Sciences*, 24, 309–82.

Reuter, M., et al. (2004). Personality and biological markers of creativity. *European Journal of Personality*, 19, 83–95.

Richerson, P. J., & Boyd, R. (1998). The evolution of human ultrasociality. In I. Eibl-Eibesfeldt & F. K. Salter (Eds.), *Indoctrinability, Ideology, and Warfare* New York: Berghahn Books.

Riedl, K., et al. (2012). No third-party punishment in chimpanzees. *Proceedings of the National Academy of Sciences of the USA*, 109(37), 14824–29.

Rieppel, O. (2005a). Modules, kinds, and homology. *Journal of Experimental Zoology B. Molecular and Developmental Evolution*, 304, 18–27.

Rieppel, O. (2005b). Monophyly, paraphyly, and natural kinds. *Biology and Philosophy*, 20, 465–87.

Rolls, E. T. (1999). *The brain and emotion*. Oxford: Oxford University Press.

Rolls, E. T. (2005). *Emotion explained*. Oxford: Oxford University Press.

Rolls, E. T. (2007). A computational neuroscience approach to consciousness. *Neural Networks*, 20, 962–82.

Rosslenbroich, B. (2009). The theory of increasing autonomy in evolution: A proposal for understanding macroevolutionary innovations. *Biology & Philosophy*, 24(5), 623–44.

Rosslenbroich, B. (2014). *On the origin of autonomy: A new look at the major transitions in evolution*. History, Philosophy and Theory of the Life Sciences, 5. Dordrecht: Springer.

Routtenberg, A., & Lindy, J. (1965). Effects of the availability of rewarding septal and hypothalamic stimulation on bar pressing for food under conditions of deprivation. *Journal of Comparative and Physiological Psychology*, 60, 158–61.

Rozin, P., & Vollmeke, T.A. (1986). Food likes and dislikes. *Annual Review of Nutrition*, 6, 433–56.

Rubenstein, J. L., et al. (1999). Genetic control of cortical regionalization and connectivity. *Cerebral Cortex*, 9, 524–32.

Rubin, D. C. (1986). *Autobiographical memory*. New York: Cambridge University Press.

Rubin, D. C., & Skulking, M. (1997). The distribution of autobiographical memories across the lifespan. *Memory & Cognition*, 25, 859–66.

Ryan, R. M., & Deci, E. L. (2000). Intrinsic and extrinsic motivations: Classic definitions and new directions. *Contemporary Educational Psychology, 25*, 54–67.

Sahney, S., et al. (2010). Rainforest collapse triggered Pennsylvanian tetrapod diversification in Euramerica. *Geology, 38*, 1079–82.

Savage, L. J. (1954). *Foundations of statistics.* New York: Dover.

Savage-Rumbaugh, S. (1987). A new look at ape language: Comprehension of vocal speech and syntax. *Nebraska Symposium on Motivation, 35*, 201–55.

Savage-Rumbaugh, E. S., et al. (2001). *Apes, language, and the human mind.* Oxford: Oxford University Press.

Sazima, I. (2008). Playful birds: Cormorants and herons play with objects and practice their skills. *Biota Neotropica, 8*, 259–64.

Schacter, D. L. (1996). *Searching for memory.* New York: Basic Books.

Schall, J. D. (2001). Neural basis of deciding, choosing and acting. *Nature Reviews Neuroscience, 2*, 33–42.

Schank, R., & Abelson, R. (1977). *Scripts, plans goals and understanding: An inquiry into human knowledge structures.* Hillsdale, NJ: Erlbaum.

Scherer, K. R. (1992). What does facial expression express? In K. Strongman (Ed.), *International Review of Studies on Emotion. Vol. 2.* Chichester: Wiley, 139–65.

Scherer, K. R. (1999). Appraisal theory. In T. Dalgleish & M. J. Power (Eds.), *Handbook of cognition and emotion.* Chichester: Wiley, 637–63.

Scherer, K. R., et al. (2001). *Appraisal processes in emotion: Theory, methods, research.* Oxford: Oxford University Press.

Schleidt, W. M., et al. (1984). A proposal for a standard ethogram, exemplified by an ethogram of the bluebreasted quail. *Coturnix chinensis. Zeitschreift für Tierpsychologie, 64*, 193–220.

Schneider, W., & Shiffrin, R. M. (1977). Controlled and automatic human information processing: I. Detection, search, and attention. *Psychological Review, 84*, 1–66.

Schultz, W. (2002). Getting formal with dopamine and reward. *Neuron, 36*, 241–63.

Schwarzer, R. (2008). Modeling health behavior change: How to predict and modify the adoption and maintenance of health behaviors. *Applied Psychology: An International Review, 57*, 1–29.

Seligman, M. E. P., & Hager, J. L. (1972). *Biological boundaries on learning.* New York: Appleton-Century-Crofts.

Semendeferi, K., et al. (1997). The evolution of the frontal lobes: A volumetric analysis based on three-dimensional reconstructions of magnetic resonance scans of human and ape brains. *Journal of Human Evolution, 32*, 375–88.

Semendeferi, K., et al. (2001). Prefrontal cortex in humans and apes: A comparative study of area 10. *American Journal of Physical Anthropology, 114*, 224–41.

Sharot, T., & Phelps, E. A. (2004). How arousal modulates memory: Disentangling the effects of attention and retention. *Cognitive, Affective, & Behavioral Neuroscience, 4*, 294–306.

Sheffield, F. D., & Roby, T. B. (1950). Reward value of a non-nutritive sweet taste. *Journal of Comparative and Physiological Psychology, 43*, 471–81.

Sheldon, K. M., et al. (2001). What is satisfying about satisfying events? Testing 10 candidate psychological needs. *Journal of Personality and Social Psychology Bulletin, 80*, 325–39.

Sherry, D. F., & Schacter, D. L. (1987). The evolution of multiple memory systems. *Psychological Review, 94*, 439–69.

Sherwood, C. C., et al. (2009). *Evolution of the brain: In humans—specializations in a comparative perspective.* New York: Springer Verlag.

Shiffrin, R. M., & Schneider, W. (1977). Controlled and automatic human information processing: II. Perceptual learning, automatic attending, and a general theory. *Psychological Review*, 84, 127–90.

Shillito, J. F. (1963). Observations on the range and movements of a woodland population of the common shrew *Sorex araneus*. *Proceedings of the Zoological Society London*, 140, 533–46.

Shultz, S., & Dunbar, R. (2010). Encephalization is not a universal macroevolutionary phenomenon in mammals but is associated with sociality. *Proceedings of the National Academy of Sciences*, 107(50), 21582–86.

Siiter, J. R. (1999). *Introduction to animal behavior*. New York: Brooks/Cole.

Sillen-Tullberg, B., & Møller, A. P. (1993). The relationship between concealed ovulation and mating systems in anthropoid primates. A phylogenetic analysis. *The American Naturalist*, 141, 1–25.

Silvia, P. J. (2006). *Exploring the psychology of interest*. New York: Oxford University Press.

Siviy, S. M. (1998). Neurobiological substrates of play behavior: Glimpses into the structure and function of mammalian playfulness. In M. Bekoff & J. A. Byers (Eds.), *Animal Play: Evolutionary, Ecological, and Comparative Perspectives* Cambridge: Cambridge University Press.

Skinner, B. F. (1938). *The behavior of organisms: An experimental analysis*. Englewood Cliffs, NJ: Prentice Hall.

Sloman, A. (2001). Beyond shallow models of emotion. *Cognitive Processing: International Quarterly of Cognitive Science*, 2, 177–98.

Smith, P. K. (1982). Does play matter? Functional and evolutionary aspects of animal and human play. *Behavioral Brain Sciences*, 5, 139–84.

Smuts, B. (1985). *Sex and friendship in baboons*. Boston, MA: Harvard University Press.

Spencer, A. N. (1989). Chemical and electrical synaptic transmission in the Cnidaria. In P. A. V. Anderson (Ed.), *Evolution of the First Nervous Systems* New York: Plenum, 33–53.

Sperber, D. (2000). Metarepresentations in evolutionary perspective. In D. Sperber (Ed.), *Metarepresentations: A Multidisciplinary Perspective* Oxford: Oxford University Press, 117–37.

Spinka, M., et al. (2001). Mammalian play: Training for the unexpected. *Quarterly Review of Biology*, 76, 141–68.

Squire, L. R. (1986). Mechanisms of memory. *Science*, 232, 1612–19.

Staddon, J. E. R. (2003). Adapative behavior and learning (2nd electr. ed). <http://psychandneuro.duke.edu/research/labs/staddon-lab>

Stanovich, K. E. (1999). *Who is rational?: Studies of individual differences in reasoning*. Mahwah, NJ: Erlbaum.

Stanovich, K. E. (2004). *The robot's rebellion: Finding meaning in the age of Darwin*. Chicago: University of Chicago Press.

Stanovich, K. E. (2009). Distinguishing the reflective, algorithmic, and autonomous minds: Is it time for a tri-process theory? In J. Evans & K. Frankish (Eds.), *In Two Minds: Dual processes and beyond* Oxford: Oxford University Press, 55–88.

Sterelny, K. (1990). *The representational theory of mind: An introduction*. Oxford: Basil Blackwell.

Sterelny, K. (1998). Intentional agency and the metarepresentation hypothesis. *Mind and Language*, 13, 11–28.

Sterelny, K. (2003). *Mind in a hostile world*. Oxford: Oxford University Press.

Stich, S. (2001). Plato's method meets cognitive science. *Free Inquiry*, 21, 36–38.

Stoytchev, A., & Arkin, R. (2001). Combining deliberation, reactivity and motivation in the context of a behavior-based robot architecture. *Proceedings of IEEE International Symposium on Computational Intelligence in Robotics and Automation (IEEE CIRA 2001)*. Banff, Canada.

Streidter, G. F. (1998). Progress in the study of brain evolution: From speculative theories to testable hypotheses. *The Anatomical Record*, 253, 105–12.

Streidter, G. F. (2005). *The principles of brain evolution*. Sunderland, MA: Sinauer Associates.

Suddendorf, T., & Busby, J. (2003). Mental time travel in animals? *Trends in Cognitive Sciences*, 7, 391–96.

Sugrue, L. P., et al. (2005). Choosing the greater of two goods: Neural currencies for valuation and decision-making. *Nature Reviews Neuroscience*, 6, 363–75.

Suhler, C. L., & Churchland, P. S. (2009). Control: Conscious and otherwise. *Trends in Cognitive Science*, 13, 341–47.

Sun, R., et al. (2005). The interaction of the explicit and the implicit in skill learning: A dual-process approach. *Psychological Review*, 112, 159–92.

Swanson, L.W. (2000). What is the brain? *Trends in Neuroscience*, 23, 519–27.

Swanson, L. W. (2003). *Brain architecture: Understanding the basic plan*. Oxford: Oxford University Press.

Szathmáry, E., et al. (2006). The evolution of information in the major transitions. *Journal of Theoretical Biology*, 239(2), 236–46.

Szathmáry, E., & Fernando, C. (2011). Concluding remarks. In B. Calcott & K. Sterelny (Eds.), *The Major Transitions Revisited* Cambridge, MA: MIT Press, 301–10.

Tangney, J. P., et al. (2007). Moral emotions and moral behavior. *Annual Review of Psychology*, 58, 345–72.

Thelen, E., & Smith, L. B. (1994). *A dynamical systems approach to the development of cognition and action*. Cambridge, MA: MIT Press.

Thompson, K. V. (1998). Self assessment in juvenile play. In M. Bekoff & J. A. Byers (Eds.), *Animal Play: Evolutionary, Ecological, and Comparative Perspectives* Cambridge: Cambridge University Press, 221–42.

Thompson, E., & Varela, F. J. (2001). Radical embodiment: Neural dynamics and consciousness. *Trends in Cognitive Sciences*, 5(10), 418–25.

Thorndike, E. L. (1901). Animal intelligence: An experimental study of the associative processes in animals. *Psychological Review Monograph Supplement*, 2, 1–109.

Thrun, S., et al. (2006). Stanley: The robot that won the DARPA Grand Challenge. *Journal of Field Robotics*, 23(9), 661–92.

Tien, J. H., et al. (2004). Dynamics of fish shoals: Identifying key decision rules. *Evolutionary Ecology Research*, 6, 555–65.

Timmermans, B., et al. (2012). Higher order thoughts in action: Consciousness as an unconscious re-description process. *Philosophical Transactions of the Royal Society B: Biological Sciences*, 367(1594). 1412–23.

Tinbergen, N. (1951). *The study of instinct*. Oxford: Clarendon Press.

Tinbergen, N. (1963). On aims and methods of ethology. *Zeitschrift fur Tierpsychologie*, 20, 410–33.

Toates, F. (1986). *Motivational systems*. New York: Cambridge University Press.

Tolman, E. C. (1948). Cognitive maps in rats and men. *Psychology Review*, 55, 189–208.

Tomasello, M. (2014). The ultra-social animal. *European Journal of Social Psychology*, 44(3), 187–94.

Tomkins, S. S. (1962). *Affect, imagery and consciousness*. New York: Springer Verlag.

Tooby, J., & Cosmides, L. (1989). Adaptation versus phylogeny: The role of animal psychology in the study of human behavior. *International Journal of Comparative Psychology*, 2, 175–88.

Tooby, J., & Cosmides, L. (1990). The past explains the present: Emotional adaptations and the structure of ancestral environments. *Ethology and Sociobiology*, 11, 375–424.

Tooby, J., & Cosmides, L. (1992). The psychological foundations of culture. In J. H. Barkow et al. (Eds.), *The Adapted Mind: Evolutionary Psychology and the Generation of Culture* Oxford: Oxford University Press, 19–136.

Topál, J., et al. (2006). Reproducing human actions and action sequences: 'Do as I do!' in a dog. *Animal Cognition*, 9, 355–67.

Tracy, J. L., & Robins, R. W. (2004). Show your pride: Evidence for a discrete emotion expression. *Psychological Science*, 15, 194–97.

Truppa, V., et al. (2011). Same/different concept learning by capuchin monkeys in matching-to-sample tasks. *PLoS One*, 6(8), e23809.

Tulving, E. (1985). How many memory systems are there? *American Psychologist*, 40, 385–98.

van den Heuvel, O., et al. (2005). Frontal-striatal dysfunction during planning in obsessive-compulsive disorder. *Archives of General Psychiatry*, 62, 301–09.

Vehanen, T. (2003). Adaptive flexibility in the behaviour of juvenile Atlantic salmon: Short-term responses to food availability and threat from predation. *Journal of Fish Biology*, 63, 1034–45.

von Neumann, J., & Morgenstern, O. (1944). *Theory of games and economic behavior*. Princeton: Princeton University Press.

Vossbeck-Elsebusch, A. N., & Gerlach, A. L. (2012). The relation between disgust-sensitivity, blood-injection-injury fears and vasovagal symptoms in blood donors: Disgust sensitivity cannot explain fainting or blood donation-related symptoms. *Journal of Behavior Therapy and Experimental Psychiatry*, 43(1), 607–13.

Wagner, G. P. (1996). Homologues, natural kinds and the evolution of modularity. *American Zoologist*, 36, 36–43.

Wagner, G. P. (2000). What is the promise of developmental evolution? Part I: Why is developmental biology necessary to explain evolutionary innovations? *Journal of Experimental Zoology*, 288, 95–98.

Wagner, G. P., & Altenberg, L. (1996). Complex adaptations and the evolution of evolvability. *Evolution and Development*, 50(3), 967–76.

Wagner, W., & Wagner, G. P. (2003). Examining the modularity concept in evolutionary psychology: The levels of genes, mind and culture. *Journal of Cultural and Evolutionary Psychology*, 1, 135–65.

Walker, R. (1999). 'Niche selection' and the evolution of complex behavior in a changing environment: A simulation. *Artificial Life*, 5(3), 271–89.

Wang, R. F., & Spelke, E. S. (2002). Human spatial representation: Insights from animals. *Trends in Cognitive Sciences*, 376, 376–82.

Watson, J. D., & Crick, F. H. C. (1953). A structure for deoxyribose nucleic acid. *Nature*, 171, 737–38.

Watts, A. G. (2003). Motivation: Neural substrates. In M. A. Arbib (Ed.), *The Handbook of Brain Theory and Neural Networks*. 2nd ed. Cambridge, MA: MIT Press, 680–83.

Wayner, M. J., & Zellner, D. K. (1958). The role of suprapharyngeal ganglion in spontaneous alternations and negative movements in *Lumbricus terrestris*. *Journal of Comparative and Physiological Psychology*, 51, 282–87.

Wegner, D. (2002). *The Illusion of the conscious will*. Cambridge, MA: MIT Press.

Wegner, D. M., & Bargh, J. A. (1998). Control and automaticity in social life. In D. Gilbert et al. (Eds.), *Handbook of Social Psychology* (4th ed.) New York: McGraw-Hill, 446–96.

Weiner, B. (2013). *Human motivation*. Psychology Press.

Weismann, A. (1889). *Essays on heredity and kindred biological subjects*. Oxford: Oxford University Press.

Wellman, H. M., et al. (1990). *The child's theory of mind.* Cambridge, MA: MIT Press.

Wells, M. J. (1968). Sensitization and the evolution of associative learning. In J. Salánki (Ed.), *Neurobiology of Invertebrates* New York: Plenum Press, 391–411.

West-Eberhard, M. J. (2003). *Developmental plasticity and evolution.* Oxford: Oxford University Press.

White, R. W. (1959). Motivation reconsidered: The concept of competence. *Psychological Review,* 66, 297–333.

Whiten, A., et al. (1999). Cultures in chimpanzees. *Nature,* 399, 682–85.

Whiten, A., & Byrne, R. W. (1991). The emergence of metarepresentation in human ontogeny and primate phylogeny. In A. Whiten (Ed.), *Natural theories of mind: Evolution, development and simulation of everyday mindreading.* Oxford: Blackwell, 267–82.

Wilkinson, A., et al. (2009). Visual and response-based navigation in the tortoise. Geochelone carbonaria. *Animal Cognition,* 12, 779–87.

Wilkinson, A., & Huber, L. (2012). Cold-blooded cognition: Reptilian cognitive abilities. *Oxford Handbook of Comparative Evolutionary Psychology,* 1–8.

Willer, R. (2009). Groups reward individual sacrifice: The status solution to the collective action problem. *American Sociological Review,* 74, 23–43.

Williams, Z. M., et al. (2004). Human anterior cingulate neurons and the integration of monetary reward with motor responses. *Nature Neuroscience,* 7, 1370–75.

Williams, H. L, et al. (2008). Autobiographical memory. In G. Cohen & M. A. Conway (Eds.), *Memory in the Real World (3rd ed.).* Hove, UK: Psychology Press, 21–90.

Wilson, E. O. (1975). *Sociobiology.* Cambridge, MA: Belknap Press.

Wilson, T. (2004). *Strangers to ourselves: Discovering the adaptive unconscious.* Cambridge, MA: Belknapp.

Wilson, M., & Daly, M. (1985). Competitiveness, risk taking, and violence: The young male syndrome. *Ethology and Sociobiology,* 6, 59–73.

Wiltschko, R., & Wiltschko, W. (2003). Avian navigation: From historical to modern concepts. *Animal Behaviour,* 65, 257–72.

Winter, D. G. (1996). *Personality: Analysis and interpretation of lives.* New York: McGrawHill.

Wise, R. A. (2004). Dopamine, learning and motivation. *Nature Reviews Neuroscience,* 5, 1–12.

Wisenden, B. D., & Millard, M. C. (2001). Aquatic flatworms use chemical cues from injured conspecifics to assess predation risk and to associate risk with novel cues. *Animal Behaviour,* 62, 761–66.

Wolfe, J. L. (1969). Observations on alertness and exploratory behavior in the eastern chipmunk. *American Midland Naturalist,* 81, 249–53.

Wong, R. (2000). *Motivation: A biobehavioural approach.* Cambridge: Cambridge University Press.

Wood, J. N., & Grafman, J. (2003). Human prefrontal cortex: Processing and representational perspectives. *Nature Reviews Neuroscience,* 4, 139–46.

Wood, W., & Neal, D. T. (2007). A new look at habits and the habit-goal interface. *Psychological Review,* 114(4), 843.

Wood, W., et al. (2002). Habits in everyday life: Thought, emotion, and action. *Journal of Personality and Social Psychology,* 83, 1281–97.

Wood-Gush, D. G. M., & Vestergaard, K. (1991). The seeking of novelty and its relation to play. *Animal Behaviour,* 42, 599–606.

Yamada, H., et al. (2013). Coding of the long-term value of multiple future rewards in the primate striatum. *Journal of neurophysiology,* 109(4), 1140–51.

Yarkoni, T., et al. (2011). Large-scale automated synthesis of human functional neuroimaging data. *Nature Methods,* 8(8), 665–70.

Yin, H. H., & Knowlton, B. J. (2006). The role of the basal ganglia in habit formation. *Nature Neuroscience, 7*, 464–76.

Zacher, P. (2000). *Psychological concepts and biological psychiatry: A philosophical analysis.* New York: John Benjamins.

Zacks, J. M., & Tversky, B. (2001). Event structure in perception and conception. *Psychological Bulletin, 127*, 3–21.

Zentall, T. R., et al. (2008). Concept learning in animals. *Comparative Cognition & Behavior Reviews, 3*, 13–45.

Zentall, T. R., & Galef Jr., B. G. (2013). *Social learning: Psychological and biological perspectives.* New York: Psychology Press.

INDEX